WOMEN TRAVELERS ᴵᴺ EGYPT

WOMEN TRAVELERS IN EGYPT

——FROM THE EIGHTEENTH——
TO THE TWENTY-FIRST CENTURY

Edited by
DEBORAH MANLEY

The American University in Cairo Press
Cairo   New York

The editor and publisher are grateful to the following for permission to use material in this book: Little Brown and Company for excerpts from *Down the Nile Alone in a Fisherman's Skiff* by Rosemary Mahoney; the family of Bettina Selby for excerpts from her *Riding the Desert Trail by Bicycle to the Source of the Nile*. Every reasonable effort has been made to contact copyright holders. We apologize to and thank any authors or copyright holders who we have not been able to properly acknowledge. If a work in copyright has been inadvertently included, the copyright holder should contact the publisher.

All the illustrations in this book are from *The Nile Boat, or Glimpses of the Land of Egypt* by W.H. Bartlett (London: Arthur Hall, Virtue, and Co., 2nd ed., 1850). Reproduced courtesy of the Rare Books and Special Collections Library, the American University in Cairo.

First published in 2012 by
The American University in Cairo Press
113 Sharia Kasr el Aini, Cairo, Egypt
420 Fifth Avenue, New York, NY 10018
www.aucpress.com

Dar el Kutub No. 7416/12
ISBN 978 977 416 570 2

Dar el Kutub Cataloging-in-Publication Data

Manley, Deborah
      Women Travelers in Egypt: From the Eighteenth to the Twenty-first Century/ Deborah
   Manley. —Cairo: The American University in Cairo Press, 2013
      p.   cm.
      ISBN 978 977 416 570 2
      1.   Women Travelers—Egypt
      I. Title
      910.92

1 2 3 4 5   17 16 15 14 13

Designed by Jon W Stoy
Printed in Egypt

Contents

Introduction

Lady Tobin, traveling through Egypt with her husband in 1853, wrote about keeping a journal—the record upon which her account of her journey would depend:

I quite agree with Miss Martineau that one of the greatest nuisances in travelling is keeping a journal. One is far more disposed to lie down and rest after a fatiguing ride of eight or nine hours on a camel, beneath a burning sun; than—having made a hasty toilette—to take out one's writing materials. I persevered, however, and rejoice that I did so.

We can rejoice also for it was upon such journals that travelers wrote the books which we can still read, enjoy—and learn from—today. In this book the accounts are linked together by the journey rather than time. Thus, a traveler in, say, 1824 may stand side by side with a traveler in the late twentieth century and share their response to Egypt.

1

Most men set out to travel with a purpose—for many their purpose was, and is, related to work rather than leisure. In the past women needed a purpose to justify their travels more than did men—for, unless they had enough money of their own, they had to ask for either male or female permission. Some women travelers were invited to make up numbers in a group or to accompany their husbands, but then quite often wrote a book of their travels—and thus became the traveler still remembered, while the men of their party are remembered only as a presence. Eliza Fay, Anne Katherine Elwood, Harriet Martineau, Amelia Edwards, M.L.M. Carey, and others in this collection were such travelers.

As we wander through the writings on travel in Egypt, we see both how different and how similar men's and women's accounts can be. When we read a man's account, the author is usually the 'hero' and any accompanying ladies are backdrop only. In the women's accounts the Egyptian crew often come forward to front of stage. The dragoman (or 'tour leader' and guide) usually moves to prime position, arranging everything for the whole party.

Early European travelers in Egypt, such as Danish Captain Frederik Norden, in 1737, were 'explorers' rather than travelers or tourists, but even then a lady was a member of the party. Some of the earlier women travelers, such as Eliza Fay or Sarah Lushington, were passing through Egypt—with their husbands—en route for India or returning from the East, rather than taking the long, long route around the Cape of Good Hope. But it was they who wrote the accounts of their journeys—often offering useful advice to future lady travelers. In 1836 the wealthy American couple, the Haights, traveled very widely in 'the Old World,' and were among the first American 'tourists' on the Nile. Again it was Mrs. Haight who wrote of their journeying.

By the mid-nineteenth century some women were traveling far and wide in their own right—and sometimes on their own. Two who came to Egypt were from Central Europe: the Viennese widow Ida Pfeiffer in the early 1840s, and the German countess Hahn Hahn a few years later, both traveling first to Syria, as the whole of the eastern Mediterranean lands were then called, to visit the 'Holy Land', then onward to Egypt and up the Nile. By mid-century the political economist Harriet Martineau traveled with a small group first through Egypt and then to Sinai and Petra. But even at that time the main guide book to the country, *Murray's Guide*, gave no advice to women travelers on the clothes they might need or the items they would be wise to bring. Some of them, like Mrs. Carey in 1861, brought her maid to look after her needs, but also gave good advice on what to bring. Others, including Martineau, attended to their own washing and ironing. All depended on the local guides to oversee their needs—this was particularly true of travelers like Isabella Bird when she traveled through the Sinai Peninsula, and was cared for with great tenderness by her Bedouin guides when she fell ill.

Perhaps the woman traveler who had the most long-term impact both on Egypt and on travel to Egypt was Amelia Edwards. She came almost by chance, having been disappointed by the weather in southern Europe in 1873, but she was so dismayed by the way the ancient treasures of Egypt were being ransacked by travelers and Egyptians alike that, on her return to England, she worked to set up the Egypt Exploration Society to organize 'digs' in a legal and orderly manner, and she funded the first Professorship of Egyptology in Britain.

By the latter half of the nineteenth century—and the coming of Thomas Cook and his Nile steamers—most travelers to Egypt—such as Norma Lorimer in 1907–1908—had become 'tourists,' seeing Egypt from a big, highly organized ship, much as most tourists do today. Yet even now there are a few travelers who, like Bettina Selby and Rosemary Mahoney, at the end of the twentieth century, went to Egypt with almost as much sense of adventure as the earlier travelers.

One of the great differences between the female and male travelers was that the women could meet the women of Egypt. Some of the women started as 'travelers' but then lived in Egypt for several years, and would have spoken Arabic and thus have had further insights into Egyptian life. Sarah Belzoni came with her husband but spent much time independent from him. Mary Whately, teacher and missionary in Egypt from the 1870s, met both the poorest women along the Nile and the richest women in the harems of Cairo. Ellen Chennells was employed by the Egyptian royal family to educate the harem. Sophia Poole, sister of the famous Edward Lane, lived among the women of Cairo for many years—and became an object of other travelers' interest in her own right. And the women travelers were able to observe, meet, and converse with local women more than the men could.

The best time for traveling in Egypt is during the winter months in Europe. This was particularly true when the annual inundation of the Nile made it less attractive for sailing. Many early travelers who spent many weeks upon the journey, would spend New Year's Eve in Egypt and, thus, the date of their diaries changed from the old year to the new.

I have myself been privileged to travel up the Nile on a modern day *dahabiya* similar to those on which most of the women traveled, and I can understand fully the pleasures they had and the Egypt they saw and brought to us in their writings.

1

Alexandria, the Delta, and Suez

Before the days of flight, travelers to Egypt arrived either through Alexandria or, the Red Sea, to cross the desert to the Nile, or, when the Suez Canal opened, and the railway had been built to Cairo, taking that route. Alexandria was to many travelers their first experience of Egypt and, after their journeying down the Nile, the flat coastline at Alexandria was their last sight of Egypt.

Early women travelers were provided with very little advice in the guidebooks about what they should bring with them—attention was focused on the needs of the 'gentlemen travelers.' Even the fourth edition of Murray's Guide of 1873 ("revised on the spot") would need to have been interpreted for women. In the section "Clothing and mode of life" we read that "Invalids coming to Egypt should always wear flannel next to the skin." Nothing was said about any requirement for a woman to be politely covered out of respect for local society. By 1901 Murray's Hand-book to India, Burma and Ceylon (an area with a similar climate) acknowledged the needs of the

5

'ladies.' "A lady," they were told, "cannot better than provide herself with thin skirts of tussore, silk or some such material, and thin flannel or silk shirts. Ladies should have a jacket and shawl, and a very thin dust-cloak." Another suggestion was for "a loose warm cloak to wear before the sun rises." In fact, just as today, "the secret of dressing is to begin the day in things that can be thrown off as the heat increases."

Men would need "Two tweed suits, one of lighter texture than the other." Flannel shirts were thought best for health—and "convenience of washing." The head, Murray advised, should be well protected. But, of course, in those days ladies wore hats whenever they left the house. For footwear, "brown leather boots and shoes will be found useful up the Nile." Presumably this applied to both sexes. "Coloured glass spectacles with gauze sides afford great relief to the eye from the glare of the sun, and a blue or green veil is sometimes useful for the same purpose." Anne Katherine Elwood certainly wore a veil on her visit to the Pyramids in 1823.

A useful suggestion for those going to India was that "linen and underwear for at least three days should be taken"—to give time for washing and ironing. In India—and probably in the hotels of Cairo—"there was a considerable amount of dining out" and, therefore, a lady, "unless she intends to eschew society" should be provided with several evening dresses. Riding habits for ladies should not be forgotten—and Anne Katherine Elwood wore hers in Egypt on her way to India.

Of course, as well as those colored glass spectacles (favored by Harriet Martineau) "A good sun hat is an essential." The 'terai'—two soft felt hats fitting one over the other—was recommended. In India you were advised to have bedding "to take with you everywhere" and no doubt this was necessary too on the Nile. "A waterproof cover to wrap the bedding in must not be omitted." By 1929 Baedeker's Egypt recognised that many travelers were women, and advised for the 'cool season' to take light tweed suits, a cardigan, and a moderately warm overcoat; for warmer weather, Baedeker advised for "ladies" one light and one warmer costume of wool or other woollen material, several jumpers (we would probably now say 'sweaters') or blouses (we would say shirts) and white or fadeless washing frocks (dresses).

Baedeker also advised not to forget "writing and sewing materials, a small medicine chest, a thermometer, pocket-compass, binoculars, electric torch, drinking cup, a large flask or thermos, and a body belt" (wrapped around one's middle for warmth). Cameras should not, Baedeker advised, be too large. Photographic material were available everywhere. Films could be developed and printed in the larger towns.

Would-be lady travelers surely turned to each other for advice or sought out the advice of their acquaintances who had been to Egypt—but none, except Mrs. Carey, with her invalid companions, seems to have acknowledged this or recommended anything to other future travelers. The advice given in the guides about not drinking too much, was, to be sure, not directed at the ladies.

How the People Made Egypt and the Nile, 1875
Mary Whately
At Cairo, where I live, which is near the middle [of Egypt] there are sometimes four or five showers in the year, sometimes more, but rarely; in the upper provinces only one or two; nothing would grow therefore if the vegetation depended on rain, and though there are heavy dews, these would be quite insufficient; the sun is so powerful that the whole land would be one vast sandy desert, dry and barren, were it not for the wonderful river Nile.

At a certain season every year this river begins to rise gradually; it is supplied from the mountains where it has its source very far off in the middle of Africa, where rain falls copiously at a regular time of year. When it has reached the greatest height (which is ascertained by careful measurement, persons appointed for the purpose watching day and night as the time draws near), the dams which have been artificially made are cut or broken through, and the water overflows the low lands all over the country and fills the numerous canals which cross it in every direction. It would certainly overflow its banks naturally and without this artificial help as soon as the height of those banks had been reached by the water, but much of the country would then be untouched, and some lands get more water than they needed.

From very ancient times the Egyptians knew how to regulate the flow and manage it so that (except on occasions of sudden and excessive rise which now and then make a flood in some places) the land should be properly watered; and their various conquerors had the wisdom to let the natives, who were accustomed to it, have the direction of their great river and its canals. It is probable that the irrigation was much more extended in old times, and that, instead of being as now a strip of cultivated land on each side of the river and the sandy desert beyond—as is the case in a large part of the middle and southern provinces—the canals were more numerous and a far wider tract under cultivation. However, the canals are increasing under the present government, and the famous "sweet water canal" of Suez is alone a proof of what water can do in Egypt.

As we have seen, contemporary nineteenth-century guide books gave very little advice on what women needed to take to Egypt, but Mrs. Carey added from her own experience to this meager advice . . .

What You Need to Bring, 1861
M.L.M. Carey

The Arabs wash well enough, but the iron is beyond them; and therefore the choice for Europeans must frequently be between a lady's-maid, a couple of irons for their own use, or doing without an iron at all.

With no more than the usual stock of linen required at home; a few *common* dresses for the river; the lightest possible shawl or mantle for the daytime; plenty of warm wraps for the night; round hats, neckhandkerchiefs, veils, gauntleted gloves, and large, lined umbrellas, to guard the white skin against the unscrupulous burning of the Egyptian sun; two pair of strong boots for the desert and temple excursions; light ones to baffle mosquitoes at all hours of the day; galoshes, for the mud on the banks of the Nile; elder-flower water for the eyes and the complexion; a preparation of zinc—one grain to ten drops of water—one drop of which applied to the corner of the eye on the point of a fine camel's-hair brush, and repeated night and morning, is an *infallible cure* on the first symptoms of the dreaded Ophthalmia; a large quantity of quassia, to destroy the flies; thermometers and guide books—Murray, Wilkinson, Warburton, etc; and, finally, as there are no M.D.s on the Nile, a good book and a box of medicines—homoeopathic, of course—we considered ourselves armed against all emergencies.

Mrs. Carey also had advice on how to protect oneself from the nuisance of mosquitoes . . .

There is an art in arranging mosquito curtains, as in everything else, and if it is not well understood, these protections are useless. When properly gathered round on the frame round the top of the bed, no mosquitoes can penetrate during the day. A short time before retiring to rest, a vigorous flapping with a fly-flapper or towel should be resorted to, the curtains instantly dropped and carefully tucked in all round. If one small aperture is left, farewell to sleep! Although the Arab servants are supposed to go through these manoeuvres in a masterly style, we always found it necessary to repeat them again for ourselves just before getting into bed. In this last operation, too, unless you are very expert and expeditious, the mosquitoes are on the watch, and will be sure to accompany you. At about sunset these little tormentors of our race congregate upon the window-panes in large numbers. A few moments spent in destroying them at this time will be well repaid. The slightest stroke of a handkerchief puts an end to their fragile existence, and renders that of the traveller so much the more endurable for one day.

Arriving in Egypt, 1779
Eliza Fay

Mrs. Fay and her husband were to travel through Egypt on their way to India where he would work for the East India Company.

23rd July, 1779 We are now off Alexandria, which makes a fine appearance from the sea on a near approach; but being built on low ground, is, as the seamen say "very difficult to hit." We were two days almost abreast of the Town. There is a handsome Pharos or light-house in the new harbour, and it is in all respects far preferable; but no vessels belonging to Christians can anchor there, so we were forced to go into the old one, of which however we escaped the dangers, if any exist.

On the next day the Fays set out to see the local sights.

Having mounted our asses, the use of horses being forbidden to any but musselmens, we sallied forth preceded by a Janizary, with his drawn sword, about three miles over a sandy desert, to see Pompey's Pillar, esteemed to be the finest column in the World. This pillar which is exceedingly lofty, but I have no means of ascertaining its exact height,* is composed of three blocks of Granite; (the pedestal, shaft, and capital, each containing one). When we consider the immense weight of the granite, the raising such masses, appear beyond the powers of man. Although quite unadorned, the proportions are so exquisite, that it must strike every beholder with a kind of awe, which softens into melancholy, when one reflects that the renowned Hero whose name it bears, was treacherously murdered on this very Coast, by the boatmen who were conveying him to Alexandria; while his wretched wife stood on the vessel he had just left, watching his departure, as we may naturally suppose, with inexpressible anxiety. What must have been her agonies at the dreadful event! Though this splendid memorial bears the name of Pompey, it is by many supposed to have been erected in memory of the triumph, gained over him at the battle of Pharsalia.[†]

Leaving more learned heads than mine to settle this disputed point, let us proceed to ancient Alexandria, about a league from the modern town; which presents to the eye an instructive lesson on the instability of all sublumary objects. This once magnificent City, built by the most famous of all Conquerors, and adorned with the most exquisite productions of art, is now little more than heap of Ruins; yet the form of the streets can still be discerned; they were regular, and many of the houses (as I recollect to have read in Athens) had fore-courts bounded by dwarf walls, so much in the manner of our Lincoln's Inn Fields,[**] that the resemblance immediately struck me.

First Impressions, 1826
Anne Katherine Elwood

Mrs. Elwood—an imaginative young lady—and her husband stayed with the British Consul General in Alexandria and ventured out around the city.

---

[*]   The height of the column with its base and Corinthian capital rises 27 meters; the shaft has a circumference of 9 meters and is of pink Aswan granite. (Michael Haag, *Discovery Guide to Egypt*, 1990.)

[†]   Pompey's Pillar was wrongly named such by the Crusaders. It was raised in honor of Diocletian at the very end of the fourth century. (Haag's *Discovery Guide to Egypt*.)

[**]   Lincoln's Inn Fields is an area of London near the Law Courts and very much inhabited by the legal profession.

The road, if road it could be called, was rough, and passed over innumerable hillocks of sand and rubbish. We met several Arab parties. The women hid their faces, and they were riding camels! "An Arab wife," exclaimed Selim, who was acting the part of cicerone, and anxiously showing off his English, for my edification. In a narrow, a very narrow, place, we came suddenly upon a string of loaded camels, which it was necessary for us to pass, and they stretched out their ugly necks one way, and they stretched them out the other, and they looked half-determined to eat me up, as they, stalked, stalked, stalked on close to me, so close that I could have touched them. Charles called out, "Do not be afraid!" and the Janissary told me not to mind; however, I could but think of them very monstrous-looking creatures, and I sincerely wished myself safely in England.

At last we reached Mr Salt's country house (the British consulate), which was built very much in the Italian style, with one long sala in the middle, upon which all the other apartments opened, and with a flat-terraced roof. We were received by the Consul with the utmost civility, but I thought of the Arabian Nights, when, clapping his hands, a black slave made his appearance,* fortunately, however, not with a scimitar to cut off our heads, with which Zobeide treated the Caliph Haroun Al-Raschid and the three Calendars, but bearing refreshments.

From the window we looked over a garden of date-trees and saw Pompey's Pillar; over a dusty, brown and undulating plain we beheld Cleopatra's Needle. A Turkish mosque rose in front—camels with their Arab drivers slowly stalked by, and donkeys with Turkish riders sitting cross-legged on their backs. "'Twas strange 'twas passing strange" to see these objects; what we had so often read, and heard, and talked of; we could scarcely believe our own identity!

Entering Alexandria, 1842
Sophia Poole

The old or western harbour of Alexandria (anciently called Eunostos Portus) is deeper and more secure than the new harbour (which is called Magnus Portus). The former, which was once exclusively appropriated to the vessels of Muslims, is now open to the ships of all nations; and the latter,

---

* It seems unlikely that this was a slave as Salt greatly disapproved of slavery, and it is more likely that the idea suited Mrs. Elwood's lively imagination from her reading of the tales of the Arabian Nights!

which was "the harbour of the infidels", is almost deserted. The entrance of the old harbour is rendered difficult by reefs of rocks, leaving three natural passages, of which the central has the greatest depth of water. The rocks occasion a most unpleasant swell, from which we all suffered, but I especially; and I cannot describe how gratefully I stepped on shore, having passed the smooth water of the harbour. Here already I see so much upon which to remark, that I must indulge myself by writing two or three letters before our arrival in Cairo, where the state of Arabian society being unaltered by European innovations, I hope to observe much that will interest you with respect to the condition of the native female society.

The streets, until we arrived at the part of the town inhabited by Franks, were so narrow that it was extremely formidable to meet anything on our way. They are miserably close, and for the purpose of shade the inhabitants have in many cases thrown matting from roof to roof, extending across the street, with here and there a small aperture to admit light; but the edges of these apertures are generally broken, and the torn matting hanging down: in short, the whole appearance of the streets, for where the sun is excluded by the matting, the deep shade produced by the manner in which the houses are constructed is most welcome in this sunny land; and, indeed, when we arrived at the Frank part of the town, which is in appearance almost European, and where a wide street and a fine open square form a singular contrast to the Arab part of the town, we scarcely congratulated ourselves; for the heat was intense, and we hastened to our hotel, and gratefully enjoyed the breeze which played through the apartments.

Landing in Egypt

From the hotel Sophia Poole watched the people passing in the street—in every variety of costume . . .

I can scarcely describe to you the picturesque attraction of the scene. Among the various peculiarities of dress, feature, and complexion, which characterize the nature of Africa and the East, none are more striking than those which distinguish the noble and hardy western Bedawee, enveloped as he is in his ample woollen shirt, or hooded cloak, and literally clothed suitably for a Russian winter. You will believe that my attention has been directed to the veiled women, exhibiting in their dull disguise no other attraction than a degree of stateliness in their carriage, and a remarkable beauty in their large dark eyes, which, besides being sufficiently distinguished by nature, are rendered more conspicuous by the black border of kohl round the lashes, and by the concealment of the rest of the features. The camel-drivers' cries "O'a," "Guarda,"and "Sakin," resound every where, and at every moment, therefore, you may imagine the noise and confusion in the streets.

In the open space before the hotel there are long trains of camels laden with water-skins, or with bales of merchandise, winding slowly and cautiously along even in this wide place, while their noiseless tread, and their dignified (I might almost say affected) walk, at once distinguished them from all other beast of burden.

I believe I have already seen persons of almost every country bordering on the Mediterranean, and I can convey but a very imperfect idea of such a scene. The contrast between the rich and gaudy habits of the higher classes, and the wretched clothing of the bare-footed poor, while many children of a large growth are perfectly in a state of nudity, produced a most remarkable effect. The number of persons nearly or entirely blind, and especially the aged blind, affected us exceedingly, but we rejoiced in the evident consideration they received from all who had occasion to make room for them to pass. I should imagine that all who have visited this country have remarked the decided respect which is shown to those who are superior in years; and that this respect is naturally rendered to the beggar as well as the prince. In fact, the people are educated in the belief that there is honour in the hoary head, and this glorious sentiment strengthens with their strength, and beautifully influences their conduct.

Many of the poor little infants called forth painfully my sympathy: their heads drooped languidly; and their listless, emaciated limbs showed too plainly that their little race was nearly run; while the evident tenderness of their mothers made me grieved to think what they might be called on to endure.

Desiring to see the Obelisks before the heat of the day, we set out early, and having passed the great square, we entered the field of ruins, and found a number of peasants loitering among the miserable huts, while a few children, in a state of nudity, and extremely unsightly in form, were standing or sitting in the entrances of their dwellings. . . .

Among the mounds we observed the mouths of some of the ancient cisterns; each, with few exceptions, having the hollowed marble base of an ancient column placed over it. The cisterns seem to have extended under a great part of the ancient city; and there remain a sufficient number of them open and in good repair for the supply of the modern town. They have arched or vaulted roofs, which are supported by columns or by square pillars, and some of them have two or three ranges of pillars and arches, one above another, and are very extensive.

We saw little worthy of remark until we reached the Obelisks, which are situated at an angle of the enclosure, almost close to the shore of the new harbour; I mean those obelisks called Cleopatra's Needles. Each is composed of a single rock of red granite, nearly seventy feet in length, and seven feet and a half wide at the base. And here I wondered, as so many have done before me, that the ancient Egyptians contrived to raise such solid masses, and concluded that their knowledge of machinery, of which they have left such extraordinary proofs, must have been remarkable indeed.

Women's Experiences, 1858
Emily Anne Beaufort

> *Arriving in Alexandria and, like others, looking out on the great square of Alexandria, Miss Beaufort and her sister found Egypt very strange, noisy and, perhaps, unexpected. They also found that women travelers could face particular problems . . . although few others speak of such problems.*

The noise without seem to us pretty well balanced by the confusion we immediately fell into within; ladies travelling alone were certainly a legitimate prey to the hosts (I use the word advisedly) of dragomans, old and young, experienced and inexperienced, from the master of eight or ten languages to the stammerer in all but one; natives of every country within three thousand miles, and of every degree of intelligence or stupidity, who obtruded themselves on our notice, at all hours of the day, walking into our *salon*, or not finding us there, coming straight into our bedroom without knocking; as well as cooks and waiters, each with his packet of dirty, thumbed, faded, torn letters of recommendation, which each entreated us to read on the spot at once—all these creatures besieging us one after another, all day and every day during the whole time we remained in Alexandria.

We found several kind, though new, friends in Alexandria, and were induced by their advice to change our plans and to take a boat at once, instead of waiting till we reached Cairo, which is by far the pleasantest plan; but we had fixed our minds upon securing a dragoman of whom we had heard much in England, Achmet Adgwa, and he would not separate himself from his own boat, or leave Alexandria until it was let to some one else; for the latter contingency we could not, of course, wait, and we therefore put an end to the hopes of all our besiegers and closed with him, after inspecting every boat on the Mah'moudieh Canal over and over again, until we were too glad to be obliged to decide finally.

And a beautiful boat our *dahabieh* was; from first to last we thought her the best and most comfortable boat on the Nile.* Our great sail was the largest on the river . . .

Landing in Egypt, 1873
Marianne Brocklehurst
Saturday, November 29, 1873 Great scrimmages. We land at Alexandria, get through the custom house with our new dress improvers on, and behold the Egyptians—first impressions never to be forgotten of the crowds in the streets, the strange and many coloured dresses, the dark faces and white turbans, the fine stately men and veiled and mysterious women. It is almost a shock to plunge so suddenly into the Old World and its fashions which have not yet passed away.

---

* They hired the *dahabieh* in Alexandria, but it is described with other Nile boats later.

We are well lodged at Hotel Abat and presently take a drive round by
Cleopatra's Needle and Pompey's Pillar, by groves of grand old date trees,
many still loaded with fruit, up shocking bad roads where the dust and jog-
gling are not to be thought of by reason of the sunshine, the avenues of 'Eastern' trees, the strings of camels, the picturesque people, the little mosks, the
weird burial grounds, the bright bazaars, and the dahabeeyahs, which we go
to see on the Canal.

Sunday, November 30, 1873 We go by railway to Cairo. We pass Lake Meri-
oti's mud villages, Bedouin encampments, see strange birds, cranes, ibises,
camels ploughing, the fellah at his daily drudgery, and last, towards sunset,
the Pyramids afar, then Cairo with its minarets and domes, and then again
the crowd, with Nubians, Arabs, Persians and even a snake charmer charming
on the pavement, wisely with the fangs extracted from his twisting friends,
and so to Hotel Shepheard, where we take up our abode.

Coming into Alexandria, 1925
Annie Quibell
As the steamer warps its way into harbour one small boat after another puts
out to meet it, decked with the flags of every hotel in Cairo and Alexandria;
amid a babel of noise and the distant waving of handkerchiefs and hats from
the crowded quay. If one is arriving in the East for the first time, it is rather
lively and amusing, but amusement is soon merged in unpleasant excitement when the rush of porters and hotel touts comes on board, and most
people, tired and bewildered with the din and the fighting with wild beasts
to get their luggage through the Customs, are thankful to subside into a
comfortable hotel, or better still, to catch the train to Cairo and get done
with it. So Alexandria is only thought of as a port to land or to leave from
and hardly counts as part of Egypt. Indeed, with only a short time to dispose of, it is best to treat it so, for other things are much more interesting
and much more strange.

From the Windsor Hotel, Alexandria, 1907
Norma Lorimer
Alexandria is Italian—not Oriental. No matter if Pompey's Pillar stands
there—a column not erected by the great Pompey, let me mention, but by a
prefect of Egypt called Pompeius, in the year 312 A.D. No matter if the
minaret of mosques are the first things you see as you enter the bay, in Alexandria you do not feel you are in Egypt, you do not feel the sense of Islam.

In the city there are catacombs, and in them one great tomb, which is entirely without parallel in all Roman-Egypt. If you know your southern Italy well, you will while in Alexandria, feel yourself to be in one of her white cities on the shores of the Mediterranean. The presence of things Mohammedan is very slight, so slight that only now and then are you suddenly brought back to the fact that you are in a city of Oriental people, a people of Islamic faith. This happens when the blue-frocked *fellahin*, so similar in characteristic to their Sicilian brothers who live across the expanse of blue, drop their burdens of white stones on the white sea front and give themselves up in reverence to Allah. Many times in the day they will kneel in prayer, no matter where, but always mindful that their faces are turned towards the Kaaba of Mecca.

From my balcony I can see the exquisite curve of the sickle-shaped bay which is called the East Port. The two ports of Alexandria are separated by a causeway which Ptolemy the First built to connect the island of Pharos. . . . The bay on the east was called the Great Harbour, and the one on the west Eunostos. The west harbour is the busy one, the one you enter in landing at Alexandria. It has a breakwater a mile and three-quarters long, running out into it. It is the east bay I know best, and shall always remember with ecstasy. In my memory it will ever lie all glittering blue and white in the sunshine, all calm and at rest under the immense night-sky of moon and stars.

I shall never forget that last night; I could hear the stillness; it forced itself upon my ears and unnerved my senses—the moon hung like a globe of pale light above the medieval port of Kait Bey. That white fort, which stands today a beautiful ruin, sea-girt and flower-strewn, was built in the fifteenth century on the site of the ancient Pharos of Alexander's city, which in its day was built on the site of the Temple of Isis.

As today, one of the sights of Alexandria often visited by travelers and tourists was 'Pompey's Pillar.' Sometimes the British sailors (known as 'tars') from visiting ships used their skills learned climbing the masts of their ships to scale the monument.

Seeing the Sights, 1884
Constance Gordon Cummings
It consists of a single block of rose-coloured granite, sixty-four French feet in height, and eight feet, four inches in diameter. The pedestal is about ten feet high, and is also of granite. The column is surmounted by a capital somewhat in a Corinthian style. Several sailors have been on its top, as appears from the names of ships written in large black letters at various elevations. About the middle of the shaft I remarked the following inscription:

H.M.S.
GLASGOW
MARCH 1827

And on the ornament on the top of the column "George Canning," written in very legible characters. The tars must have had some difficulty getting up, the surface of the column being as smooth as polished marble. I could see no ancient inscription on any part—nor even the traces of one. In all my wanderings I have seen nothing in the shape of a monument that combined so much beauty and solidity as that of Pompey's Pillar.

The Pacha's Palace, 1861
M.L.M. Carey
The Palace is situated near the entrance of the Harbour. Its rooms are very handsomely furnished and hung with damask, and the floors beautifully inlaid with different kinds of wood. They are for the most part staterooms, in which the Pasha receives his own and foreign officers, and visitors. Our guide Mohammed's version was, that in one he "held his Parliament," in another his "Church," and in a third he showed the divan upon which he reposes for a time after dinner, leaning back against one pillow, whilst two other very large ones are placed in front, upon each of which, Mohamed said, one leg reclines, "*because he is so fat.*" And this was uttered in a tone of intense admiration! The chandeliers in two of the apartments are magnificent, and come from Paris; indeed, all the decorations are of French workmanship. The Hareem is close by: and the ladies walk in the surrounding garden. The Pashas are allowed four wives by the Koran, but Mohammed told us confidentially that they owned about sixty or seventy.

A Visit from Cairo, 1861
Ellen Chennells

Employed as a governess by the Pasha's family, Miss Chennels was visiting Alexandria from Cairo on the occasion of the return of the Pasha from Constantinople.

Great preparations were being made for illuminating the town in honour of his Highness's return. The whole front of the hotel was hung with coloured lamps. They were at every window, and this reconciled me in some measure to having a back room, as I should have been kept awake the whole night by the glare and heat, as well as the noise below on the Grande Place. The illuminations were to last for three nights!

The paving of the Grande Place was at last finished, and it looked very handsome. It is of great breadth, and still greater length. All down the centre is a promenade with a double row of trees on each side, and between this centre and the houses is again a broad carriage-road and excellent pavements. To the east are several handsome streets, which connect it with the roads leading to Ramleh, and to the Mahmoudieh Canal.* All the chief people of Alexandria have houses either on the canal or at Ramleh.

The English colony is a large one, and we made many acquaintances. One friend introduced another, and we soon formed a large social circle, so we hoped our stay may be prolonged, if only we could be at Ramleh and not at Alexandria. The great want of this last town is a marine promenade. It is close upon the sea, but the whole coast of the town is taken up by the backs of wretched houses. The shore is neither beach, sands, nor shingle, such as we have in England, but a loose substance in which you sink; and every opening to the sea is contaminated by bad drainage.

On the 14th, as I went down to breakfast, a prodigious firing of guns announced that the Mahroussah had entered the harbour. Presently after there was military music, and a number of soldiers passed down the Grande Place to meet his Highness at the landing-place. Then another volley told us that the Khedive had landed.

---

* This canal was built in the time of Pacha Mehemet Ali to join Alexandria to the Nile.

Onward to Cairo, 1836
Sarah Haight

*The journey the Haights (the first American 'tourists' to
Egypt) expected to last two days went on for six . . .*

We found that our boat had gone some hours, and the agent of the company
had supplied our order with a little *kanjee*, which, as he said, had the recommendation of being new, and not requiring to be sunk to rid it of vermin before it was fit to use. There being a fine north wind at the time, we naturally
supposed that we could run the short distance to Cairo in a day and a half; so
we made a virtue of necessity, and embarked cheerfully, with an assurance
from the agent that only six hands were necessary, as we should not have to
tow the boat a mile. We ran on a few hours in gallant style, stemming the
current at the rate of five or six miles per hour. When sundown came, the
wind fell; and then it is the duty of the crew to get out with their tow-line
and drag the boat along the shore, taking advantage of the eddies. No such
thing, however, with us. Our captain gave the order for supper; and as after
that an Arab must sleep, and there is no waking him without the whip, we lay
quietly moored alongside the bank all night; next morning there was no wind;
the men dragged during the morning at one mile per hour.

Onward to Cairo, 1988
Bettina Selby

*Bettina Selby is a modern traveler—rather than a tourist—
who has cycled her way around much of the world.*

It was from this Mediterranean coast that I planned to start my journey. I
thought I would ride in a leisurely manner along the seaboard of the delta,
from Alexandria to Port Said, seeing all the famous places that had been a
legend to me for so long. Only after that would I head south to begin the
4500-mile trek which would eventually take me deep into the heart of Africa,

where the Nile has its high, remote beginnings. So I did not linger in Cairo, for I would explore it later when my route led me back to it in a week or two. Instead I headed straight down to Alexandria on the desert road—and suddenly, from a pleasant temperature of 80°F I was plunged into a cold, wet world, no better than that I had left behind in England.

The winter storms were early. Huge waves came crashing in over the Corniche; the sky was a lowering dark greyish purple; water flowed dankly down the sides of buildings and gushed out of broken drainpipes and blocked gutters. It was all depressingly monochrome; only at night was the greyness relieved, when the sky was lit up along the seaward horizon with noisy displays of forked lightning.

Somewhere beneath the wet cobblestones lay the lost remains of Alexander the Great. "Uneasy will be the city where his body lies" had said the chief priest of Memphis, refusing its burial and instructing the bearers to return with it to Alexander's own city. It is not the only treasure that lies below the nineteenth century Frenchified town. Cleopatra's fabulous library had been housed here, and one of the seven wonders of the ancient world, the Tower of Pharos, had lighted the way for ships sailing into its two fine harbours. It was a city that had vied in greatness and scholarship with Athens and Byzantium. From here Ptolemy had mapped the world and decided upon the source of the Nile, and here Euclid had founded his school of mathematics. Art, philosophy, and theology had all flourished here for centuries until the tide of barbarism swept over it and its splendid buildings were broken up to become quarries for lesser ones. Now, occasionally, a crack opens and a remnant of the Graeco-Roman world breaks surface. One of these, a small pretty Roman theatre, had recently been unearthed and as I stood looking at it from the shelter of an open shed where the excavators' shovels were kept, I realised that in this dismal wintry weather I could get no feeling at all of that brilliant vanished world; it needs sunshine to dream of Alexander.

Through the Delta towards Cairo, 1779
Eliza Fay

Early travelers would cross the land to the Nile and then sail up the river from Rosetta to Cairo, until the canal link was built from Alexandria to the Nile.

Rosetta is a most beautiful place, surrounded by groves of lemon and orange trees; and the flat roofs of the houses have gardens on them, whose fragrance perfumes the air. There is an appearance of cleanliness in it, the more gratifying to an English eye, because seldom met within any degree, so as to remind us of what we are accustomed to at home. The landscape around was interesting from its novelty, and became peculiarly so on considering it as the country where the children of Israel sojourned. . . .

You will readily conceive that, as I drew near Grand Cairo, and beheld those prodigies of human labour, the Pyramids of Egypt, these sensations were still more strongly awakened; and I could have fancied myself an inhabitant of a world, long passed away; for who can look on buildings, reared (moderately computing the time) above *three thousand years ago*, without seeming to step back as it were, in existence, and live through days, now gone by, and sunk in oblivion "like a tale that is told."

Situated as I was, the Pyramids were not all in sight, but I was assured that those which came under my eye, were decidedly the most magnificent. We went out of our way to view them nearer, and by the aid of a telescope, were enabled to form a tolerable idea of their construction. It has been supposed by many that the Israelites built these Pyramids, during their bondage in Egypt, and I rather incline to that opinion; for, altho' it has lately been proved that they were intended to serve as repositories for the dead, yet each, being said to contain only one sarcophagus, this circumstance, and their very form, rendered them of so little comparative use, that most probably, they were raised to furnish employment for multitudes of unfortunate slaves; and who more aptly agree with this description, than the wretched posterity of Jacob?

Women of the Delta, 1827
Anne Katherine Elwood

In our walks, the women in the villages, and on the banks, eyed us with the most intense curiosity. Some of them were much ornamented with gold, and their veils were tied up between the eyes with a string of small silver bells. Their chief occupation appeared to be the drawing and carrying of water; the children, generally in a complete state of nature, were frequently much frightened at our appearance, and one of them, on meeting us, ran quickly away, crying out "Mamma, Mamma," in as broad a tone as any Scotch boy could have done.

The men laughed good-naturedly, but not disrespectfully at our foreign appearance, and turned away their eyes, exclaiming, "Haram!" One

morning I found myself suddenly caught hold of, and turning, in some degree of alarm, I beheld a woman in the blue dress of the country, completely
veiled, offering her hand, and exclaiming, at the utmost pitch of her voice,
"Salamat! Salamat!" I returned the salutation, and gave her my hand in return, upon which she made signs for me to follow her to her house, in a village at a little distance, but I was afraid of accompanying her, as the
invitation did not extend to C. (her husband). She, however, offered her
hand to him in a very friendly manner, and seemed very well pleased at his
putting some piastres into it.

Alexandria to the Nile, 1849
Florence Nightingale
Here we are, our second step in Egypt. We left Alexandria on the 25th [No-
vember] at 7 o'clock a.m. We were towed up the Mahmoudieh Canal by a
little steam-tug to Atfeh, which we reached at 5 p.m. The canal perfectly
uninteresting; the day gloomy. I was not very well so stayed below from
Alexandria to Cairo. At Atfeh, we were seventy people on board a boat built
for twenty-five. . . . Then first I saw the solemn Nile, flowing gloomily; a
ray of sun shining out of the cloudy horizon from the setting sun upon him.
He was still very high [during the inundation]; the current rapid. The
solemnity is not produced by sluggishness, but by the dark colour of the
water, and enormous varying character of the flat plain, a fringe of date trees
here and there, nothing else. By six o'clock p.m. we were off, the moon shining, and the stars all out.

On board our steamer, where there is no sleeping place, but a ladies' cabin,
where you sit round all night, nine to the square yard, we have hardly any
English, no Indians, for fortunately it is not the transit week.* Our condition
is not improved physically, for the boat is equally full of children, screaming
all night, and the children are much fuller of vermin; but mentally it is, for
the screams are Egyptian, Greek, Italian and Turkish screams and the fleas,
etc. are Circassian, Chinese and Coptic fleas.

---

*   Travelers to and from India transited Egypt to and from Suez by the 'overland'
     route. Her reference to 'Indians' is to these travelers to and from the sub-continent.

The Impact of the Nile, the Canals and the Weather, 1880
Mary Whately

Mary Whately had been visiting and living in Egypt for
some years when she wrote.

When I first came here, the whole region where the modern town of Is-
maila stands was nothing but a sandy waste, inhabited by gazelles and
desert foxes. Now the great work of the new canals—the salt water one
connecting the Mediterranean and Red Seas, and the sweet water one
which conducts the Nile water—have combined to make a delightful spot;
gardens rose like magic, grapes and even strawberries grow where twenty
years ago burning dry sand and pebbles lay, and thickets of feathery bamboo and flowering shrubs meet the eye and look the more attractive from
the waste all round. "The parched land shall become a pool, and the thirsty
land springs of water." Would that those who laboured in that wondrous
canal had known the blessed spiritual refreshing of which the entrance of
the water into the desert land affords so beautiful a type!

But to return to the river: its rise does not begin till summer, and during
the winter it is gradually shrinking and retiring. The winter of Egypt is
very unlike our English ideas of that season; there is comparatively very
little cold; the sights are indeed sharp, and sometimes a cold wind blows,
but you would say it cannot be very severe when frost is almost an unknown
thing. Some labourers in the country near Cairo once found a very thin
film of ice, at daybreak, on some shallow water channels, and reported that
the water was bewitched and would not flow! So very rare was the wonder
that none of them had ever seen such a thing before. . . . The sun is generally warm at midday, and the people seek out sunny corners to sit in, especially the old; and now and then a party of labourers will light a fire of
brushwood and sit round it in a field. . . .

By the middle of May, the intense heat of summer has usually set in and
the fields look dry and brown—unless watered with much labour from the
canals; the very weeds, except the thistles, which seem to need scarcely any
water, are withered up . . .

For the native of the soil, I do not think that great heat is the cause of
as much suffering among the poor as great cold. The Egyptian . . . does
not mind heat, and prefers summer in general to winter; if he has to labour

hard, of course he must be greatly fatigued in the hot weather, but at any rate his family do not suffer with him. Cold falls *most* heavily on little children and aged persons, while these in the hot weather here sit in the shade of their mud walls, and as they do not mind dust and vermin, which abound, they appear happy in their way—and certainly the comforts within their reach are cheap. Fuel and warm clothes, as you know too well, are not.

First Sight of the Pyramids, 1846
Harriet Martineau

Till 3 p.m., there was little variety in the scenery. I was most struck with the singular colouring—the diversity of browns. There was the turbid river, of vast width, rolling between earthy banks; and on these banks were mud villages, with their conical pigeon-houses. The minarets and the Sheikhs' tombs were fawn-coloured and white; and the only variety of these shades of the same colour was in the scanty herbage, which was so coarse as to be almost of no colour at all. But the distinctness of outline, the glow of the brown, and the vividness of light and shade, were truly a feast to the eye. At 3 o'clock, when approaching Werdan, we saw spreading acacias growing out of the dusty soil; and palms were clustered thickly about the town; and at last we had something beyond the banks to look at—a sandy ridge which extends from Tunis to the Nile.

When we had passed Werdan, about 4 p.m., Mr E. came to me with a mysterious countenance, and asked me if I should like to view the Pyramids. We stole past the groups of careless talkers, and went to the bows of the boat, where I was mounted on boxes and coops, and shown where to look. In a minute I saw them, emerging from behind a sand hill. They were very small; for we were still twenty-five miles from Cairo; but there could be no doubt about them for a moment; so sharp and clear were the light and shadow on the two sides we saw.

I had been assured I would not be disappointed in the first sight of the Pyramids; and I had maintained that I could not be disappointed, as of all the wonders of the world, this is the most literal, and, to the dweller among mountains, like myself, the least imposing. I now found both my informant and myself mistaken. So far from being disappointed, I was filled with surprise and awe: and so far was I from having anticipated what I saw, that I felt as if I had never before looked upon anything so new as those clear and vivid masses, with their sharp blue shadows, standing firm and alone on their expanse of sand.

In a few minutes, they appeared to grow wonderfully larger; and they looked lustrous and most imposing in the evening light. This impression of the Pyramids was never fully renewed. I admired them every evening from my window at Cairo; and I took the surest means of convincing myself of their vastness, by going to the top of the largest; but this first view of them was the most moving: and I cannot think of it without emotion.

Between this time and sunset, the most remarkable thing was the infinity of birds. I saw a few pelicans and many cormorants; but the flocks—I might say the shoals—of wild ducks and geese which peopled the air, gave me a stronger impression of the of the wildness of the country, the foreign character of the scenery, than anything I had yet seen.

Towards Cairo and Arriving, 1855
Lady Tobin

The sun rose in all his glory the following day upon a lovely scene. Scarcely a cloud was in the sky, the Nile was covered with boats and rafts, and many five palms and sycamores grew on either bank, some of which reared their tall heads out of the river, so high was the inundation. The small towns with their minarets, and the mud villages, looked most picturesque as we approached them, but were sadly disappointing in reality. Their inhabitants seemed poor and wretched in the extreme, and the children ran around quite naked.

On Wednesday, October 12th, the Pyramids were in sight. Wonderful and mysterious creations! They stood distinct in the desert before us. No other object was there to turn our attention from their clear outlines. We were not even in motion, for the wind had become directly contrary.

As we approached the capital, the scenery became more and more interesting. The palace of Shoobra was pointed out to us on our left. At noon we came to anchor at Boulak, the port of Cairo, and immediately despatched Antonio to secure donkeys. He soon returned with the number required, and we were thereby enabled to mount them without being torn in pieces by rival competitors.

We ladies found ourselves ill at ease on the Arab saddles just at first; but speedily learnt to think them as comfortable as any others, though not so safe—according to *our* mode of riding—as they are for Egyptian women, who sit astride upon them.

We passed quickly through some narrow streets; up the broad road that leads from Boulak direct to Cairo; and entered the city, by the Uzbekeeh gate, into the immense square of that name, which contains about 150,000 square feet. It is laid out partly as a garden, partly in fields; and trees are planted along the banks of the canal which surrounds it; a road runs through the centre. We were shown on our left the house in which [the Frenchman] Kleber was murdered. On the one side of the Uzbekeeh is the Copt quarter; on another that of the Franks [foreigners], where the best hotels are situated.

Grand Cairo, though bereft of her ancient grandeur, is still, even in her decay a noble city. Many were the objects of interest that attracted our gaze as we proceeded.

Setting Out by Train, 1907
Norma Lorimer
In the busy station which was in the wildest confusion, congested by a shipload of passengers of all nationalities embarking themselves on one small train for Cairo, I saw a stately Arab spread out his prayer mat close to the wall of the stationmaster's office, the one spot free from luggage, and commence his evening prayer. As though alone in the desert or before the sacred *mihrab* of a mosque, he stood for some moments at the end of his mat with folded hands and closed eyes. He seemed to be listening to some voice speaking to his ears alone, then suddenly he dropped to his knees and touched the mat three times with his forehead. For at least ten minutes he prayed, now in perfect silence, now in chanting monotones, with that peculiar intonation which is intimately connected with the Koran as a curate's voice is associated with the litany. The engines shrieked, the European passengers lost their manners and their seats in their noisy nervousness about their luggage, but that unmindful Moslem prayed on. At the very last moment, when the guard, and the engine-driver, and the stationmaster, and I think the stoker and the porters, had all agreed with each other by mystical signs and glances that the train might make a start, he picked up his mat, put on his shoes and shouldered his *goullah* of unbaked clay. On his back was a sweeping bundle of green sugar-cane, a brown-and-white bag full of only an Eastern could have told what, and a meek black kid, which with Christian resignation allowed its legs to be tied together round his neck. With that scorn of hurry which gives the Arab his 'Christ-like' dignity, he walked across the platform and stepped majestically into the slowly moving train. I was lost in admiration.

2
Cairo

The great, sprawling city of Cairo has always amazed the traveler—with its beauty, with the crush of humanity through its narrow, winding streets and, later, along the great boulevards, with its amazing variety. The travelers—in the past—enjoyed the markets, visited the ladies of the harems, ventured into the baths, and looked onward up the Nile where they were to travel.

Cairo was—and is—the highlight of any visit to Egypt. Although, of course, much has changed since many of these accounts were written, it has for centuries been a great throbbing city—but, like most cities, a city both with much beauty and excitement and much poverty and hardship. Everywhere there are people—once crushed into the narrow crowded streets along with donkeys and camels, now crowded with endless traffic. Travelers then as now threaded their way through the crowds to admire the city with its splendid architecture, fine views from the surrounding hills, its splendid great mosques and wondrous bazaars bursting with color and choice.

The travelers were—as travelers today are—often overwhelmed by the city.

The Rose of Cities, November 1849
Florence Nightingale

No one ever talks about the beauty of Cairo, ever gives you the least idea of this surpassing city. I thought it was a place to buy stores at and pass through on one's way to India, instead of its being the rose of cities, the garden of the desert, the pearl of Moorish architecture, the fairest, really the fairest, place of earth below. It reminds me always of Sirius; I can't tell why except that Sirius has the silveriest light in heaven above, and Cairo has the same radiant look on earth below; and I shall never look at Sirius in future years without thinking of her.

Arriving up the Nile, 1842
Sophia Poole

We shortly after arrived at Boulak, the principal port of Cairo, and with our arrival came the necessity that I and my sister-in-law should equip ourselves in Eastern costume.* There was no small difficulty in this ceremony, and when completed, it was stifling to a degree not to be forgotten. Imagine the face covered closely by a muslin veil, double at the upper part, the eyes only uncovered, and over a dress of coloured silk an overwhelming covering of black silk, extending, in my idea, in every direction; so that, having nothing free but my eyes, I looked with dismay at the high bank I had to climb, and the donkey I must mount, which was waiting for me at the summit. Nothing can be more awkward and uncomfortable than this riding dress; and if I had any chance of attaining my object without assuming it, I should never adopt it; but in English costume I should not gain admittance into many harems; besides, the knowledge that a Muslim believes a curse to rest on the "seer and the seen," makes one anxious not to expose to passers-by what they would deem a misfortune, or ourselves to their malediction.

The Countess had traveled in Syria and Palestine and crossed into Egypt from Gaza through the desert, so her arrival was from a very different direction than that of most foreign travelers. . . .

---

* Sophia Poole's brother, Edward Lane, lived in Cairo not among the foreigners but among the Egyptians, dressed as an Egyptian, and was returning to his home in that quarter.

Arriving from the Desert, 1844
Countess Hahn Hahn
I found myself again upon the old and too-well-known desert plain. How long and how broad it is, Heaven only knows—with again single cultivated spots to the right, and to the left also, again, nothing but the accustomed mountain-chain of Arabia, which bears the name Mokkatam. It must be said, however, that the plain was no longer deserted by man. The villagers were carrying to the city oranges and lemons, dates and bananas; whilst from the latter were issuing travellers, traders and merchants, trains of camels and asses, soldiers exercising their horses—in short, the further we proceeded the more apparent became the traffic that generally prevails in the neighbourhood of a large city. At length carriages too! Folks driving in European fashion! What an unusual sight! In a small *drosky*, Ibrahim Pasha, in a *coupe* with four horses, Abbas Pasha!* Running footmen were in front—a fashion now quite extinct in Europe.

On the declivity of the Mokkatam rises the citadel, the palace of the ruler of Egypt; at its feet lies the great, great city, with its obedient people. A multitude of elegant minarets shot distinctly aloft out of the indistinct throng of habitations which are surrounded, and, as it were, grown over with palms and other trees. In the foreground a row of windmills, elevated upon sand-hills, present their ungraceful forms; and single large monuments disengage themselves from the multitude of tombs visible in the extensive burying-grounds. But in the background, on the other side of the city, are one or two mighty structures. Are they hills?—They are too regular. Are they buildings? They are too gigantic. They are the pyramids of Gîzeh. They command and domineer over the picture, and attract the gaze with a magnetic power. And with justice. Like the pictures of a family in a great ancestral hall, do they begin the series of development which the human race passes through in that sphere in which the intellectual idea envelopes itself in a sensual garment, in order to make the impression which we call Art. In these creations must original faculties have been active; not material only—but also spiritual.

On Arrival from Alexandria, 1836
Sarah Haight
We first rode through a great square, next squeezed through a narrow and crowded street, then plunged under an archway into an alley so narrow as to admit only one horse at a time. Again crossing another apology for a street,

---

* The sons of the ruler (or viceroy) Mehemet Ali Pasha.

we rode directly into a house, where we groped about for ten minutes, threading dark passages, without being able to see each other, under the vaulted basements of a square of houses, and guided by the voice of the donkey boys, who piloted us through these nether regions. We emerged again into open day, and passing a huge wooden gate, we found ourselves in the Frank Quarter,* and were set down opposite a low-arched doorway, into which we were desired to walk. As we had to spend some time at Cairo, my heart failed me when I saw we were to be ushered into a stable for our abode.

Frequently, "ce n'est que le premier pas qui coute," so in this instance, after clearing the barrier of low-arched passages and double gates, we came to a spacious court, surrounded by a fine four-storey house, with beautiful and singular arabesque carvings in stone and wood. Here we found the best apartments—those that had been used for the *hareem* of the former possessor—allocated to our use.

When she woke next morning, she was delighted by the view.

Being in the highest storey of the house (always considered the best and pleasantest in Oriental houses), my apartment overlooked all the houses around . . . [She threw on a robe-de-chambre and went out onto the terrace.] Turning suddenly round, I was astonished and surprised to see the three great Pyramids, appearing so near to me that one might walk to their base, ascend to the top, and return to breakfast. This apparent proximity is caused first by their vast height, and secondly by the extreme transparency of the medium through which they are viewed. It was to me a glorious sight, and as gratifying as it was unexpected . . .

At the early hour at which I first saw the Pyramids, the western horizon had yet its deep blue tinge of departing night; and the light, cream-coloured stone of those gigantic masses being lighted up by the rising sun, they stood in extraordinarily bold relief against the western sky.

---

*   Cairo was divided into districts which were closed at night by gates. The 'Frank Quarter' was the quarter in which the foreigners lived—'Frank' being the popular term for 'foreigners.'

Up the Nile with the Viceroy, 1861
Ellen Chennells

*Accompanying one of her pupils, the English governess was
arriving on the royal yacht from Alexandria.*

. . . the steam was got up, and proceeding up the river, the Dar-el-
Memlekeh (Royal Abode), as Cairo was originally called, burst into view.

At that distance, like all Eastern cities, it looks most beautiful, pleasing
and charming. Then it appears to great advantage, with its hundreds of
white tapering minarets, whose fairy-like points rise majestically towards
the sky. Soon we catch a glimpse of its oriental-looking houses, with their
exquisitely interlaced Mushrebeehs; then loom forth palm and sycamore
trees, all of which have a most picturesque effect, and yet, knowing as I well
do, every nook and crook of it, I could not help comparing it in my own
mind to a vain old dowager of *haut ton*, who had had herself made beautiful
by means of all the appliances of art and cosmetics. Such a haughty dame,
viewed at a distance, looks most beautiful; and as she enters a drawing room

Entrance to the El Azhar

with that grace and elegance which appears to be the prerogative of high birth, a murmuring is heard among the gay throng, and the ear of the listener catches the words, "What a charming creature!" But when you draw near to the object of that adulation, Heaven help us—to use a vulgarism— what a take in! . . . Well, so it is with Grand Cairo, for as soon as it is entered a nausea affects you, the sight becomes disgusted with its filthiness. Those houses, which look at a distance so pretty, are covered with dust, and ruinous in appearance; those balconies so beautifully sculptured are borne up by wooden supporters; the serpentine winding streets are full of filth and dirt; mangy dogs are stretched full length across them, basking in the mid-day sun, who never move an inch for horses, donkeys, or camels . . . Nevertheless, people never hurt them . . . and prize them for their usefulness, since they are the scavengers of all the cities and villages . . .

Our Rides through Cairo, 1836
Sarah Haight

The first thing to be done was for Mustafa to engage a certain number of sprightly donkeys by the week, with such a set of donkey-boys as would agree to make themselves clean and tidy, and keep so.

Then, after counting out to his highness a given number of piastres to pay out-door expenses, or for such matters as we might have occasion to purchase during our rides, together with *backshee* to be distributed at all times, of all of which the *spendidor* keeps a correct account, . . . we set out upon our first voyage of discovery through the town, old Mustafa leading the van, and we all in Indian file behind him. When we got into a thronged street, this worthy of ours, in order to clear the way, never compromised his dignity so much as to speak to the *canaille*, but with his silver-headed bamboo staff of office and insignia of authority, he laid about him on the shoulders, heads and faces of all who happened to be in the way. Our whole passage through every crowded street was opened by these blows, none of them of the most gentle kind, for I sometimes thought they would have cracked some of the shorn crowns of the poor camel drivers and water-carriers. All our remonstrations were of no avail with him. He would, in spite of us, proceed *en regie*, and perform his official duties . . .

First Impressions, November 4, 1845
Isabel Romer

This morning I awoke in a new world! The sun, the bright sunshine of Egypt, streamed in golden rays through the curtains of the vast projecting window of my bedchamber; strange, unwonted noises were heard in the street below, and roused me from my dream of home; I jumped out of bed, not quite sure where I was, and, throwing open the casement, my eyes were greeted with such Oriental groupings that soon convinced me of my whereabouts, and riveted me to the spot. Early as the hour was, the space before the hotel was already full of life, and movement, and noise (for nothing here is done quietly). Near the door were kneeling two camels laden with stones, and growling vehemently; notwithstanding the blows rained upon them by their drivers, they would not get up—they had been overloaded or badly loaded, and refused to rise until their burthens should be more equitably disposed of; and this, their firm determination, they conveyed to their task masters by sounds and gestures not to be misunderstood. . . . And they were right, the sagacious brutes! for the men, finding the violent measures availed them nothing in such a dispute, decided upon lightening their loads; and no sooner was that done than the camels arose and cheerfully stalked away, turning their patient heads from side to side, and meekly looking down with half-closed eyes upon their drivers, as though they had never been at issue with them.

In the centre of the place were gathered together twenty or thirty donkeys, all ready caparisoned for hire, with high-fronted saddles covered with red morocco and carpets spread over them, fit to carry gentleman or lady; and their noisy drivers standing by, vociferating among themselves as Arabs only can do, their dark slender limbs covered merely with a blue cotton shirt, the sleeves of which are gracefully drawn up with cords that cross the shoulders, their swarthy faces surmounted by a voluminous white turban, scarcely one among them possessing two eyes, such are the ravages of ophthalmia in this clime!

And lo! immediately facing my window rises the tall minaret of a neighbouring mosque, and from its upper gallery sounded the deep-toned cry of the Muezzin calling the Faithful to prayer—sounds long unheard by me, yet well remembered, and bringing with them happy associations of my first wanderings in the East!

So Much for an Artist to See, 1899
E.M. Merrick

Miss Merrick watched the swirling crowds of Cairo with the eyes of an artist, and recorded what she saw in words and pictures.

It was always a moving scene, and the novelty of dresses and faces perfectly enchanting. But when I went into the bazaars I was even more charmed, and could quite agree with one of the Royal Academicians, who told me I should find a picture at every corner. I made many rapid sketches there, and often before I could reach my room with them on return to the hotel they were sold. Water-carriers, with their quaint water-skins and brass cups, which they banged together; Bedouins on their camels; donkeys, with attendant donkey-boys—I made them all sit for their portraits, with more or less success. And in making sketches in Cairo I nearly always found the Arabs kind and courteous, anxious to lend me a chair; and sometimes, in the bazaars, inviting me to sit inside their little shops out of the way of the inquisitive crowd which always gathered round, and bringing me a cup of Persian tea or coffee. "Backsheesh" was very often asked if I was suspected of making a sketch of one of them, but they always were amused and laughed if I suggested they should give *me* "backsheesh" for painting *them*.

First Impressions, 1876
Mathilda Bethune-Edwards

When I left England little more than a fortnight ago, the weather was wintry; every one was wrapt to the chin in furs, and fires were blazing on every hearth. We were now wearing the thinnest summer clothing to be had, it was much too hot to stir out after ten o'clock in the morning, and the only way to enjoy life was to lie perfectly still, with Lane's *Modern Egyptians* in your hand, and a bottle of Nile water within reach.

My chief amusement during those hours of imprisonment were the birds and flowers of our garden. From five to nine or ten o'clock in the morning we could have doors or windows open, and the bullfinches were so tame that they would sing on the very threshold. The singing lasted all day long. What with the palm-trees and rose-bushes and the bulbuls I fancied myself in some garden of Eastern story.

The principal work of the house was done by handsome Nubians dressed in bright blue cotton garments reaching from head to foot, who on hearing the accustomed clapping of the hands, would answer the summons with a good natured "Esh-tereed?" "What do you want?" The garden and the birds, and the beautiful Nubians, made up a picture which every now and then the shrill voice of the hotel director would spoil. He was not at all a disagreeable person otherwise, but he had a habit of screaming out to the servants in the harshest tones of a very harsh voice, which was quite out of keeping with the scene. If I lived a hundred years I could not forgive him . . .

Cairo Seen by a Resident, 1873
Marianne North
I confess to having looked at Egyptian things from a purely picturesque point of view, and was scolded for this by the Cairo clergyman's wife: "Dear, dear, like all travellers, you wander hither and thither and see nothing with a proper object, everything from a false point of view. I suppose you never consider that on the precise spot where those Mameluke tombs stand the Israelites made their bricks without straw!" And her husband took us to the top of a hill and showed us the *very* stone on which Moses stood to count the Israelites as they passed out of Egypt! At any rate fine views were still to be got there, and the Nile valley and pyramids of Ghizeh and Dakkarah seemed a perfect sea of green vegetation, with but little desert in proportion. We picked up quantities of fossilised sea-shells on that hill top, and my suggestion that they might have been the remains of a picnic the Jews had before they started, was not received favourably; yet it was difficult the good man who, when a doctor in India, had stayed through a terrible time of cholera, taking care of the people when all others had fled.

The Scene from my Balcony, 1907
Norma Lorimer
However long I stay in Cairo, this quarter of the Ezbekiyeh will always maintain a paramount place in my vision of the city. It is so strange, so picturesque, so unceasingly amusing, so changingly changing, so simple and yet so depraved. For the first three days I thought I should never leave my balcony. Why should I? Here was the most delightful feast of colour and oriental happenings you could ever hope to find. Here the Egypt of the Pyramids, the Egypt of the tombs of the kings and of the Sphinx, was forgotten—and the city of the Caliphs did not matter. Let them wait; here was the East, the East I loved the most, the East of poverty and simplicity. . . .

How could I ever tire of watching the life that flows and loiters along that wide pavement? The wall is broad enough to afford on its flat top excellent quarters for the stock-in-trade of the various merchants, who sell anything from Roman Catholic church bric-a-brac to exquisite Oriental embroideries, whose value they know less about than the quality or use of the European trousers and coats that hang from the points of the high railings. You have to leave the pavement now and then, for decency will not allow you to disturb the circle of brown-limbed donkey-boys—as slim and active in their one white garment as the athletes of old Greece—who squat around a circular tray raised a few feet from the ground, covered with tempting viands.

Countless little blue bowls full of various pickles and savoury morsels cover the round table, which is always arranged with a fascinating delicacy and refinement. Each customer buys a piece of bread from the bread vendor close by, who carries a stack of it on his head with the balance of an acrobat. It is scone-shaped, but so raised in the baking that it is quite hollow inside; he makes a pouch of it by tearing an opening in it, and then selects from each blue bowl a morsel of what his stomach most desires. The *bonnes bouches* are stowed away in the bread pocket, to be eaten at leisure.

Passing in the Streets, 1852
Ida Pfeiffer

Many of the streets were so narrow, that when loaded camels meet, one party must always be led into a by-street until the others had passed. In these narrow lanes I continually encountered crowds of passengers, so that I really felt quite anxious, and wondered how I should find my way through. People mounted on horses and donkeys tower above the moving mass; but the asses themselves appear like pigmies beside the high, lofty-looking camels, which do not lose

A Street in Cairo

their proud demeanour even under their heavy burdens. Men often slip by under the heads of the camels. The riders keep as close as possible to the houses, and the mass of pedestrians winds dexterously between. There are water-carriers, vendors of goods, numerous blind men groping their way with sticks, and bearing baskets with fruit, bread, and other provisions for sale; numerous children, some of them running about the streets, and others playing before the house-doors; and lastly, the Egyptian ladies, who ride on asses to pay their visits, and come in long processions with their children and negro servants.

Let the reader further imagine the cries of the vendors, the shouting of the drivers and passengers, the terrified screams of flying women and children, the quarrels which frequently arise, and the peculiar noisiness and talkativeness of these people, and he can fancy what an effect this must have on the nerves of a stranger. I was in mortal fear at every step, and on reaching home in the evening felt quite unwell; but as I never once saw an accident occur, I at length accustomed myself to the hubbub, and could follow my guide where the crowd was thickest without feeling uneasy.

The streets, as they may be properly called, the lanes of Cairo are splashed with water several times in a day; fountains and large vessels of water are also placed every where for the convenience of the passers-by. In the broad streets straw-mats are hung up to keep off the sun's rays.

The population of Cairo is estimated at 200,000, and is a mixed one, consisting of Arabs, Mamelukes, Turks, Berbers, Negroes, Bedouins, Christians, Greeks, Jews, etc. Thanks to the powerful arm of Mehemet Ali, they all live peacefully together.

The Streets of Cairo, 1842
Sophia Poole

❧

As in many other matters, women's descriptions of customs and places are often more detailed than those of male travelers. Often they would have sat and watched, rather than taking an active part in whatever was going on. Mrs. Poole's description, for example, of the streets of Cairo is more detailed and closely observed than that of the great majority of male travelers. This account of the street patterns of Cairo enables us to understand the present layout of the city beyond the fast-moving traffic of the modern roads.

❧

The streets are unpaved and very narrow, generally from five to ten feet wide. Some are even less than *four* feet in width; but there are others as much as forty or fifty feet wide, though not for any great length. I must describe the streets under their different appellations.

A *sharr*, or great thoroughfare street, is generally somewhat irregular both in its direction and width. In most parts the width is scarcely more than sufficient for two loaded camels to proceed at a time; and hence much inconvenience is often occasioned to the passenger, though carriages are very rarely encountered.

All burdens are borne by camel, if too heavy for asses; and vast numbers of the former, as well as many of the latter, are employed in supplying the inhabitants of Cairo with the water of the Nile, which is conveyed in skins, the camel carrying a pair of skin bags, and the ass a goat-skin, tied round at the neck. The great thoroughfare-streets being often half obstructed by these animals, and generally crowded with passengers, some on foot, and others riding, present striking scenes of bustle and confusion, particularly when two long trains of camels happen to meet each other where there is barely room enough for them to pass, which is often the case. Asses are in very general use, and most convenient for riding through such streets as those of Cairo, and are always to be procured for hire.

They are preferred to horses even by some men of the wealthier classes of the Egyptians. Their paces are quick and easy; and the kind of saddle with which they are furnished is a very comfortable seat. It is a broad, particoloured pack-saddle. A servant generally runs with the donkey; and exerts himself, by almost incessant bawling, to clear the way for his master. The horseman proceeds with less comfort, and less speed—seldom beyond the rate of a slow walk; and though preceded by a servant, and sometimes by two servants to clear his way, he is often obliged to turn back: it is, therefore not often that a numerous cavalcade is seen in the more frequented streets.

A *darb*, or by-street, differs from a *sharr* in being narrower, and not so long. In most cases, the *darb* is about six to eight feet wide, is a thoroughfare, and has, at each end, a gateway, with a large wooden door, which is always closed at night. Some darbs consist only of private houses; others contain shops.

A *harah*, or quarter, is a particular district consisting of one or more streets or lanes. In general a small quarter contains only private houses, and has but one entrance, with a wooden gate, which, like that of the *darb*, is closed at night.

The sooks, or markets, are short streets, or short portions of streets, having shops on either side. In some of them, all the shops are occupied by persons of the same trade. Many sooks are covered over-head by matting, extended upon rafters, resembling those I observed at Alexandria, and some have a roof of wood. Most of the great thoroughfare streets and many by-streets consist, for the most part, of a succession of *sooks*.

Many of the *khans* of Cairo are similar to the *sooks* just described, but in general, a *khan* consists of shops or magazines surrounding a square or oblong court.

Encounters in the Streets, 1826
Anne Katherine Elwood

. . . We saw Turks on donkeys, and Mamelukes on horseback, "pride in their port, defiance in their eye," riding down every one before them, purposely and offensively sticking out their tremendous shovel-shaped stirrups; one Chieftain, in particular, seemed to wish to evince in what utter contempt he held the Franks [foreigners]; but when he saw a *female* among the party, it is impossible to describe the change that instantaneously took place in his whole demeanour; the proud and contemptuous air with which he surveyed the gentlemen, was to me altered to one of the most perfect courtesy and civility; and the most polished Frenchman could not have rained in his steed with more grace, or have expressed more gentlemanly regret at my being annoyed or alarmed, by my donkey accidentally running against his horse. Though it was evident he held the Christians in abhorrence, he saw that I was a *woman*, and he treated me with deference and respect. Indeed, I must say for the Turks, in general, whatever their other faults may be, that their manners towards our sex far exceed those of our countrymen in courtesy, as their graceful costume surpasses that of the Franks in magnificence and grandeur.

Then we saw women mounted on camels, riding on immense saddles, towering aloft in the air, and shrouded in their black cloaks, looking really very tremendous and awful.

Woman to Woman, 1828
Sarah Lushington

Coming to Cairo northwards down the Nile from Luxor, having crossed the desert from the Red Sea, Mrs. Lushington was, despite her initial hesitation, and her criticism of women's dress, more prepared for Cairo than others.

I felt some nervousness at the idea of riding through the crowded streets at noon; but there proved no just cause of apprehension from the people, who, though they looked intently, and one or two Turks made observations to each other, offered not the slightest incivility.

I believe the women I met eyed me with as much interest as I regarded them. They resembled friars more than women; appearing generally coarse and fat, riding *en cavalier*, and enveloped in a loose, shapeless garment of black silk, which covered the head as well as the figure, and on the forehead joined a piece of white linen which descended in a peak to the waist, and which without sticking close, concealed the face like a mask. Two holes were cut in this for eyes, sometimes so large that one might guess at the character of the face beneath; and the cloth, from the forehead down to the tip of the nose, was adorned with a row of sequins, or other ornaments. Altogether the whole dress was grotesque and ugly.

Many streets were so narrow that, but for the blows of the donkey drivers, I think I should have been squeezed to death by the camels and their loads. Men, horses, donkeys, and camels, all hurried on, without the least regard to whom or what might be in their way, and yet all appeared to escape with safety.

Chaos in the Streets—Day and Night, 1876
Mathilda Bethune-Edwards

Driving is slow work in a narrow street without pavements, and as crowded as a London thoroughfare. Every moment our wheels put somebody's toes in jeopardy, and every moment we are in danger of getting our carriage wheels locked; the donkey-boys shriek and brandish their sticks; the street-waterer, with his pig-skin* on his back, squirts right and left, stirring not an inch for anybody; the blue-robed Fellaheen woman, with her baby on her shoulder, moves on with stateliness; the pedestrians, for the most part wearing every conceivable shade of purple, crimson, green, and yellow, go on and take no heed; now some rich man's equipages heralded by the wild, beautiful figure of his sais, or groom, who runs forward, waving a staff over his head, and crying, "Out of the way! out of the way!" his long white sleeves fluttering like the wings of a bird, his gold-embroidered vest flashing for a second, and then vanishing; now we are

---

* The water-carrier would have had a goat-skin rather than pig-skin carrier.

brought to a standstill, blocked by donkeys, carriages, fruit-vendors, water-vendors, heavily-burdened street-porters, and English dog-carts, and a string of camels.

Then, as the evening wears on, the press of vehicles and donkey-riders increase, and the scene becomes magnificent, but not quite what we had expected. Here are European equipages and toilettes that look fresh from Hyde Park or the Bois de Boulogne, Oriental picturesqueness and delicious combinations of colour side by side with chimney-pot hats, crinolines, and other crude inventions of modern millinery. Alas! the chimney-pot hat has reached the land of the Pharaohs, and the high-heeled boot has penetrated into the harem! By-and-by, where shall we seek for a vestige of those charming inventions of bygone ages which have so embellished and beautified, instead of disfiguring and caricaturing, the human figure. It is hard to say.

The Streets of Cairo, 1988
Bettina Selby

Coming to Egypt by bicycle, Bettina Selby's experiences were different from but also similar to those of earlier travelers.

I was only ever run into in the streets of Cairo by drivers reversing, at which they were particularly inept. When going forward they behaved more like bicyclists, weaving in and out wherever they saw a gap, but although they also kept up a continuous blaring of horns, they did not seem to have any real malice towards other road users. This was a comfort, even if the effect is much the same, I prefer to be knocked down as a result of someone's lack of skill, rather than their aggression. Parking was often three deep and a large number of men were kept employed juggling vehicles around so that those trapped against the kerbs could be released. To keep the pavements free of cars, the pavements have been raised to a height which made them practically unscaleable, so pedestrians joined the traffic in the narrow space left in the centre of the road. It says much for the vigilance of my guardian angel that I cycled around Cairo, day and night, for a couple of weeks without adding to the city's prodigal accident figures.

The City at Night, 1870
Mary Whately

Formerly each district of the city had an arched doorway to the chief of the narrow little streets of the quarter, and a huge massive wooden door, which was locked after a certain hour at night; and if by a rare chance I had been to see friends, and was returning after ten o'clock, my servant had to arouse the doorkeeper, who was asleep on a bench beside this great door, and get him to unlock it; often a quarter of an hour was spent in waking him up and waiting by persons who returned late. Many of these doors are now taken away in the making of the new streets, and the largest thoroughfares in the city (though only these) are lighted now with gas. Formerly we had to take a lamp if going out even the shortest distance after sunset; but even now it is needful if going to a wedding, for instance, or any visit to a native family out of the broad highway.

The little old-fashioned lamps were of prepared paper or calico, made to fold up flat and go in a man's pocket, a piece of wax taper being carried with them. These are still found, but glass lanterns are more common with persons of the better sort, who generally make a servant (or slave boy if they are natives) walk in front carrying it. In the narrow lanes of a great part of the city, where rubbish is always found, and where the half-wild dogs are crouching about among the dust-heaps, and stones encumber the path, it is necessary to pick the way very carefully if walking at night, and the lamp is usually held as *low* as possible, in order to throw light on the path for a few steps before the person walking. This is no doubt an old custom. Formerly, when no gas was found in Egypt, I used to watch from my window in the city passengers returning home in the short winter evenings, and each one carrying his lantern, or his servant, if a rich man, holding it before his feet, and think of the comparison in the Psalm, "Thy word is a light unto my *feet* and a lantern to my *path*." Just light for the way, step by step, is all we expect as the little lantern throws its ray on the rough footpath . . .

Seen and Met along the Way, 1853
Lady Tobin

Shopping again the next morning—a slow process in the East, where the seller not only makes a point of demanding for his goods at least three times their value, but appears perfectly indifferent as to whether the purchases are eventually made or not!

While impatiently awaiting the result of one of these bargains, my attention was attracted towards a water carrier, of whom I would gladly have made a sketch. His figure, already bent by age, stooped still more under the weight of the elegant, long-shaped jar of porous earthenware attached to his shoulders by ropes. Within the neck of this jar was a bunch of orange leaves. He held two or three brightly polished copper cups in one hand, into which he poured the water.

Of the Bazaars, that for shoes is most showy, with its gay colours and embroidered slippers. As we returned to the European quarter we passed several handsome old Mosques; they are generally painted externally in horizontal stripes of red and white. We met two marriage processions; and unless some of the covered baskets were empty, which I understand is not infrequently the case, the brides must have been endowed with noble *trousseaux*. We also met a party of Hadji carrying banners and burning incense.

Our Neighbours, May 25, 1863
Lucie Duff Gordon

The street and the neighbours would divert you [She was writing to her husband.] Opposite lives a Christian dyer who must be a seventh brother of the admirable barber. The same impertinence, loquacity, and love of meddling in everyone's business. I long to see him thrashed, though he is a constant comedy. My delightful servant, Omar Abou-el-Hallaweh (the father of sweets)—his family are pastry cooks—is the type of all the amiable *jeune premiers* of the stories. I am privately of opinion that he is Bedr-ed-Deen Hassan, the more that he can make cream tarts and there is no pepper in them. Cream tarts are not very good, but lamb stuffed with pistachio nuts fulfils all one's dreams of excellence. The Arabs next door and the Levantines opposite are quiet enough, but how *do* they eat all the cucumbers they buy of the man who cries every morning as "fruit gathered by sweet girls in the garden with the early dew."

The more I see of the back-slums of Cairo, the more in love I am with it. The oldest European towns are tame and regular in comparison, and the people are so pleasant. If you smile at anything that amuses you, you get the kindest, brightest smile in person; they give hospitality with their faces, and if one brings out a few words, "Mashallah! what Arabic the Sitt Ingleez speaks." The Arabs are clever enough to understand the amusement of a stranger and to enter into it, and amused in turn, and they are wonderfully unprejudiced. When Omar explains to me their views on various matters, he adds: "The Arab people think so—I know not if right," and the way in which the Arab merchants worked the electric telegraph, and the eagerness of the Fellaheen for steam-ploughs, are quite extraordinary. They are extremely clever and nice children, easily amused, easily roused into a fury which lasts five minutes and leaves no malice, and half the lying and cheating of which they are accused comes from misunderstanding and ignorance. . . .

Plague! June, 1843
Sophia Poole

There has been an alarm of plague in Cairo, and several of the great harems have been in quarantine. The apprehension has been induced by the fearful murrain which has raged during nine months, as a similar misfortune has proved in former years the forerunner of a severe pestilence.

At El-Mansoorah (near the Damietta branch of the Nile), the cases of plague have not been few; and while on this subject I must tell you an extraordinary fact, which will show you that it is even possible to extract sweet from one of the bitterest of human draughts. Some Russians have been at El-Mansoorah for the purpose of studying the disease. As a means of discovering whether it be contagious or not, they have employed persons to wear the shirts of the dead, and paid them five piastres a day for so doing. This was a considerable salary, being equal to a shilling a day! Now when the poor of this country consider half a piastre per day a sufficient allowance for each person, and maintain themselves well, in their own opinion, on this trifling sum, you can conceive how charmed they might be with the liberal offers of these Russian gentlemen, were it not for the risk they incurred.

Risk, however, they did not imagine. The poor flocked to the physicians from all parts of the town, and *entreated* to be permitted to wear the plague-shirts. One old man urged his request, saying, "I am a poor old man, with a family to maintain; do not refuse me; by your life, let me wear the shirt." The women crowded round the house where they imagined benefactors had taken up their quarters, to bless then for having undertaken to support them, their husbands and their children: and when the chief of these adventurous gentlemen found the dwelling thus surrounded, he walked forth among them, and, taking off his hat, made a courteous bow to his dark-eyed visitors; whereupon they made the air resound with the shrill *zaghareet*,* or cries of joy.

Not one of the shirt-wearers died . . . but one of the physicians died . . .

It is a singular and sad fact, that during our few month's sojourn here this country has been visited by three of its peculiar plagues—murrain, boils and

---

* A trilling sound made with the tip of the tongue against the teeth.

Interior of a House

blains (or common pestilence), and locusts. The first has destroyed cattle to an almost incredible amount of value; the second has not been so severe as it usually is; but the locusts are still fearfully eating the fruits of the ground. In the gardens of Ibraheem Pasha (Mehmet Ali's eldest son) and others, the peasants are employed to drive them away by throwing stones, screaming, beating drums, etc.

Visiting a Harem, February, 1843
Sophia Poole

An introduction from Mrs. Lieder, wife of the longtime resident Church Missionary Society* priest, Mrs. Poole was delighted to be able to visit Egyptian ladies in their homes.

---

*   The Church Missionary Society (CMS) was a mainly British Protestant society which sent pastors or ministers to work with Christians across the world throughout the nineteenth century. It still works in many countries today.

When we arrived at the house of Habeeb Efendee, and had passed the outer entrance, I found that the harem apartments, as in other houses of the great in this country, are not confined to the first and other floors, but form a separate and complete house, distinct from that of the men. Having passed a spacious hall, paved with marble, we were met at the door of the first apartment by the elder daughter of Habeeb Effendee, who gave me the usual Eastern salutation, touching her lips and forehead with her right hand, and then insisted on removing my riding-dress herself, although surrounded by slaves. . . .

Mrs. Poole was then offered the traditional dishes of sweet-meats brought on silver trays and small china cups (not, as in ordinary houses, simply of silver filigree, but decorated with diamonds).

In the course of the conversation, I expressed my admiration of the Turkish language, and to my surprise, the elder of the young ladies gave me a general invitation, and proposed to become my instructress: addressing herself to Mrs Lieder with the most affectionate familiarity, she said, "O my sister, persuade your friend to come to me frequently, that I may teach her Turkish; in doing which I will learn her language, and we can read and write together."

Mrs. Poole politely refused the invitation, realising how much of her time such a project would take up.

Before our departure it was proposed that I should see their house; and the elder daughter threw her arm round my neck, and thus led me through the magnificent room which was surrounded by divans; the elevated portion of the floor was covered with India matting, and in the middle of the depressed portion was the most tasteful fountain I have seen in Egypt, exquisitely inlaid with black, red and white marble. The ceiling was a beautiful specimen of highly-wrought arabesque work, and the walls as usual white-washed, and perfectly plain, with the exception of the lower portions, which, to the height of about six feet was paved with Dutch tiles.

I was conducted upstairs in the same manner; and I could not help feeling exceedingly amused at my situation; and considering that these ladies are of the royal family of Turkey, you will see that I was most remarkably honoured.

When we rose to take our leave, the elder daughter received my riding-dress from a slave, and was about to attire me, when her sister said, "You took them off; it is for me to put them on." The elder lady partly consented, . . . and thus they dressed me together. Then, after giving me the usual salutation, they each cordially pressed my hand, and kissed my cheek. . . . Having crossed the court, we arrived at the great gate, through which I had before passed, which was only closed by a large mat, suspended before it, forming the curtain of the harem. This mat was raised by black eunuchs, who poured from a passage without, and immediately after the ladies bade us farewell, and returned, followed by their slaves. The principal eunuch ascended first the mounting platform, and placed me on the donkey, while the others arranged my feet in the stirrups; our own servants being kept in the background.

Cats about the Harem, 1862
Ellen Chennells

Miss Chennells was employed as governess to the girls of the ruling family and, living in the harem, had unusual insights as a foreigner.

It would be difficult enough for any intruders to make their way in. But nothing could keep out cats, which ran wild about the country; and as winter came on, they would dart through the gates, hide themselves in the garden, and towards evening get into the house. Now and then the nuisance would become so serious, and the dirt made by them so great, that orders were given to chase them out, and eunuchs and slaves would join in a hunt; but that was only for a day or two; in a week they were as plentiful as ever. As the spring advanced, they began to seek out comfortable nooks for coming families; and as my windows were a convenient height from the ground, and my bedroom was less of a passage than any other apartment in the palace, the cats favoured me much more frequently than was agreeable.

They were not quiet domestic animals, but frightened, rushing creatures, springing past you when you least expected it. With all my care, I had one or two families born in my room; and one day walking down the passages leading to the Princess's apartments, I found five or six parties established behind the heavy curtains which were always drawn before each door in winter. I did not find this nuisance for a long time, however, as, when I returned to Cairo in September, the weather was too warm at night for any animals to seek the shelter of a house.

Another Visit, 1844
Sophia Poole

Mrs. Poole was invited to visit the harem of the Pasha within the Citadel, high over Cairo.

The Kasr* appropriated to the hareem of the Pasha in the citadel is a noble mansion, the finest domestic structure I have seen in Egypt. The interior is on the usual Turkish plan. On the ground floor is a spacious saloon, paved with marble of a blueish white, nearly surrounded by suites of apartments, which open into it; and on the first floor are rooms on the same plan. Accompanied by my friend Mrs Lieder [wife of the Protestant pastor], I passed from the principal entrance to a large square court, and having crossed this, we found ourselves in the lower of the two saloons.

We then ascended by an ample marble staircase to the saloon on the first floor. Here a most magnificent prospect burst upon our view: three windows which are opposite to the head of the stairs, command the whole of Cairo, and the plain beyond; and every object of interest to the north and west of Cairo within the reach of our sight lay in picturesque variety before our admiring gaze; the green carpet of the Delta, and the plain of Goshen, terminating the view towards the north. I would willingly have lingered here, but our attendants were impatient to conduct us into the presence of the chief lady.

---

* Palace

We found her sitting in a room which was carpeted and surrounded by a divan, attended by three ladies. She received us with much respect and cordiality, and as I had been informed that she had the reputation of being an exceedingly haughty person, I was agreeably surprised by finding in her conversation and deportment the utmost affability and politeness. She conversed with me freely of my children, told me that her son was under twenty years of age, and introduced to my notice two nice little girls, children of the hareem, one of whom presented me with a bouquet.

Doctoring the Ladies of the Harem, 1853
Lady Tobin
The French government send one of their most talented physicians to Cairo, for the purpose of making enquiries respecting the causes and treatment of the Plague; he is recalled at the end of five years, and another takes his place. Dr Burgueres has held that appointment for more than three years, and has had abundant opportunity of studying the manners and customs of the modern Cairenes. His professional visits to the harems seem to tax his patience severely; and no wonder.

Mosque of Sultan Hassan

First, one of the eunuchs must be summoned; and after a great deal of needless parley, that individual sets off to inform the ladies that the hakim [doctor] has arrived. At the end of ten minutes—generally much longer—the eunuch comes again, with a request that the hakim will step into the adjoining room, smoke a pipe, and drink a cup of coffee—which performances cause an immense delay; besides that the poor hakim must wait another full hour, perhaps, before he is admitted into the chamber of the invalid, who remains all the time closely veiled.

Processions Past the Window, 1842
Sophia Poole

As in Alexandria, Mrs. Poole spent time at the window observing life. She and her brother lived near the busy Shubra road.

The wedding processions, in which the poor bride walks under a canopy of silk, not only veiled, but enveloped in a large shawl, between two other females, amuse me much; while the tribe before the 'destined one,' occasionally demonstrate their joy by executing many possible, and, to our ideas, many impossible feats, and the rear is brought up by the contributions of children from many of the houses *en route*. The bride must, indeed, be nearly suffocated long before she reaches her destination, for she has to walk, frequently almost fainting, under a mid-day sun, sometimes a long distance, while a few musicians make what is considered melody with drums and shrill hautboys, and attending females scream their *zaghareet* (or quavering cries of joy), in deafening discord in her train.

The funeral processions depress me. The corpse of a man is carried in an open bier, with merely a shawl thrown over the body, through which the form is painfully visible. The body of a woman is carried in a covered bier over which a shawl is laid, and an upright piece of wood, covered also with a shawl and decorated with ornaments belonging to the female head-dress, rises from the forepart. The corpses of children are carried on this latter kind of bier.

One sound that I heard as a funeral procession approached, I can never forget; it was a cry of such deep sorrow—a sob of such heartfelt distress, that it was clearly distinguished from the wail of the hired women who joined the funeral chorus. We were immediately drawn to the windows, and saw a man leading a procession of women, and bearing in his arms a little dead infant, wrapt merely in a shawl, and travelling to its last earthly home. The cry of agony proceeded, I conclude, from its mother, and could only be wrung from a nearly bursting heart. Contend against me who may, I must ever maintain my opinion, that no love is so deep, no attachment so strong, as that of mother to child, and of child to mother.

The Mecca Caravan Passes, 1826
Wolfradine Minutoli
Riding one day through the streets of Cairo, I met the great caravan returning from Mecca. The street was so thronged by it that I was obliged to wait until it had passed. It is a very curious sight, which is seen only once a year. This caravan, composed of pilgrims to Mecca, sets out from Barbary and stops at Cairo, where it encamps, then continues its journey, becoming larger as it advances, like the avalanches of the mountains of Switzerland.

The faithful who have made a vow to go and pray at the tomb of the Prophet, collect from all quarters, and place themselves under the protection of the sheik of the caravan; a privilege enjoyed exclusively by a tribe of Arabs under the command of their chief. The valuable presents that this caravan generally carried to Mecca, render this message necessary, and notwithstanding the armed force by which is escorted, it frequently happens that it is attacked by the Bedouin tribes who roam in the deserts of Libya and Arabia, and live only by rapine and plunder.

The law of Mahomet commands every true believer to perform, at least once in his life, the pilgrimage to Mecca, so that the number of persons from the confines of Asia and Africa, who undertake this dangerous and fatiguing journey, is always considerable. The caliphs of Cairo formerly enjoyed the prerogative of presenting, annually, a magnificent carpet at the tomb of the Prophet; but now the Pacha of Egypt, as the successor to their rights, has the honour of offering this rich present. At the end of the year this carpet is cut into small pieces, which are distributed among the faithful, by whom they are highly prized.

In the caravan which passed before me, I saw several women, who, by their style of travelling, appeared to me to be of high rank. A large camel sometimes carry two, in a kind of sedan chair, fastened on each side of the animal. Other females, seated in palanquins, borne by two mules, were accompanied by their slaves, and surrounded with every thing that luxury and wealth could supply; lastly, those of the poor class, with infants at the breast, were merely sitting on camels or asses, and in this manner submitted to all the hardships of this long journey. Men mounted on superb horses, with haughty looks, in splendid and singular dresses, and remarkable for the beauty of their arms—in short, a strange medley of pilgrims of all ages, sexes, and colours, attracted and engrossed my attention.

The Egyptian Museum and the Mecca Caravan, 1873
Marianne Brocklehurst

Wednesday, December 3 It is a charming collection of Old Egyptian statues— that of Shafra (Khafre) who built the Second Pyramid, most famous—mummies, gods, tablets, household goods, boats, weapons, gold and silver ornaments—bracelets of lapis lazuli and gold particularly beautiful—and other antiquities. The wooden statue of the Shepherd Man (chief of the village, it is supposed) wonderfully lifelike, 6000 years old, and the wooden statues of the King and Queen from Sakkara are quite unique and fresh, as if made yesterday. Afternoons at the bazaars. We see carpets but many of the new ones have strange wrong colours such as magenta in them. We hesitate about two long strips of secondhand Persian . . .

Thursday, December 11 . . .
We go to see the procession of pilgrims starting for Mecca. Out of the great gate come camels with palanquins and camels with riders, sheiks, priests and the like, dervishes and pilgrims on foot, flags of all kinds, regiments of soldiers, horses, holy men in many coloured garbs. The fat man who rides bareback to Mecca is the sheik of the camels. And last, the Golden Pagoda and white camel. This contains the new and sacred carpet which every year goes to replace the other ones at Mecca. We saw the Holy Sheik who on the return rides over the prostrate crowd. We saw other green turbans of the Mahomet family and were altogether greatly satisfied with this Eastern spectacle and the crowds of devotees and the faithful in general.

A Funeral Procession, 1845
Sophia Poole

Another uncommon funeral procession, that of Khursheed Pasha, late Governor of Sennar (Sudan), passed our house . . . and as it was the most remarkable of all such spectacles seen in Cairo since my arrival, I am induced to describe it to you.

It was preceded by six camels, each bearing two boxes filled with corn and dates, above and between which sat the distributor, with a stick in his hand with which to drive off the crowd that pressed upon him, making as great a clamour as though they were all starving, and strange to say, the most decently dressed were the most importunate. Then followed three camels with water, and then two buffaloes to be sacrificed at the tomb, and the flesh to be divided among the poor. These practices are always observed at the funerals of rich persons in Egypt, and I believe throughout the East. About thirty reciters of the Kur-an followed next, and about the same number of sheikhs headed a large body of Turks of the middle classes, chiefly wearing the military dress. Then followed a tribe of Chaooshes, two and two, in full uniform; after these walked about fifty grandees of all ages. Their dresses were most picturesque; the varieties of colour they displayed rendering the group they formed by far the most striking feature in the procession. . . . Some boys walked next, each bearing a Kur-an; and they were immediately followed by a crowd of men bearing incense in silver censers, filling the streets and houses with clouds of frankincense and other perfumes; while others, carrying sprinkling-bottles of silver, showered their sweet contents around them on the more distinguished of the spectators.

Then passed the bier, the appearance of which was not unusual; it was covered with a red figured Cashmere shawl, and borne by four men. The ladies, female slaves, and friends and attendants of the Hareem next followed, consisting of about twenty-five or thirty ladies mounted on high donkeys, and perhaps twenty slaves on ordinary donkeys, and a host on foot. All the last mentioned screamed and wailed so loudly that the noise cannot be easily forgotten by those who have heard as well as seen the great procession—the mingling of noises, the reciters of the Kur-an, the chanting-boys, and the wailing-women, occasion a deafening yell hardly to be imagined. The led horses of the grandees bore up the rear, and thus concluded a spectacle as singular as almost any which can be witnessed in the streets of Cairo.

From the Palace Windows, 1827
Wolfradine Minutoli

> *Mrs. Minutoli—like many other visitors—went to the Citadel with a large party and visited the newly rebuilt palace of Pacha Mohammad Ali.*

The Bazaar

The prospect commanded from the windows of this palace is truly magnifi-cent. At our feet lay the immense city of Cairo, from this elevation resem-bling a great ant-hill: in the distance the view embraced a rich plain, watered by the Nile, which had lately returned within its natural limits, and was cov-ered with the first verdure of spring, which is so brilliant in this happy cli-mate. To the west our eyes discovered those venerable witnesses of past ages, lifting their grey summits to the clouds, and seeming proud of their struggle against time; and the desert of sand, which separates the pyramids from the cultivated grounds, appears, when viewed from this elevation, to serve as a line of demarcation between life and death; between the present and the past; lastly, the remote horizon was bounded by tow chains of arid moun-tains, which enclosed this striking picture.

Khan El-Khaleelee, November, 1842
Sophia Poole

This market is often visited by modern tourists and provides real insights—on a small scale—into souks of the past.

Khan El-Khaleelee, which is situated in the centre of that part which con-
stituted the original city, a little to the east of the main street, and occupies
the site of the cemetery of the Fawatim (the Khaleefehs of Egypt),* particularly deserves to be mentioned, being one of the chief marts of Cairo. It
consists of a series of short lanes, with several turnings, and has four entrances from different quarters.

The shops in this khan are mostly occupied by Turks, who deal in ready-
made clothes and other articles of dress, together with arms of various kinds,
the small prayer-carpets used by the Muslims, and other commodities. Public
auctions are held there (as in many other markets in Cairo) twice in the week,
on Monday and Thursday, on which occasions the khan is so crowded, that,
in some parts, it is difficult for a passenger to push his way through. The sale
begins early in the morning, and last till the noon-prayers. Clothes (old as well
as new), shawls, arms, pipes, and a variety of other goods, are offered for sale
in this manner by brokers, who carry them up and down the market. Several
water-carriers, each with a goat-skin of water on his back, and a brass cup for
the use of any one who would drink, attend on these occasions. Sherbet of
raisins, and bread (in round, flat cakes), with other eatables, are also cried up
and down the market; and on every auction day, several real or pretended id-
iots, with a distressing number of other beggars, frequent the khan.

Beautiful Architecture, 1907
Norma Lorimer
These Mameluke houses of old Cairo have no rivals in Oriental domestic
architecture, or in fairy elegance and fantastic grace. In many of them the
walls of the best apartments, where the master of the house entertains his
men friends, still gleam with the iridescence of old Persian tiles, and jewel-
inlaid fountains still delight the ear with the splash of falling water.

Some of these palaces of pleasure have fallen upon evil days; I have seen
one high room which any one can find for the looking, for it is near the famous Blue Mosque, so blessed with every grace that Saracenic art could be-
stow upon it, that a little lump rose to my throat when I suddenly entered it
from the dark and disorderly staircase I had climbed to reach it. The mixture
of desolation and beauty was overwhelming—cocks and hens and large-
eared Persian rabbits were scattered about the floor.

---

* Mrs. Poole added a footnote to say that "The bones of the Khaleefehs were thrown
  on the mounds of rubbish outside the city . . ."

Gems of stained glass still glowed like uncut jewels from the lace-work of white stucco which ran in a deep frieze along the top of the brown meshrebiyeh windows, which formed one side of the gigantic apartment. Not a particle of it had been disturbed by impious hands, not one screen of the priceless meshrebiyeh had been cut out for sale—the place had been allowed to slowly drift into ruin. The youth who showed me over it said he had no money to spend upon restoring a house which was ten times larger than he could afford to use; he seemed to have no money to do more than keep body and soul together, from his delicate appearance; yet he stiffened with pride when I suggested that he should let off one or two of the splendid old rooms of the palace to wealthy Americans . . . He scorned the idea with as much hauteur as though his one cotton garment had been the richest brocade, and his palace guarded by an army of slaves.

Street Scenes, 1907
Norma Lorimer
I have seen the afternoon market under the citadel where conjurors, snake-charmers, mountebanks, fortune-tellers, whistlers, actors and musicians are every day to be found working hard for their scanty livelihood, mixed up with old rags, old brass, old iron, old household utensils, and every kind of second-hand article imaginable. This 'afternoon market' is one of the most eastern things in Cairo, but it is far too humble and unsavoury for the ordinary tourist, so it is there you see 'Kim' and his friends in all their unspoilt poverty.

I have watched for long hours the women shopping. In twos and threes they glide along, these upright, black-veiled daughters of the East, all intent on the purchase they are going to make. From their outdoor appearance you would think that five or six yards of black material of some soft stuff was all they would require for an entire outfit, a sort of black winding-sheet for head and body; but no doubt like the king's daughters of old they are glorious within. I have seen them forcing their tiny hands, with the aid of a powerful shopkeeper, through bracelets of gaily-coloured glass, suffering much pain for their pride, I can assure you.

The Cotton Bazaar—and the Water-carriers, 1914
E.L. Butcher
Very few visitors seem to know the cotton bazaar in Cairo, yet it is well worth a visit, not only because it is a very picturesque, if insanitary, place, but because it is one of the few almost perfect examples left in Cairo of a khan for travellers. In just such a place as this Our Saviour must have been

born at Bethlehem. There is the court for the animals, all driven in and herded here for the night in the days long ago, when the khan was used for its original purpose, and all round are deep arched recesses, with stone platforms in front of them, where the herdsmen and servants in charge of the animals slept. Above this and all round it, with an awning or light roof to the court, ran the rooms of the inn proper looking into the court. The only entrance to the place is through a low, narrow, arched way, which leads from the court, under the inn, to the street.

Now the arched recesses are filled with brightly coloured cottons—stripes for the men only, other patterns for the women. I discovered once that my servants were rather scandalized because I had bought myself a dress of the striped cotton which should only be worn by men. On the platforms sit the merchants with their scribes.

Behind the cotton bazaar the weavers of silk ends to cotton cloths may be seen at their work. There are many quantities of Egyptian silks; the best is very expensive, but the tourists generally buy a quality which, though half cotton, has the merit of washing well to the last. It is always woven in fine stripes, and generally in beautiful colours.

Water-carriers are a very familiar sight in Cairo, though the modern water-carts have driven them from the principal streets. They fetch the water from the Nile to the houses where the women of the family are too well off to work in the fields, or go down with their jars to the river, and they still water some small streets where the carts cannot go. A favourite form of charity for the well-to-do is to set a zeyr outside his house for the benefit of thirsty passers-by, and this he pays a water carrier to keep full regularly. The water-sellers, too, are often hired by some rich man to dispense water gratuitously to everyone for the day, generally some day of feast.

The seller carries his supply in a zeyr upon his back, with a branch of green leaves by way of a stopper. He has two brass cups which he clinks together to attract attention. He generally carries a goolla also, and it is curious to watch the demeanour one of these men in a crowd on an occasion when he has received a certain sum for the day, since he never asks nor waits for money.

Snake Charmers, 1843
Sophia Poole

You have doubtless read many accounts of the feats of Eastern snake charmers, and wondered at their skill. Very lately, a friend of ours witnessed an instance of the fascination, or rather attraction, possessed by one of these people. He was in the house of an acquaintance when the charmer arrived, who, after a little whistling, and other absurd preliminaries, invoked the snake thus: "I conjure thee, by our Lord Suleyman" (that is, Solomon, the son of David), who ruled over mankind and the Jan (or Genii); if thou be obedient, come to me, and if they be disobedient, do not hurt me!"

After a short pause, a snake descended from a crevice in the wall of the room, and approached the man, who secured it. No other snake appearing, it was decided that the house was cleared, and our friend requested the snake charmer to accompany him to his own house. He did so, and invoked the snakes in the same words. The invocation was attended by the same result; a snake descended, and in the same manner resigned itself to the snake charmer.

With regard to the snake still in our house, let us say, with the Muslims, we are thankful it is not a scorpion. Their philosophy is a lesson to us.

Visiting the Baths, 1827
Wolfradine Minutoli
The Baths, which in the East are a public amusement of women, are too well known to be dwelt upon here. These baths, which are generally situated in the bazaars, are open during several days in the week to the public in general; women of all ages, in their finest clothes, assemble early in the morning and pass here the greatest part of the day; it is a place of ren-dezvous, where they generally carry even their young children. The extreme heat of these vapour baths often obliges them, however, to lay aside not only their ornaments, but even their dress, and thus they spend the day, chatting, smoking and laughing: for the women of the East never amuse themselves so much as at these places of public meeting. Meantime, their slaves rub their limbs with a kind of paste, made of the filaments of the date-tree, which is said especially to contribute to render the skin soft and smooth, which they consider as a principal charm, or else they anoint them with pre-cious perfumes, and make their joints render them supple.

A lady of my acquaintance who visited these baths, told me that it was very singular and curious scene, but that the eye was much oftener struck by features of ugliness, than by the pleasing forms of beauty. Not having felt any inclination to visit these baths, I contented myself with seeing those in the house of Mr Rossetti [her Consul], the neatness and elegance of which are far preferable to those of the bazaars, where hundreds of women assem-ble. The ladies of the family, among whom was a grandmother, twenty-seven years of age, used them frequently.

The Bath, April, 1844
Sophia Poole

Whatever others may think of it, I confess that the operation of bathing in the Eastern manner is to me extremely agreeable; and I have found it singularly beneficial in removing the lassitude which is occasioned by the climate. It is true that it is followed by a sense of fatigue, but a delightful repose soon ensues; and the consequences, upon the whole, I find almost as enjoyable as the process itself.

The buildings containing the baths are all nearly on the same plan, and are much alike in appearance; the fronts being decorated fancifully, in red and white, and the interiors consisting of several apartments paved with marble. I will describe to you, in a few words, one of the best in Cairo, which I visited with three ladies of my acquaintance: English, Abyssinian, and Syrian.

. . . The first large apartment, or chamber of repose, in which the bathers undress previously to their entering the heated chambers, and in which they dress after taking the bath, and rest on a raised marble platform . . . on which are spread mats and carpets. . . . Each of us enveloped herself in a very long and broad piece of drapery—which, but for its size, I might call a scarf, and proceeded through a small chamber . . . to the principal inner apartment, where the heat was intense.

The plan of this apartment is that of a cross, having four recesses, each of which, as well as the central portion, is covered with a dome. The pavements are of black and white marble, and small pieces of fine red tile, very fancifully and prettily disposed. In the middle is a jet of hot water, rising from the centre of a high seat of marble, upon which many persons sit together. . . .

On entering this chamber a scene presented itself which beggars description. My companions had prepared me for seeing many persons undressed; but imagine my astonishment in finding at least thirty women of all ages, and many young girls and children, perfectly unclothed. You will scarcely think it possible that no one but ourselves had a vestige of clothing. Persons of all colours, from the black and glossy shade of the negro to the fairest possible hue of complexion, were formed in groups, conversing as though full dressed, with perfect *nonchalance*, while others were strolling about, or sitting round the fountain.

Mrs. Poole then described the various operations which the bath offered—from the almost overpowering heat which was at first oppressive but was soon relieved by "a gentle, and afterwards by a profuse perspiration." Then followed various operations . . .

The first operation is a gentle kneading of the flesh, or champooing. Next the attendant cracks the joints of those who desire to submit to this process. . . . Some of the native women after this are rubbed with a rasp, or rather two rasps of different kinds, a coarse one for the feet, and a fine one for the body; but neither of these rasps do I approve. A small coarse woollen bag, into which the operator's hand is inserted, is in my opinion preferable.

Next the head and face are covered with a thick lather, which is produced by rubbing soap on a handful of fibres of the palm-tree, which are called *leef*, and which form a very agreeable and delicate looking rubber. It is truly ridiculous to see another under this operation. When her head and face have been well lathered, and the soap has been thoroughly washed off by abundance of hot water, a novice would suppose that at least *they* were sufficiently purified; but this is not the case: two or three such latherings, and as many washings, are necessary before the attendant thinks her duty to the head and face accomplished. Then follows the more agreeable part of the affair—the general lathering and rubbing, which is performed by the attendant so gently, and in so pleasant a manner, that it is quite a luxury; and I am persuaded that the Eastern manner of bathing is highly salubrious, from its powerful effect upon the skin.

When the operation was completed, I was enveloped in a dry piece of drapery, similar to the bathing-dress, and conducted to the reposing-room, where I was rubbed and dressed, and left to take rest and refreshment, and to reflect on the strange scene that I had witnessed.

Modern Egyptian Life, 1948
Eileen Bigland

An excellent vantage point was the French window of the lesser lounge [of the hotel], as it faced directly onto the street, and it was remarkable how many and varied were the excitements could be seen from it. Several times

Cairo and the Valley of the Nile

I caught a glimpse of His Majesty driving past in a fast car escorted by soldiers in scarlet jeeps, on his way to make his devotions to one or other of Cairo's mosques. Once I saw a Coptic funeral with priests walking ahead followed by a bevy of little girls in white frocks and a fantastic hearse decorated with monstrous, foot-high purple pansies, while the mourners brought up the rear. On the Friday after the celebration of the Prophet's Birthday the street was suddenly filled with wild pipe music and from the mousky opposite came a throng of people clapping and swaying before a group of men who danced with enormous sticks held upright before them.

And there were always friends to greet. The policeman from the corner would lean on the iron railings and indulge in loud conversations, during one of which I was shocked to learn that, although a policeman had to be able to read and write, his wages were only four pounds a month.

"That doesn't leave you much margin?" I yelled above the din of the traffic. "No." He shrugged his shoulders and quoted an Egyptian proverb: "Some people eat the dates: others get the stones thrown at them."

The Finest View in the Whole World, 1849
Florence Nightingale
Oh, could I but describe those Moorish streets, in red and white stripes of marble; the latticed balconies, with little octagonal shrines, also latticed, sticking out of them, for the ladies to look straight down through; the innumerable mosques and minarets; the arcades in the insides of houses you peep into, the first storeys meeting almost overhead, yet the air with nothing

but fragrance on it, in these narrowest of narrow wynds! But there are no words to describe an Arabian city, no European words at least: for that *one* day yesterday you would have thought it worth while to make a voyage three times as long, and then times as disagreeable, as the one we made, and go back again content, and well content.

After threading these streets for miles, we came out upon the square where stands the magnificent mosque of Sultan Hassan, and above it the citadel, up which we wound, passing the palaces of Ibrahim Pacha (son of Mehemet Ali, who pre-deceased him), Nezleh Hanum, the widow of the Defterdar, till we came to the mosque built by Mehemet Ali, and not yet finished, though in it lie his bones. It is of splendid size, but tawdrily ornamented, and looks better now with the scaffolding supporting those lofty domes, than ever it will do when decorated like Drury Lane. The obnoxious female is still admitted. Mehemet Ali's tomb is covered with shawls and carpets. . . .

From the terrace of the mosque is what I would imagine is the finest view in the whole world. Cairo, which is immense, lies at its feet, a forest of minarets, domes and towers. The Nile flows his solemn course beyond, the waters being still out (it is now high Nile), and the three Pyramids stand sharp against the sky. Here Osiris and his worshippers lived, here Abraham and Moses walked; here Aristotle came; here, later, Mahomet learnt the best of his religion and studied Christianity; here, perhaps, our Saviour's mother brought her little son to open his eyes to the light. They are all gone from the body; but the Nile flows and the Pyramids stand there still.

3

The Environs of Cairo

From the great city travelers often took short expeditions out into the surrounding countryside to see the many sites close to Cairo.

The Tombs of the Mameluke Sultans, 1828
Sarah Lushington

One of the visits travelers made was to these tombs on the outskirts of Cairo.

The ultimate object of our excursion was the tombs of the Mameluke Sultans. These are situated, as it would appear, in the very heart of the Desert; and it struck me as one of the most singular features of Grand Cairo that, from the very centre of

65

Tombs of the Memlook Sultans

population, from a scene of luxuriant cultivation, we in a moment, without the slightest preparation, passed on to a plain and hills of sand. Not a tree, nor a habitation breaks the uniformity of the surface; nothing is visible but a district of graves, extending as far as the eye can reach; and, where the stones are no longer perceptible, little hillocks of sand mark the places of sepulchure.

Amidst this desolation arise the tombs of the Mamelukes. The largest is that of Sultan Beerkook and his followers. It is in the form of a square, and its walls are in excellent preservation. On one side, in an arched and vaulted room inlaid with coloured marbles, are placed his remains; at the extremity of an open gallery is a similar room, now used as a mosque. The square is embellished with a minaret and a dome. The latter especially, with the pulpit or muezzin, is cut in the most elegant and delicate fretwork stone.

The rest of the building was occupied by poor Arabs, who lived by begging, and in this dwelling safe from tax and extortion.

The Pasha's Country Palace, 1828
Sarah Lushington
As I had already seen an Egyptian garden, I looked forward to an excursion to Shoobra, the country seat of the Pasha, with little or no curiosity. Proceeding, however, by a fine road, planted on each side with acacias and sycamores, whose growth, owing to the richness of the soil, kept pace with the impatient disposition of the Pasha [Mehemet Ali], who had, at one

sweep, cut down the avenue of mulberry trees three years before, we arrived at the house, which is situated close to the Nile, and commands a fine prospect of the river and city.

The exterior of the building exhibited nothing remarkable. On ascending a terrace a few feet square, we passed through a rough wooden door, such as is fit only for an outhouse, and found ourselves in the Pasha's room of audience. It was matted, and round the wall was fixed a row of cushions, on two corners of which were placed satin pillows, marking the seat the Pasha occupied according to the position of the sun. Just over a low ledge in the door, we stepped into a small room with a bedding on the floor; this was his sleeping chamber. Surely never monarch had so little luxury or state. Thence we came at once to the magnificent suite of apartments appropriated to the chief lady of the harem. The centre of the principal formed a sort of octagon, with three recesses, all inlaid with marble. From the four corners opened four small rooms, fitted with splendid divans and cushions of velvet, and cloth of gold; and a set of marble baths completed this series of elegant apartments.

The Pasha's Garden at Shoobra, 1853
Lady Tobin
We rode to Shoobra on the afternoon of Friday, December 23rd, along a wide avenue of acacia trees, the favourite *promenade* of Cairo. The distance is four miles from the Bab-el-Hadid, which is pointed out as a place famous as the scene of a fierce encounter between Richard I and Salah-e-deen, and where there are the remains of very ancient walls.

The road gradually approached the Nile as we advanced towards the village of Shoobra, and at last ran close along the river's bank. Arrived at the outer gate of the royal pleasure grounds, where are the Pasha's stables, we dismounted; and at the end of a short avenue came to a second portal, with a very shabby lodge attached to it. The gardens are extensive, and most beautifully kept.

Chrysanthemums, roses, geraniums, and several of our greenhouse plants were in blossom; the weeping willow and the pomegranate were to be seen here and there; but the principal growth was that of the orange, lemon and citrus. One of the gardeners gave us bouquets of flowers; and some oranges, like those of Malta, produced by grafting upon the pomegranate trees.

The broad straight walks radiate from centres, and some of them are covered overhead with trellis work. We started a pretty gazelle from under some trees. The Octagon Pagoda of gaily coloured glass cost 7,000 purses—the *kees* (purse) being equivalent to £5 sterling. Its interior is fitted up as a saloon, in the centre of which is a bronze fountain, and also a candelabra of carved wood. The floor is curiously inlaid, and the part that immediately surrounds the fountain forms a circular pattern of crescents and stars. The next object of attraction was the Great Fountain *Kiosk*, or according to our guide, the Pacha's *Divan*. The erection of a gas-house for supplying the lamps has ruined the general effect of the building. An enormous marble *reservoir*, containing water four feet in depth, is surrounded by balustrades, which, as well as the columns and mouldings of the open corridors—are from Carrara, and were worked by Italians. At each of the four corners is an apartment fitted up with divans; the first we entered had a painted ceiling, plate glass windows, and splendid silk hangings; the floor and panelled walls were of inlaid wood. The framework of the chairs and tables—for there was a mixture of the European with the Oriental style—struck us as being exceedingly paltry, compared with all around them, and their own rich damask coverings. Another of these rooms contained a billiard table, and in a third was a full length portrait of Mohammed Ali—considered an excellent likeness.

Cavalcade to the Pyramids, 1826
Wolfradine Minutoli

Being desirous to behold with our own eyes the colossal grandeur of these edifices, of which a just idea cannot be formed except by being placed at their foot, we fixed a day for the excursion, with a numerous company, and all the ladies of [the consul] Mr Rosetti's family. As these ladies had to pass through a great part of the city and feared the fatigue of their large black silk cloaks, which cover half the face, they chose the Mameluke costume, and, without well knowing why, I followed their example.

Camels, carrying tents and provisions, had been sent before us early in the morning. Our little caravan, consisting of eight gentlemen in the European dress, five ladies in the Turkish costume, followed by some janissaries, negro slaves, and the Arab guides running by our side, set out, mounted on asses, in the finest weather.

Having never before worn the Mameluke dress, I found myself extremely embarrassed in passing through the streets of Cairo, as I observed that we excited the attention and curiosity of the crowd, who doubtless were surprised to see five Turks among this European company. My companions, to whom I did not dare speak, participated in my embarrassment, and we felt quite relieved when we reached the country.

We embarked at this place to cross the Nile, and admired on the passage the charming island of Rhoda, formed by two arms of this river, and adorned

The Ferry at Old Cairo

with the richest vegetation; then passing through a grove of palms which grows on the ruins of ancient Memphis, our road led through fields and pastures, intersected by numerous ditches and canals for watering the land, till nature, becoming more and more sterile and destitute of vegetation, we came to the entrance of the sandy desert which we had to cross to reach the Pyramids.

Before the Sphynx, 1824
Anne Katherine Elwood
We came into the neighbourhood of the Sphynx; *the* Sphynx, of which everyone has heard so much, and here the soil presented some immense fissures, and such heavy beds of sand, that while wrapped no doubt in some very sublime speculation, down fell my donkey, and over its head went I— I was picked up by a Bedouin Arab, who was offering me some cucumbers and melons at the moment—but, though more frightened than hurt, this *contretemps* was enough to quell my courage for the day. However, that you do not attribute my fall to my bad riding, I beg to observe that several others of the party made a similar obeisance with myself to the Sphynx, by involuntarily prostrating themselves in the dust before her. The Sphynx presented an African countenance, and her hair was dressed much in the same

style with my Nubian friends in the slave market. The sand, which at times had been cleared away, has again collected, and it was at this time nearly embedded in it.

The Vast Size of the Pyramids, February, 1844
Sophia Poole

When we were at least a mile from our journey's end, I remarked to my brother (Edward Lane), "The Pyramids do not appear so grand as I expected now we are almost close to them." Accordingly we rode on; the provoking appearance of nearness to the objects of our visit surprising me during our whole approach. At this season it occupies three hours to reach the Pyramids from Cairo, and this month, on account of its coolness, is particularly agreeable for such an excursion.

An acquaintance had arranged a place for them to camp overnight.

Our tents were pitched, our carpets spread, and our home in the desert had an air of comfort I had hardly anticipated. There is much that is homeish in carrying one's own carpet: place it where you will, in the boat or in the desert, your eyes rest upon it while thinking, and its familiar patterns afford a sort of welcome. The habit of placing a *seggadeh* (a small carpet) on the saddle enables an Eastern lady to take it wherever she may wander. When she is disposed to rest, her attendants spread it; and nothing is more refreshing during a desert excursion than to rest upon it, and take a simple meal of bread and fruit, and a draught of delicious Nile water.

Ascending the Pyramid, 1845
Harriet Martineau

Miss Martineau had sailed up the Nile to Nubia and returned to Cairo before setting off eastward to Sinai and beyond, when she made her visit to the Pyramids.

On looking up, it was not the magnitude of the Pyramid which made me think it scarcely possible to achieve the ascent, but the unrelieved succession—almost infinite—of bright yellow steps; a most fatiguing image! Three strong and respectable looking Arabs now took me in charge. One of them, seeing me pin up my gown in front, that I might not stumble over it, gave me his services as lady's maid. He turned up my gown all round, and tied it in a most squeezing knot, which lasted all through the enterprise.

We set out from the north-eastern corner. By far the most formidable part of the ascent was the first six or eight blocks. If it went on to the top thus broken and precipitous, the ascent would, I feel, be impossible. Already, it was disagreeable to look down, and I was much out of breath. One of my Arabs carried a substantial camp-stool, which had been given to me in London with a view to this very adventure—that it might divide the higher steps—some of which being four feet high, seem impracticable enough beforehand. But I found it better to trust to the strong and steady lifting of the Arabs in such places, and, above everything, not to stop at all, if possible; or, if one must stop for breath, to stand with one's face to the Pyramid. . . . The greatest part of one's weight is lifted by the Arabs at each arm; and when one comes to a four feet step, or a broken ledge, there is a third Arab behind.

I was agreeably surprised to find at the top, besides blocks standing up which gave us some shade, a roomy and even platform, where we might sit and write, and gaze abroad, and enjoy ourselves, without even seeing over the edge, unless we wished it.

In this northern direction, the green plain extends to the furthest horizon, and over to Cairo eastwards. It is dotted with villages—clusters of brown houses among palms—and watered with blue thread-like canals, and showing a faint line of causeway here and there. . . . In the midst of the sand, a train of camels, wonderfully diminutive, is winding along, and a few brown Arab tents are pitched, not far from the foot of the Pyramid.

A Thoroughly Disagreeable Process, 1852
Emily Anne Beaufort
One must however make up one's mind to purchase the interesting result of examining the Pyramids by a thoroughly disagreeable process in every way. I am most glad to have *done* it, but nothing would induce me to repeat the operation, and I would earnestly dissuade any and every lady who is not entirely sure of her own nerves and self-control, and who is not very strong, from attempting it.

The Pyramids

The only right way to get through the ordeal is to be quietly passive in the hands of the three Arabs apportioned to each visitor. When once you have commenced the real business they are good-natured and careful fellows, proud of their knowledge of half a dozen sentences in half a dozen languages, and anxious to please you; they know best how to tie up your garments so that they shall not impede your progress, and how to lift you with least exertion or disagreeableness to yourself, and the solo piece of advice I give to my countrywomen is, to *let* them lift you.

Many of the stones are four feet in height, but the Arabs lift you at one jump with more ease than a stool or any other contrivance will afford you; sometimes, too, they appear to mistake you for a doll or a swaddled baby, and you find yourself seized by the ankles as well as by the arms! Even thus passively impelled upwards, the ascent is an enormous tax upon both blood and breath. The now broken summit affords a platform of thirty-two feet square, with stones upon which and beside which you can rest comfortably; the view is fine, and interesting as being characteristic of Egypt, and should, I think, be viewed at the commencement of the traveller's stay in the country, thus taking in at one glance what you learn by slow degrees afterwards.

The Summit of the Pyramid, 1852
Ida Pfeiffer

For a long time I stood lost in thought, and could hardly realise the fact that I was really one of the favoured few who are happy enough to be able to contemplate the most stupendous and imperishable monument ever erected by human hands. At the first moment I was hardly able to gaze down from the dizzy height into the deep distance; I could only examine the pyramid itself, and seek to familiarise myself with the idea that I was not dreaming. Gradually, however, I came to myself, and contemplated the landscape which lay extended beneath me. From my elevated position I could form a better estimate of the gigantic structure, for here the fact that the base was buried in sand did not prejudice the view. I saw the Nile flowing far beneath me, and a few Bedouin, whom curiosity had attracted to the spot, looked like very pigmies. In ascending I had seen the immense blocks of stone singly, and ceased to marvel that these monuments are reckoned among the seven wonders of the world.

On the citadel the view had been fine, but here, where the prospect was bounded only by the horizon and by the Mokattam mountains, is grander by far. I could follow the windings of the river, with its innumerable arms and canals, until it melted into the far horizon, which closed the picture on this side. Many blooming gardens, and the large extensive town with its environs; the immense desert, with its plains and hills of sand, and the lengthened mountain range of the Mokattam—all lay spread before me; and for a long time I sat gazing around me, and wishing that the dear ones at home had been with me, to share in my wonder the delight.

Leaving One's Name, 1848
Countess Hahn Hahn

It was the custom for those who reached the top of the Great Pyramid to have their name carved by the accompanying Arabs.

The Dragoman had forgotten to bring with him a knife for the purpose of scratching down my name; a pleasure which, as a genuine *gamin*, I was to have, I believe, for the first time in my life. A Bedouin was down and up again in no time, brought a knife, but would give it up only upon the express condition of an extra *bakschisch*. When we told them that the Dragoman would pay them all amply below, they cried, "No, no, no, no! Giurgi no bono!," which meant that they considered us more generous. They spoke half-jestingly, half-fretfully.

We went down gaily. I placed my hands upon the shoulders of two Bedouins, suffered them to descend before me, and then sprang after them. Where the steps were so crumbled away that I could not secure a firm footing, a third, who kept behind, lifted me cautiously down. Here, two years ago, an Englishman, who had insisted on going alone, became giddy, and fell to the bottom. This I strongly suspect to be a Bedouin fable . . .

In silence we left the chamber; climbed down the ramp again a little way, to a point where another passage broke away from it. This passage was horizontal, and so low that no one could stand upright in it. It ran immediately below the higher ramp we had climbed and opened into another smaller room. It was very strange to stand in that chamber, knowing that one was somewhere high up in the very core of that vast pyramid. Masonry was not only pressing in on us on every side and from above, but below as well. At last we began to downward climb, and as a glimmer of sunlight began to filter up the walls below, the feeling of being a slightly hysterical currant in an outsize bun began to leave me. Two days later we left Cairo.

A Trip into the Interior, 1938
Mary Chubb

When we arrived at Gizeh in the afternoon, I discovered that as well as observing them from a safe distance, the plan included a trip into the interior of one of the Pyramids—the Great Pyramid to be exact. As I have, in common with many people, a horror of confined spaces, this expedition was somewhat of a nightmare. But there was nothing for it—I could not hang back at the outset of my adventures in Egypt. If the others were all going in, I must go too. So I clenched my teeth, told myself that it was unlikely that the Great Pyramid would choose that particular Tuesday afternoon to disintegrate, and plunged after the others into the small, rough aperture on the north side of the vast pile. In my ignorance I had somehow expected the tomb chambers to be at ground level, but the passage at once turned upwards and a long incline could just be made out, dimly lit by a few wide-apart electric bulbs. The passage roof was very high. Underfoot, wooden slats, nailed across the ramp, gave useful foothold. A guide went ahead, and we pressed after him, while an occasional vast bat swept in the gloom past our shrinking heads. At the top of the slope we came to the lofty King's Chamber, and at the sight of the great empty tomb, stood silently in the presence of that relic of tremendous majesty.

4
Up the Nile from Cairo

 *Part of the exciting experience of visiting Cairo was the making of arrangements for the journey southward on the Nile to Nubia. This meant negotiating at the port of Bulak for a boat with a* reis *or captain and a crew. Then provisions had to be laid in and various other arrangements had to be made. At last the new adventure began as they set off up the Nile, their sails filled by the wind from the North pushing them up the Nile against the stream. On the journey back north navigation would be dependent upon the flow of the river.*

Choosing a Nile Boat, 1873
Amelia Edwards

In the meanwhile, our first business was to look at dahabeeyahs; and the looking at dahabeeyahs compelled us constantly to turn our steps and our thoughts in the direction of Boulak—a desolate place by the river, where some two or three hundred Nile-boats lay moored for hire. Now, most persons know something of the misery of house-hunting; but only those who have experienced them know how much keener are the miseries of dahabeeyah-hunting. It is more bewildering and more fatiguing, and is beset by its own special and peculiar difficulties.

The boats, in the first place, are all built on the same plan, which is not the case with houses; and except as they run bigger and smaller, cleaner or dirtier, are alike each other as twin oysters. The same may be said of their captains, with the same differences; for to a person who has only been a few days in Egypt, one black or copper-coloured man is exactly like every other black or copper-coloured man. Then each Reis, or captain, displays the certificates given to him by former travellers; and these certificates, being apparently in active circulation, have a mysterious way of turning up again and again on board different boats and in the hands of different claimants.

Nile Boats, 1842
Sophia Poole
The boats of the Nile are admirably constructed for the navigation of that river. Their great triangular sails are managed with an extraordinary facility, which is an advantage of the utmost importance, for the sudden and frequent gusts of wind to which they are subject, require that a sail should be taken in almost in a moment, or the vessel would most probably be overset. On many occasions one side of our boat was completely under water, but the men are so skilful that an accident seldom happens, unless travellers pursue the journey during the night.

Our Dahabieh, 1844
Isabel Romer
These Dahabiehs are very graceful looking vessels, with two masts and three Lateen sails, and they are constructed with cabins for the accommodation of passengers which occupy the whole aft-part of the deck. Ours has two excellent cabins, fitted up at each side with Turkish divans, capable of being converted at night into four beds, and very neatly furnished with carpets and cushions, besides two book-shelves, well stocked with works of reference for Egyptian travellers. There is a *cabinette de toilette* beyond these, and in front is a tent or awning where the servants sleep; and I assure you that when all the doors are thrown open, our present abode has quite as consequential an appearance as many of the seaside lodging houses in England, where grand pianos are located, and quadrilles are danced in drawing rooms twelve feet long by ten.

Of course our bedding, linen, canteens (cutlery) and *batterie de cuisine* etc are supplied by ourselves, and (our dragoman) Mohammed's perfect knowledge of the outfit required for such an excursion has saved us a world of trouble, and his cleverness and good management in providing everything that he knew to be adapted to English tastes and habits, has really not left us the possibility of forming a wish.

We had wisely prepared ourselves to expect a somewhat scrambling life of it, but most agreeably have we been surprised at finding everything going on under his auspices as smoothly as though we were in the best hotel on shore.

Our crew consists of a Reis, or captain, a pilot, and fourteen Arab sailors, besides which we have a Cairene cook, who is quite an artist, and our trusty interpreter Mohammed, making in all eighteen Mussulmans, to whose tender mercies we have consigned ourselves for the next six weeks. We welcome the coolness of night . . . To us, indeed, it is but comparative, for in July the nights are only less hot than the days. When August comes the suffocation seems increasing, a sort of still breathless heat prevails: this shows the river is at its height. The water is not good to drink at this time, unless filtered or boiled; the peasants do not, however, take this trouble, and drink it as it is.

At last, about the fifth or sixth or August (sometimes several days later), the great day comes when the Nile is cut. The watchers who for a week or more have relieved each other night and day, measuring incessantly to ascertain the moment the right height has been reached, give the news, and immediately the dam is removed and the water flows; not all at once over the country, but at first over the lower lands, and then entering the canals, by degrees waters all the country.

All the coasts of the river are at once flooded, of course, and the effect on the landscape is wonderful to see. Where you saw yesterday a great brown dry field, reaching from the highroad all the way to the river banks, is now a shallow lake glistening in the sun, the little villages with their groups of palm trees peeping out like islands from the water. The pools and brimming canals look very beautiful and refreshing after the long, sultry heat; not that it less hot, rather I think more oppressive in some respects, but the moisture is something delightful to look at; and everyone is so happy. The poor women, who had to toil along a weary way to fill their great pitchers, now laugh and sing as they trip down to the watercourse close at hand; the children spend most of their day in the river or the canals—occasionally, however, getting drowned therein; the great buffaloes stand up to their horns in water, giving contented puffs to show their enjoyment; everywhere reed and rushes spring

Departure of the Kangia from Old Cairo

up with wonderful speed; water birds sport in the places lately full of dry clods and choking dust; the brilliant kingfisher darts after his prey . . .

Ploughing is done by oxen or buffaloes, as is the threshing or treading out of the corn. For this business a man sits in a sort of wooden chair without legs, and with some simple machinery under it, which crushes the corn as the oxen draw it about on a space of hard beaten earth; the feet of the animals and the machine together knock out the grains. Winnowing is done with a shovel, tossing up the corn on a breezy day. They leave the grain out in heaps till it is sold, the climate being so dry.

The Seasons of the Nile and the Inundation, 1875
Mary Whately

> *Unlike many travelers Mary Whately both lived and traveled in Egypt so had experience of the seasons of the year, and watched the life of the peasants.*

As the season heated up in 'Spring' . . . the clover disappears, the cattle having eaten it, and having, poor things, nothing but dry food to look forward
to for several months; the hot winds begin to blow, the corn rapidly gets
yellow, and is reaped in April (I speak here of Middle Egypt). By the middle
of May, the intense heat of summer has usually set in and the fields look dry
and brown—unless watered with much labour from the canals; the very
weeds, except the thistles, which seem to need scarcely any water, are withered up, and man most literally eats bread in the sweat of his brow if he has
to labour in the field. . . .

In July, the heat is at its greatest height and the river at its lowest—everything seems panting and parched; the ground is so hot that one can scarcely
endure to lay a bare hand on its surface, and it appears as if one walked into
a furnace if obliged to be out in any part of the day except the early morning
and late evening. These are very lovely—the pure dry air seems to make
every object stand out and look as if painted in rich and delicate hues, but
like all earthly beauties these fair colours soon fade; as the hours advance a
whitish haze of intense heat seems to settle over everything, and then "the
hireling earnestly desireth the shadow." Well may the weary hired labourer
long for the shadow, which sets him free to throw himself down and rest,
and bathe his burning brow in the waters of the little channel, and enjoy
the comparative coolness of the water.

A Prayer on Starting, 1842
Sophia Poole
A custom which is always observed by the Arab boat-men at the commencement of a voyage much pleased me. As soon as the wind had filled our large
sail, the Reyyis (or captain of the boat) exclaimed, "El-Fat-hah." This is the
title of the opening chapter of the Kur'an (a short and simple prayer), which
the Reyyis and all the crew repeated together in a low tone of voice. Would
to Heaven that, in this respect, the example of the poor Muslim might be
followed by our countrymen, that our entire dependence on the protecting
providence of God might be universally acknowledged, and every journey,
and every voyage, be sanctified by prayer.

Starting Out, 1873
Amelia Edwards
Happy are the Nile travellers who start thus with a fair breeze on a brilliant
afternoon. The good boat cleaves her way swiftly and steadily. Water-side
palaces and gardens glide by, and are left behind. The domes and minarets

of Cairo drop quickly out of sight. The mosque of the citadel, and the ruined fort that looks down upon it from the mountain ridge above, diminish
in the distance. The Pyramids stand up sharp and clear.

We sit on the high upper deck, which is furnished with lounge chairs, tables
and foreign rugs, like a drawing room in the open air, and enjoy the prospect
at our ease. The valley is wide here and the banks are flat, showing a steep
verge of crumbling alluvial mud next to the river. Long belts of palm groves,
tracts of young corn only an inch or two above the surface, and clusters of mud
huts relieved now and then by a little whitewashed cupola or a stumpy minaret,
succeed each other on both sides of the river, while the horizon is bounded to
right and left by long ranges of yellow limestone mountains, in the folds of
which sleep inexpressibly tender shadows of pale violet and blue.

Presently, when it is quite dusk and the stars are out, we moor for the
night at Bedreshayn, which is the nearest point for visiting Sakkarah. There
is a railway station here, and also a considerable village, both lying back
about half a mile from the river; and the distance from Cairo, which is reckoned at fifteen miles by the line, but is probably about eighteen by water.

Such was our first day on the Nile . . .

Fellow Passengers, 1873
Marianne North

All three men smoked continually all the evening, and were consequently
happy, till I felt myself becoming as dry as a red herring; but smoking is a
blessed invention and peacemaker amongst men, and I highly approve of
it, so we all got on tolerably together, and my father's health improved every
day. Mr S. confessed to me that the Frenchman went to bed clothes and all,
and that his toilette in the morning consisted of a thorough brushing downwards with the same brush, beginning with his hair, then his green velvet
coat, and lastly his dear shining boots, *c'est tout, voila!* He made himself of
use in the scolding way, and disapproved from the first of the coffee, which
he called *de l'eau sale.* He also complained that if he could not get filtered
water to wash in, he would not wash his 'figure' at all. He was told that
Madame used that of the Nile for hers. "Madame was too good to complain,
and besides she was an Englishwoman, bah!"

My father's cabin came like a fretful porcupine from the quantity of pins
and nails he hammered all over it, and we used to say that if the vessel took
to rolling at night we should find him minced up in the morning; mine was
perfectly comfortable, and when my waterproof was spread over my bed it
made a capital wash-stand, and on it I painted all day when not on land.

Measuring the Land, 1875
Mary Whately

The arable land is not in Egypt divided by hedges, as in England; measurement is the only thing to decide the limits of the different fields, though of course trees, canals etc, serve as landmarks to the eye. The measurement is made by a reed of a certain length, and in writing of deeds and leases it is always said so many 'reed lengths.'

I was struck years ago by first seeing a man measuring ground in this way; he had a long smooth reed of the kind before described in his hand, and laid it down and lifted it up, making a running leap with great dexterity, and thus went on springing from measure to measure quickly, yet as it seemed accurately. Another man accompanied him, walking behind—at a much slower pace, however. Perhaps you may recollect, in the measuring of Ezekiel's temple, the reed of six cubits long and the height and breadth of different parts being said to be 'one reed'. So this is one among the many things that remain unchanged from the old days.

Encounter on the Banks of the Nile, 1861
Ellen Chennells

I heard the beating of the darra-bouka, then the voice of a female who was also on the river bank attracted my attention. Leaving the Grand Pasha in the Kiosk, I hurried through an avenue, and just as I had reached its extremity, I caught sight of a beautifully gilded *cangia* which was being rowed rapidly along the Nile by eight boatmen dressed in crimson silk shirts. Suddenly they rested on their oars which gave me an opportunity of examining the bark. The deck was covered with thick Smyrna carpets, and there doubled up upon a large blue satin cushion was a veiled lady of rank; perhaps she was one of the Egyptian princesses, for everything about her, even to her rich and elegant costume, denoted her to be no ordinary personage; the beautiful and richly decorated cangia, her superb costume, the attire of the boatmen, the black slaves who surrounded her, all proclaimed her rank.

Two gaunt Abyssinian eunuchs were seated at the prow, wearing snow white turbans, as in days gone by. In all probability that graceful lady had taken it into her head to make a morning aquatic excursion. A slave coquettishly dressed in an azure blue velvet jacket, embroidered with silver, held in her hand the tar whose sounds I had heard, and which I had mistaken for the darrabouka; another, attired in a crimson jacket, richly embroidered with gold, now began to sing in that distinct yet soft voice so peculiar to the denizens of Africa. She was warbling a love ditty, for in the East the women chant nothing else. I stopped, and sitting myself down upon the stump of an old tree, caught her words.

The loveliness of the scene around, and the stillness of the air added additional charms to the beauty of the group on board the *cangia*. The Nile was as calm as an inland lake, and in its waters were reflected the shady avenues of Roda, formerly the favourite resort of the Cairenes in Mahomet Ali's time to enjoy the luxury of roaming about this beautiful place.

In the Mud, 1873
Marianne North

We were continually sticking in the mud, and then all the men jumped into the water, wearing their turbans but throwing aside all their other rags, to push and pull us off again; and once at sunset another beside ours was stranded, and all the neighbouring population was in and out of the river trying to get them off again. The hour of prayer had come, and our saint and some others began at once, just where they were, up to their knees in water, going through all the devotions due to Mahomet. They looked picturesquely black against the orange sky, all reflected in the damp sands and calm river. It was a wonderful study in form and colour.

Another pretty scene was that of the men taking their supper every night, when they would sit round a fire and boil up their broken bits of hard brown bread with an onion and some peas in a large pot, and helped themselves out of it alternately with three fingers hollowed out like a spoon, shaking off back into the pot between each helping what they could not get into their mouths; the little low fire lit up their dark faces most magnificently.

Our Boat from Luxor, 1827
Sarah Lushington

Mrs. Lushington, having crossed the desert from the Red Sea, hired a boat from Luxor to sail north up the Nile. It was far less attractive than the Cairo boats, having probably been used as a freight carrier, but she made what she could of it.

Our servant had the whole morning been cleaning the *maash* selected for us, from the mud and dirt, which adhered to it as least two inches thick.

The outside had already dispelled any illusions I might have had of its resemblance to Cleopatra's galley, but when I entered it, I confess I was quite dismayed. A common coal barge on the river Thames would have afforded better accommodation. Two small cabins in the stern, the wooden partitions besmeared with dirt, every plank divided, some entirely broken out, admitting sun, wind, and rats, and the lowness of the ceiling, which did not allow me standing upright, made me look round in hopeless discomfort.

Few minutes, however, elapsed before our tent was dismantled, the walls thrown over the top of the boat, and a projecting pole added, which, with the help of our trunks for a platform, and a carpet over them, formed a sort of verandah. We nailed table-cloths on the ceiling and sides of the cabin, and the openings most exposed to cold I closed with little coloured mats, which I happened to have brought with me from India. The carpet was spread; our two little brass camp beds soon looked like sofas, and it was no small gratification to me to see a clean, comfortable, nay, almost pretty habitation instead of the dirty dismal hole I had entered an hour before.

A Thousand Mile Journey, 1847
Harriet Martineau

Our object, like that of Egyptian travellers generally, was to sail up the river as fast as the wind would carry us, seeing by the way only as much as would not interfere with progress of the boat. It was the season when the north wind prevailed; and this advantage was not to be trifled with the voyage of a thousand miles, certain as we were of the help of the current to bring us back. We were therefore to explore no pyramids or temples on our way up; and to see only so much of the country as we could get a glimpse of on occasion of the wind, or other accidental delays. To this there was no objection in our minds; for we found at once that in going up the Nile in any manner we should meet with as much novelty and interest as we could bear. The face of the country was enough at one time. To have explored the monuments immediately would have been too much. Moreover, there was great advantage in going up quickly while the river was yet high enough to afford some view of the country. In returning, we found such a change produced by the sinking of the waters only a few feet, that we felt that travellers going up late in the season can hardly be said to have seen the country from the river. At all times, the view of the interior from the Nile must be very imperfect, and quite insufficient to justify any decision against the beauty of the great valley. This arises from the singular structure of the country. Everywhere else, where a river flows through the centre of a valley, the land either slopes from the base of the hills down to the river, or it is level. In Egypt, on the contrary, the land rises from the mountains up to the banks of the Nile; and where, as usually happens, the banks are higher than the eye of the spectator on the deck of his boat, all view of the interior, as far as the hills, is precluded. He sees nothing but the towns, villages, and palm-groves on the banks, and the mountains on the horizon. My attention had been directed upon this point before I went by the complaints of some read-ers of Eastern travels that, after all their reading, they know no more what the Egyptian valley looked like than if it had never been visited. As this fail-ure of description appeared to regard Egypt alone, there must be some pe-culiar cause for it: and thus we found it.

The remedy was, of course, to go ashore as often as possible, and to mount every practicable eminence. I found this so delightful, and every wide view that I obtained included so much that was wonderful and beautiful, that mounting eminences became an earnest pursuit with me. I carried com-pass and note-book, and I noted down what I saw, from eminence to emi-nence, along the whole valley, from Cairo to the Second Cataract. Sometimes I looked abroad from the top of a pylon, sometimes from a rock on the banks; sometimes from a sandy ridge of the desert; sometimes from a green declivity of the interior; once from a mountain above Thebes, and once from the summit of the Great Pyramid. My conclusion is that I differ entirely from those who complain of the sameness of the aspect of the coun-try. The constituent features of the landscape may be more limited in num-ber than in other tracts of country of a thousand miles: but they are so grand and so beautiful, so strange, and brought together in such endless diversity, that I cannot conceive that any one who has really seen the country can complain of its monotony. Each panoramic survey that I made is now as distinct as the images I retain of Niagara, Iona, Salisbury Plain, the Valais and Lake Garda.

By Road, 1948
Eileen Bigland

She left Cairo after nightfall and was soon past the suburbs when they met a camel caravan coming into Cairo market with their produce.

From then on the procession seemed endless. Motor vehicles were rare indeed, and the few we saw were broken down at the roadside with their perspiring drivers scrabbling vainly inside the bonnets or endeavouring to mend punctures while a crowd of gesticulating white-clad figures stamped around them giving much useless advice in raucous voices, and past them plodded the camels, the water-buffalo, the donkeys and the families to whom these animals belonged.

Under each donkey cart hung a small charcoal brazier as a primitive form of tail-lamp, and at times, looking ahead I could see these glowing jewel-bright, like long strings of rubies looped along the road.

The water-buffalo drew bigger carts and great loads, and sometimes whole families sprawled across the produce in the abandonment of sleep. . . . The camels had all the arrogance of their species. Heads held high and with an expression of ineffable disdain on their faces, they swayed forward, occasionally giving a vicious snap at anyone who threatened to get in their way. Slung from their backs were enormous panniers weighted down with the fruits of the earth, and I noticed that the fellahin in charge of the camels put on a certain swagger, a conscious superiority of mien— and well they might, for did not possession of a camel stamp you as a man of property?

On and on came the long train of pack-animals, the dust swirling and eddying about their feet, the white or striped gallabiyehs of their owners billowing around them, the fire-flies darting to and fro above their heads; and about twenty five kilometres out of Cairo we parked our wagon up a side lane that ran through a gap in the trees to a canal, and sat down by the roadside to watch.

Along the River on a Breezy Winter Day, 1875
Mary Whately

The banks are not green in general, nor flowery—the inundation prevents that, making a fresh bank every year—and yet there is a great deal of beauty; the clear air and brilliant sun make *everything* beautiful, in fact, and the groups of palms are a delight to the eye. Fields of bright green clover and young corn reach as far as the eye can see on one side, on the other a range of cliffs, sometimes high, sometimes low, barren, and dry; but their yellow and white rocks take wonderful colours, in the sunset especially. Little villages dot the coast, some all among palm-trees, others with only a few standing up like sentinels among the low mud dwellings; here and there a little grove of gum-arabic trees grow near the river on a raised path-

way, and as the sky grows red with the evening light, and the sun sinks behind golden clouds, troops of peasants are seen on this same high pathway,
driving their buffaloes and cows from the pasture, and shepherds with large
flocks of goats.

It is customary (and safest) to moor the boats at night, so we draw up to
shore, and are soon made fast to a peg driven in the earth. A number of
men, wrapt in mantles of brown goats' hair, or wool, are seated on the bank;
one or two are still at their evening prayers, kneeling and touching the
ground with their heads, then standing, then kneeling again, and all the
while repeating the Moslem form of prayer . . .

Employment of Our Time, 1827
Wolfradine Minutoli

To give my readers an idea of the manner in which we spent our days, when
they did not afford any thing particularly interesting in the study of antiquities, I will give them a sketch of our occupations and amusements.

We rose very early, because the extreme coolness of the nights and the
evening dews are very prejudicial to the eyes, obliged us to retire betimes.
After our breakfast, which consisted of coffee and buffaloes' milk, which we
never had any difficulty to procure, my husband and Dr Ricci, provided
with fowling-pieces, and myself, attended by my little negro,* went on
shore: while the gentlemen were occupied in their sport, I amused myself
with botanising.

Met along the Way, 1875
Mary Whately

*Mary Whately, who lived in Egypt for several years and trav-
eled regularly on the Nile, was more familiar with the lives
of the people met along the way than most other travelers.*

---

*   The Minutolis bought a young slave boy who accompanied them on their journey
and returned with them to Germany.

Almost every woman comes into market with a load on her head of some kind—either a pitcher of sour milk, or a *skin* of the same, with lumps of butter in it, or a basket of eggs or fowls, cheese or dates, leeks or onions, or any vegetables in season. There is little except provisions of a common kind, cattle etc, and a few coloured prints, and pieces of unbleached calico, thread, etc sold in the market; scarcely anything of show or luxury, unless it be a few tiny looking-glasses, and clumsy combs, and red handkerchiefs in a corner. It is only in late years that a few plates and dishes are occasionally found in the houses of the wealthier farmers; the coarse red pottery of the country, made in a sort of pan, being the only earthen vessels in most village dwellings, and even these are not numerous. I used to wonder in those early days how they drank (not having spoon nor cup), till I saw them lift a pitcher of considerable weight (though much smaller than that carried on the head to *bring* water) and *pour* the draught from a height into their throats. I tried to do the same, but early habit being wanting, I only succeeded in watering my clothes plentifully, without getting more than a drop or two in the right direction.

The countrywomen are by no means as carefully veiled as the townspeople, and a greater many of the poorer ones have no face-covering at all; but if they have to speak to a man, most will draw the muslin veil across the mouth and nose, holding it with one hand, or in the teeth, if both hands are busy weighing cheese or dates.

The Nile Day—Tracking and Sailing, 1873
Amelia Edwards

Thus the morning passes. We sit on deck writing letters; reading; watching the sunny river-side pictures that glide by at a foot's pace and are so long in sight. Palm-groves, sand-banks, patches of fuzzy-headed dura, and fields of some yellow-flowering herb, succeed each other. A boy plods along the bank, leading a camel. They go slowly; but they soon leave us behind. A native boat meets us, floating down side-wise with the current. A girl comes to the water's edge with a great empty jar on her head, and waits to fill it till the trackers have gone by. The pigeon-towers of a mud-village peep above a clump of lebbek trees, a quarter of a mile inland. Here a solitary brown man, with only a felt skull-cap on his head and a slip of scanty tunic fastened about his loins, works a shaduf, stooping and rising, stooping and rising, with the regularity of a pendulum. It is the same machine which we will see by and by depicted in the tombs at Thebes; and the man is so evidently an ancient Egyptian, that we find ourselves wondering how he escaped being mummified four or five thousand years ago.

By and by, a little breeze springs up. The men drop the rope and jump on board—the big sail is set—and away we go again, as merrily as the day we left Cairo.

That night, having sailed on till past nine o'clock, we moor about a mile from Beni Souef, and learn with some surprise that a man must be despatched to the governor of the town for guards. Not that anything ever happened to anyone at Beni Souef, says Talhamy; but the place is supposed not to have a first rate reputation. If we have guards, we at all events make the governor responsible for our safety and the safety of our possessions. So the guards are sent for; and being posted on the bank, snore loudly all night long, just outside our windows.

Creating a Flag, 1873
Marianne North

Travelers usually flew a flag—sometimes to show their nationality; sometimes to tell other travelers who they were—having registered their emblem in Cairo.

The Shadoof

At Minieh we landed, and I bought some red and white calico, and then some more white to be dyed blue (that colour is never kept in stock, as the natives prefer having it fresh), and I set to work to make a Union Jack. When we started my father had refused to have one, thinking it would hurt the Frenchman's feelings, but now to his horror he found that he had hoisted the tricolour on board, and as both he and Achmet talked of buying slaves, my father thought it was time we had the English flag over our heads to render such traffic illegal; so we soon had a very remarkable specimen of that noble ensign, to which the French flag had to give place.

Nile Days—on the S.S. *Ramses the Great*, 1907
Norma Lorimer

It is delightful to think that we are going to do nothing all day today but enjoy the Nile—do nothing but feel the spell of Egypt—do nothing but sit under a shady awning, where a cool breeze always drifts from the bows of the boat, and watch the procession of Egypt pass along the green margin of the river's banks—do nothing but watch the fierce sunlight play on the amber sands. To be cool oneself and watch a hot world at work, what a luxury! what unconscious arrogance in the pleasure! yet is not enjoyment like all else merely relative? If there was nothing else to watch all day but the antics of our Soudanese crew, it would be sufficient for me. There is the ostrich-feather broom boy who watches for a speck of dust to brush away, and the brass boys who lift up rugs and mats to find some hidden treasure in the way of knobs to polish, indeed there is a boy with a grinning smile and flashing teeth for every mortal occupation you can imagine. I often wonder if there is a special crew kept to do nothing but say their prayers, for there is always a group of black-skinned Soudanese in white drawers on their knees in the bows of the boat. Perhaps Thomas Cook and Son recognise how valuable they are for "off days" on the Nile for tourists to kodak.

I was waked by the flush of the sunrise which flooded my room, and which called me to be up and doing—to watch the beginning of the new day.

It scarcely looked like a new day, except for its rosy, youthful light and the chill in the air, for all the world on the banks seemed to be doing exactly what it was doing last night when the lights went out; nothing had changed, it seemed as though only darkness had fallen over the land and had shut out all sights and sounds of man.

The End of the Day, 1914
E.L. Butcher

Towards evening the flocks and herds stream back to their village in charge of the herdsmen, often a small child or an old man, who walks along spinning wool in a primitive manner. The women have, many of them, been at work all day, but they have still their water to fetch from the river or the nearest canal. A group of these slight, erect figures in their trailing garments, each with an enormous jar poised upon her head, making the way to the water through the sunset glow, is one of the most picturesque sights in Egypt.

Among the picturesque objects to be seen in the provinces are the domed white tombs outside the villages or by the roadside. The earliest of these cover the bones of long-forgotten Christians, but for some centuries it has been customary to bury Mohammedan 'saints' in this way. In the case of a religious beggar—one who has chosen a certain spot where he sits all day in rags chanting appeals to Allah, and to the public in His name—it has been customary to bury him on the same spot which he hallowed by his presence in life. When this happened to be among the palms, just at the entrance to a village, the result was a picturesque object which harmed no one; but as the towns spread and grew, these tombs which, once built, were of course inviolable, became a very great inconvenience and obstruction to traffic.

The Bird Life of the Nile, 1873
Amelia Edwards

The birds are new and we are always looking out for them. Perhaps we see a top-heavy pelican balancing his huge yellow bill over the edge of the stream, and fishing for his dinner—or a flight of wild geese trailing across the sky towards the sunset—or a select society of vultures perched all in a row upon a ledge of rock, and solemn as the bench of bishops. Then there are herons who stand on one leg and doze in the sun; the strutting hoopoes with their legendary top-knots; the blue and green bee-eaters hovering over the uncut dura. The pied kingfisher, black and white like a magpie, sits fearlessly under the bank and never stirs, though the tow-rope swings close above his head and the dahabeeyah glides within a few feet of the shore. The paddy-birds whiten the sandbanks by hundreds, and rise in a cloud at our approach. The sacred hawk, circling overhead, utters the same sweet, piercing, melancholy note that the Pharaohs listened to of old.

Meeting Crocodiles, 1845
Isabel Romer

Yesterday was marked by us with a white stone, as being the date of our first personal introduction to live crocodiles! I was summoned from my cabin to behold the monstrous reptiles basking on a bank of sand in the river; there were three of them—one enormously large—I should say at least fifteen feet long, and the two others evidently young things. A double-barrelled gun was immediately discharged at them, which caused the little ones to shuffle away into the water in a great fright; but the old fellow treated the salute with superb contempt, and after a second or two that showed he was accustomed to stand fire, waddled in leisurely after them, appearing to be quite conscious that the shot might have been fired at the citadel of Cairo with the same effect as against his own impenetrable scales.

The Egyptian Beetle, 1873
Amelia Edwards

It was, I think, the afternoon of this second day, when strolling by the margin of the river, that we first made the acquaintance of that renowned insect, the Egyptian beetle. He was a very fine specimen of his race, nearly half an inch long in the back, as black and shiny as a scarab cut in jet, and busily engaged in the preparation of a large rissole of mud, which he presently began laboriously propelling up the bank. We stood and watched him for some time, half in admiration, half in pity. This rissole was at least four times bigger than himself, and to roll it up that steep incline to the point beyond the level of next summer's inundation was a labour of Hercules for so small a creature. One longed to play the part of *Deus ex machina*, and carry it up the bank for him; but that would have been a denouement beyond his power of appreciation.

We all know the old story of how this beetle lays its eggs by the river's brink; encloses them in a ball of moist clay; rolls the ball to a safe place on the edge of the desert; buries it in the sand; and when his time comes, dies content, having provided for the safety of his successors. Hence his mythic fame; hence all the quaint symbolism that by degrees attached itself to his little person, and ended by investing him with a special sacredness which has often been mistaken for actual worship.

Assiout Shawls, 1907
Norma Lorimer

Yesterday we called at Assiout, which to the tourist on the Nile means one thing—"spangled shawls." When I set out from London there was one thing

I knew I should not do in Egypt, and that was to buy a silver or gold spangled shawl. I did not know where they were to be found or how much they
cost, but I knew that they were Egyptian and that I hated them.

Imagine my surprise when I suddenly saw the whole bank of the Nile,
as we approached the landing stage at Assiout, glittering and gleaming and
alive with spangled shawls!

The bargaining began directly the boat got near enough to the landing-
stage for the sound of voices to carry. You would have thought that without
a gold or silver spangled shawl no Cook's tourist could enter the temple of
Denderah, which we are to see on Monday. Our first temple!

First View, 1827
Sarah Lushington

> *Mrs. Lushington was passing through Egypt from the Red
> Sea on her way home from India. Each year, before the open-
> ing of the Suez Canal, many travelers passed through the
> Red Sea and traveled to the Nile and Luxor before turning
> north up the Nile on their way from India towards home.*

While I was leisurely travelling along, thinking only of our arrival at Luxor,
one of the party who had preceded us, called to me from a rising ground to
turn to the left, and having gone a few hundred yards off the road, I beheld,
unexpectedly, the temple of Karnak. It was long after I reached my tent ere
I recovered from the bewilderment into which the view of these stupendous
ruins had thrown me. No one, who has not seen them, can understand the
awe and admiration they excite even in unscientific beholders. When I compare the descriptions of Denon and Hamilton, I find them essentially correct yet without giving me any adequate idea of the glorious reality.

Arriving at Luxor, 1873
Amelia Edwards

Coming on deck the third morning after leaving Dendereh, we found the
dahabieh decorated with palm-branches, our sailors in their holiday turbans, and Reis Hassan *en grande tenue*: that is to say in shoes and stockings,
which he only wore on very great occasions.

"Neharak-sa'id—good' morning—Luxor!" said he, all in one breath.

It was a hot, hazy morning, with dim ghosts of mountains glowing through the mist, and a warm wind was blowing.

We ran to the side; looked out eagerly; but could see nothing. Still the Captain smiled and nodded; and the sailors ran hither and thither, sweeping and garnishing; and Egendi, of whom his worst enemy could not have imputed the charge of bashfulness, said "Luxor—sheep—all right!" every time he came near us.

We had read and dreamt so much about Thebes, and it had always seemed so far away, that but for this delicate allusion to the promised sheep, we could hardly have believed that we really drawing nigh unto those famous shores. About ten, however, the mist was lifted away like a curtain, and we saw to the left a rich plain studded with palm-groves; to the right a broad margin of cultivated lands bounded by a bold range of limestone mountains; and on the farthest horizon another range, all grey and shadowy.

"Karnak—Gournah—Luxor!" says Reis Hassan triumphantly, pointing in every direction at once.

But when going up the Nile most dahabiehs did not stop at Luxor on the way—they sailed on towards Nubia, using the wind to drive them, and returned to Luxor later with the flow of the stream.

Met on the Nile, 1827
Wolfradine Minutoli

Some days after we met several boats filled with negro slaves of both sexes, coming from Darfur and Sennaar, and laden besides with elephant's teeth, ostrich feathers, gold dust, parrots, etc. The people who are engaged in this traffic are called *gelaps*; they generally carry off children by force or by stratagem, and even frequently purchase them of the parents themselves. Not being accustomed to this sight, we felt at the view of these poor wretches, deprived of their liberty and forced from their native land, a sentiment of pity which would not have been so lively if we had known the state of destitution and misery which they experience in their own country.

The Turks* are generally humane towards their slaves, who, besides, enjoy the protection of the laws in a special manner; for they have a right to demand to be resold whenever their condition becomes unhappy, and their masters venture to ill-treat them, which makes their situation almost equal to that of our servants in Europe. A great number of these Negroes are employed in guarding the harems.† The Pacha of Egypt, who is very magnificent in all his presents, sometimes sends several hundreds at once to the Grand Seignor.** The negresses are particularly employed within doors; most of them are very intelligent, and learn with facility all sorts of female work.

The Europeans, who dare not have white slaves in Egypt, have now obtained the right of purchasing black ones; hence all the rich families at Cairo generally have some in their service. We ourselves purchased a boy whom we afterwards brought to Europe, and who gave proofs of the happiest natural disposition. This child, who learned several languages in a short time, told us in the sequel in what manner he had been carried off with several of his brothers and sisters, while they were all at play in a garden.

To the Great Oasis of the Libyan Desert, May, 1908
Norma Lorimer

What actually fired us into going to the oasis was the fact that before the Oasis Company laid their railway across the desert, it used to take, by the shortest route, sixty hours on camel, that was from Gorgah, a distance of one hundred and twenty miles.

The route from Esneh is one hundred and thirty-eight miles; and the route from Assiout, which is part of the road by which slaves were formerly brought into Egypt from Darfur and Kordofan, is one hundred and six miles from the Nile. The journey generally takes five to six days by camel.

We left Cairo at 6:30 p.m., had a most comfortable bed and dinner on board the train, and arrived at the Western Oasis at about sundown next evening. It seemed almost incredible that we could have done that same six days' journey by camel in that short space of time on a train, and have done it too as easily and comfortably as though we had been travelling from Paris to Nice.

---

*   By 'Turks' she means the people of the Turkish Ottoman Empire under whose rule Egypt was at this time.
†   Some travelers reported that male slaves were castrated en route to Cairo—and these might be the ones who worked as guards in the harems.
**   The Grand Seignor was the Sultan in Constantinople

The *wagon-lits* in Egypt are very cool and comfortable, for they are built of wicker-work, and everything about them is extremely modern and well planned to alleviate the trials of a dusty journey.

Harvest, January 1874
Marianne North

About Silsilis they were harvesting their dourra (millet), rather a dwarf variety, but the heads well filled. They generally cut the ears off first, and then the straw, but some people cut down the whole plant at once, and in all cases they thresh it out on the spot. Camels and donkeys were eating their fill of it, and there seemed to much shedding and waste of the grain, though the straw did not look ripe.

The threshing process was very picturesque; two buffaloes and three cows we saw in one place driven in a circle over the dourra, while a boy with a rake gathered back the ears which had been pushed out of reach of the animals' feet; the beasts were muzzled—an unnecessary precaution, as there were plenty of small boys with nothing to do but to look after the cattle, all the younger children being unclothed because of the heat.

Lupins, with blue and white flowers, were the common crop of the Nile mud close to the water's edge, and looked very pretty. Wheat was also a good deal dibbled in on such spots, with a kind of broomrape growing amongst it, no doubt a parasite, as all of that family are. The date palms often grew in clusters of seven or more one root-centre, and their curves and feathery tops were most elegant.

5
Nubia and Beyond
and Turning North

Taking advantage of the wind from the north, travelers pushed on past Luxor toward Nubia. South of Aswan, before the building of the so-called 'British dam' at the turn of the twentieth century, travelers had the alarming experience of being taken through the cataracts by the Reis of the Cataract and his men. Then came the much loved island of Philae, other temples and the villages of Nubia and the great excitement of reaching the vast temple of Abu Simbel. Many travelers went on toward the second cataract and the great Rock at Abusir, where many carved their names—or had them carved—to celebrate the end of the journey.

Then they turned north again and traveled with the flow of the river.

Approaching Nubia, 1861
M.L.M. Carey

As we approach the scenery of the cataracts, very fine palm-trees again greet the eye, the hills begin to assume a darker hue, and the sandstone gives place to the granite rock. A few Roman ruins crown the top of the hills on the eastern bank as we proceed. On the western, the sand of the desert lies thickly strewn upon the rocks. Here was the island of Kubanieh, and the home of our Reis. He landed, and was surrounded by a very respectable body of black relatives, for they are Nubians; and before parting he left a basket full of presents for his mother. Each man of the crew, whose home lay on our way, was allowed to pay it a visit, and to rejoin the dahabeeh at the next village at which we stayed for the night. These people never meet their friends empty-handed, and Mohamed had provided a large box to contain his presents for his friends. They were frequently handsome, such as a fez, some coffee cups, or a silk handkerchief, and he received many in return, in the form of dates, sugar-canes, and sheep.

At half-past four P.M., Saturday, Dec. 15th we reached Assouan, the ancient Syene; and here 'Cousin Phil' and the whole party turned out for a walk. I stay on the bank fishing, Mohammed squatted at my side, musing and meditating on the lovely romantic scenery, and on the remains of past glory and grandeur.

But I must not forget the beautiful approach to Assouan. Here begins the actual rocky scenery of the Cataracts, and river appears enclosed as in a basin, or like the opening of a harbour, with lofty hills on either side. The island of Elephantina is in front, and small islands, with the most brilliant patches of vegetation, stud the water. Palm-trees, sont, young barley, and lupines of brilliant emerald green growing on every little scrap of earth (the deposit of the river), between the picturesque masses of granite and porphyry, of which the islets are composed.

In some cases a great number of large, ancient stones are heaped up, as though placed there in preparation for a building; in others they stand erect, singly, and covered with hieroglyphics. Here they assume all kinds of fantastic shapes, human figures, skulls, or old castles; there they are cut into huge plain blocks bearing the marks of the wedges used to detach them from the larger mass, and lying about as though waiting to be laid in the spot for which they were originally designed. Some of these masses are of enormous size, and we noticed one which had every appearance of having been destined for an Obelisk.

To Far Syene, 1873
Marianne North

A brisk wind made us unfurl our big sail, and carried us in a few hours to Assouan—the far Syene, now a collection of mud huts and bazaars full of strange wild people from the interior, selling ostrich feathers and elephants' tusks; we noticed fifty skin packages, each containing four of these tusks, lying on the shore for shipment, and so heavy that my father and Mr S. could not lift one of them, though using all their united force; slaves were also said to be sold here, but it was illegal and was not done openly. Enormous granite boulders were strewn about the river all round us, some of them covered with hieroglyphical inscriptions, and the channel was narrowed by the island of Elephanta. We spent the morning there among a most amusing crowd of little imps with three tufts on their heads, like the clown Grimaldi, with some leather fringe and glass beads for their sole clothing; they had at first but one word in their mouths—"baksheesh," but were not otherwise annoying; they roared with laughter at the sketch Mr S. made of them and me, it set their tongues free, and they chattered like monkeys; I imitated them, which made them mimic me in return, and we parted excellent friends, and lost the hateful word 'baksheesh' altogether.

Nubian women are often handsome, very fond of ornaments, and like showing them off; one grand lady at Korosko had three gold wheels with coral pendants in her forehead, a gold nose-ring like a double trumpet, two necklaces, one of shuttle-shaped onyx stones with coral and silver between, and splendid silver bangles on arms and wrists. Another had gold and silver rings and coins plaited in her innumerable tails of hair, which gave me the idea of never being undone, but simply soaked with castor oil occasionally; she was sitting on the steps of a sakkiah or native machine for raising water, flogging the beast who turned it, and her baby was seated near her on the sand, a perfect lump of black flies, and so completely hidden by them that one could only discover it was a baby by its general shape and happy childish noises.

Sun and Water, 2006
Rosemary Mahoney

Aswan's desert air seems to caress the town with warm promise, lending vividness and meaning to the manifestations of poverty and human struggle that would elsewhere be considered ugly. The piles of garbage, the heaps of smouldering ashes, the scatterings of broken glass, the architectural rubble, the human excrement, the sun-bleached plastic shopping bags and rusted tin cans that seem to ring all Egyptian villages and besmirched every empty plane between them are, in Aswan, softened by the sheer volume of sun and water, colour and air. Here, fishermen's houses cobbled together out of mud bricks and rusted tin cans appear somehow more ingenious than slovenly, more fascinating than dispiriting.

In a little village near the Old Cataract Hotel, I stepped on a scrap of shaggy bath mat in the road and realised with a start that it bore in one of its corners a yellowed set of jaws studded with two rows of brittle teeth. In another corner it had a moth-eaten tail. It was not a mat at all but the flattened carcass of a dog, a mud-caked rope tied round one hind leg, tongue hanging out like a twisted strip of leather. It had been there a long time. I walked on, fine beige dust splashing up round my ankles with each step, and knew that the thing I had just stepped on would have had a considerably more disturbing effect on me in a cold and rainy climate.

Nubian Afternoon and Evening, 1861
M.L.M. Carey

Thursday, December 27th. We sailed on with a side wind, the thermometer still the same, 85° and 110°, yet the awning was not allowed to be raised. Selina took refuge in the cabin, and, for want of better occupation, sketched its interior; Cousin Phil fell asleep on the divan, inside his umbrella; I sat by, and, having secured the four corners of my writing paper, with some fragments of 'Memnon' and the 'Cataracts', proceeded to write, with a pen in one hand, umbrella in the other, my mother's neutral-tint spectacles to keep off ophthalmia, and a veil tucked under my chin, but ineffectual to baffle the undaunted flies. It certainly was writing under difficulties.

Here a Nubian paddled across on a boat made of three bundles of cane, tied together, and floated on the water. We stopped at a small village, to bargain for a calf which was discovered there; but the price was too high for the dragoman's purse; so the calf was allowed to live a little longer, and we to go without the intended veal.

At four p.m. the '*Cairo*' stopped at Sabooa. The hills on the eastern shore were suffused with a deep, rich purple colour, contrasting beautifully with the bright yellow sand on the western side. A golden sunset soon glowed behind the lions of the temple, and the silver moon, nearly at the 'full', rose in the clear blue vault above. We did not land this evening, but the crew jumped on shore, and, with amusing avidity, started hopping and jumping matches on the mud-bank, with all the ardour of schoolboys. Even the fat,

heavy-looking dragoman surprised the company by the high springs in the
air with which he led off the fun.

Nubia, 1858
Emily Anne Beaufort
Our eyes opened the next morning on a gay and pretty scene: instead of
the yellow hills and smooth sandbanks of Egypt, strange black, shining
rocks popped up in the very middle of the stream—an old Saracenic wall
or fortification stretched down to the river's edge on the north, as if to
shut out Egypt from our sight, while in the narrow channel between the
east side and the green island of Elephantine four dahabiehs besides our
own were moored, with the Pasha's steamer, which had towed up Lord
Dufferin's boats. The high sandy bank was shaded with palm-trees and
covered with gaily-saddled donkeys, riding-camels, tame ostriches, and
crowds of Nubians offering spears, daggers, bows and arrows, pieces of
ivory and sandal-wood, ostrich feathers and eggs, silver bracelets, clay cups
and vases, savage-looking necklaces and head-dresses of shells, strips of
rhinoceros- and hippopotamus-hide, leopard skins, mats, and baskets of
dates for sale.

It was tempting to linger among them, but we had business to settle:
besides which a ride, our first ride in the desert, was more tempting still.

The Nubian Women, 1827
Wolfradine Minutoli
We . . . visited . . . the charming Isle of Elephantina, covered with a groves
of palms, and a luxuriant vegetation. The complexion of the natives, after
having passed through gradations of colour, was, at Syene, of a black and
chocolate hue. The women of Nubia do not veil themselves with the same
strictness as the Egyptians. The young girls wear a small apron, with leather
fringes, and adorned with shells. They are very ingenuous and simple in
their manners; and any infraction on the established laws is punished by the
father of the family with the utmost rigour.

The Nubians grease their hair in a very disagreeable manner; they use
for this purpose oil obtained from the plant called Palma Christi, which
they cultivate with much care, and which we found growing round all their
huts; they then divide their hair in an infinite number of small tresses, so
tightly braided that they generally last for their whole life. Hence we may
easily judge the neatness of the head-dress. Like the negresses, they have a
taste for tinsel and glass beads.

When we landed on the island of Elephantine, the women and children flocked about us with a cordiality which we had not before met with: they eagerly brought us many little antiquities which they had found on the island, in exchange for which we gave them glass beads, knives, and small looking-glasses, for which they expressed their satisfaction by a thousand demonstrations of joy and gratitude.

The most perfect confidence was soon established between us; they chatted and laughed together, showing two rows of teeth as white as ivory. The figure of the young women appeared to me charming; their skin was as soft as satin, in spite of the burning sun to which they are constantly exposed. I believe that the oil with which they anoint their hair and part of their bodies, contributes to produce this effect. I had occasion to admire their courage, for I saw several of them cross the Nile sitting astride upon the stem of a date tree, with an oar in their hands, without appearing to be afraid of crocodiles; who, by seizing one of their legs, might easily have dragged them to the bottom.

Coming to and Leaving Assouan, 1874
Marianne Brocklehurst

Thursday, January 15 The scenery here is quite changed. Great granite rocks are piled up on each side of the river and form an island, Elephantine, in the middle. We pass it on the right as we enter into the bend for Assouan. It is very curious and pretty here. We first see the deep golden, almost orange sands and sand drifts of Nubia, contrasting with the dark granite rocks very strangely.

We go to bazaar in Assouan, buy curious Nubian baskets, spears, 'Madame Nubia' (as they call the peculiar fringe worn by the girls but not by the women now and which constitutes full dress with bracelets and another fringe attached for silver earrings for the head, a Kohl bag, ostrich feathers, antelope horns and other savage articles. We hold palaver with the handsome Governor under the sycamore tree and smoke with him and present our letter of introduction and receive permission to go up the Cataract in due time.

We all start from Assouan at nine,* sail up the river a mile or two by the islands and rocks—granite rocks which are heaped up on either side and

---

* Miss Brocklehurst and a friend were traveling with Amelia Edwards and her group.

Approach to Philae

remind us of Cornwall and Scilly. Some have hieroglyphics cut on them, cartouches (that is, ovals containing the name of a king) showing that their majesties went up the Cataract, or did not go up, as it happened. On arriving at the first bab or gate of the Cataract, we find a heavy strong current flowing over dangerous rocks and we do not find the 300 men promised by the sheik ready for us, so for these gentlemen we have to wait an hour or two. . . . At last the *Philae*, which is first, gets into tow and a pretty row there is. Most of the Arabs scream, everybody directs, a great many look on and a few pull at the ropes, which are cleverly arranged on both sides of the dahabeeyah, as well as the chief rope in front, a breakage being dangerous work amongst these sharp rocks and rushing water. After a bit, the great ship struggles up and it is our turn next and then the Mansoura's.

All manage to get up the Bab and a few hundred yards further, our boats swarming with these Arabs who have us in possession. And then, though the wind is good and it is broad daylight, these doughty Arabs strike work for the day. There is nothing for it but to take a walk to the pretty village of Mahatta, half way to Philae, and Philae, the object of our desire, is but five miles from Assouan and we are likely to be four or five days getting there!

It was Monday, 19 January before Miss Brockleburst could write thankfully in her journal: "At last the Philae gets towed up the Great Bab, after breaking her rope once and nearly getting smashed. We will do the same thing, barring the breakage, and anchor soon after. The next day she wrote: . . . We anchor under the beautiful little temple of Isis at Philae . . . "

Assouan, 1844
Countess Hahn Hahn

Goods sent by water from Wadi Halfa to Cairo must be unloaded in Messid and again shipped in Assuan, after camels have conveyed them from one harbour to another. Gold-dust, elephant's teeth, and ostrich feathers are the principal articles of commerce from the interior of Africa; so we are informed by a French merchant who is established in Assuan, and who has just returned from Dongola with a caravan of six and forty camels (all his own), whither he had carried European wares of every possible kind—stuffs, implements, glass and bronzes. The black slaves are another and important article of merchandise.

Camels in these countries are invaluable beasts; without them merchants and travellers could not stir. I acknowledge their merits, but I am heartily glad that I have no longer occasion to avail myself of them. Here, as in Messid, they lie in large numbers on the banks of the river, with bales of goods about them, close to the tents or huts of palm leaves in which the owners or the drivers live, until arrangements are made for the further journey. What genuine oriental pictures! The merchants sitting with their pipes under palm-trees, the extended camels, the bales of goods with spices and other fine things; down by the shore, the vessels with their long sail-yards; and then the Nile with the black rocky masses of Elephantina, Bab and Philae! Or there advances, perhaps, a caravan of slim, swarthy Nubians, whose deep-red turbans and white shawls, thrown round the head and shoulders, very well become them.

Philae, with its double pair of entrances, with the long columnar porticoes, with the various temple-halls, which at first are free and open, but the nearer you approach the interior, the holy of holies, become darker and more secret—Philae could witness even now, if the rubbish were removed, some portions completed, and the magnificent ascent from the Nile by the obelisk restored, the celebration of the mysteries of the great goddess to whom the temple was dedicated. It is still, in the midst of its devastation, distinguished by such solemn and sublime a character, that its figures of gods, with sparrow-hark heads and horns of cows, appeared to me, in connection with them, like the feverish and sickly dreams of a great and mighty spirit.

Assouan, 1907
Norma Lorimer

Moslem Assouan is delightful, as all unspoilt Moslem things are. It has an Arab cemetery, which lies in exquisite solitude alone in the desert. It was this Arab cemetery, which did not come into Cooks' tourists' programme of the day ashore, which told me that there were sweeter and better things in Assouan than all the Greco-Roman remains of dynastic rock-hewn tombs in Nubia. I saw this cemetery only for a few minutes, but it took me into the heart of the Moslem world. For a brief moment only I was alone with the sky, death, and the desert—a stolen moment in which I travelled far beyond the margin of the world, deep into the kingdom where thought loses itself in infinity. This little cemetery told me that Assouan is not composed of one huge hotel and a street full of ostrich-feather shops. It showed me that if you turned your back on the Nile and that most entrancing view, which in spite of its golden shores and waving palms does not speak to you of Egypt but of some dream-place which has no sacred link with the past, you will find yourself face to face with Africa, with unclaimed Africa and "golden-treasured Nubia."

Stretched out before you lie the white-domed tombs of sheikhs, as graceful in the new brilliancy of the tropics as the fairy kiosks of Aladdin's palace, yet sad with that tender sadness which hovers round lonely desert tombs; and beyond them, in the valley, the great caravan route of the desert, which is no less than the ancient bed of the Nile. Along this road, if you wait but one half-hour, you will see a strange procession of travellers—a procession which will show you that you are very deep in Africa, that the Nubia which you hoped to see is here!

Rowing South from Elephantine Island, 2006
Rosemary Mahoney

The author traveled by herself, rowing a small boat.

The further up river I went, the more the islands seem to multiply in the distance, each one more beautiful, isolated and exotic than the last. But with every island I passed, the current grew stronger, the river rockier and more complicated, seeming to divide itself into a dozen separate creeks. As I approached the top of each island, I had to struggle mightily to surmount the surge of water that the head of the island had diverted. Going higher on this part of the river was a bit like climbing a mountain. (Florence Nightingale had referred to this place as "the staircase.") Every major step was a struggle, interspersed with moments of blessed rest. I picked my way, crablike, backward up the river. I rested by wedging my oar behind an island rock or tree trunk, and it was only then that I had time to look around and see where I was. The islands were uninhabited, supported no man-made structures, and offered a pristine glimpse of what the Nile was like thousands of years ago; the grasses and plants that were here had remained unchanged for aeons.

Exotic birds—reed larks, olivaceous warblers, little green bee-eaters—perched on swaying reeds a mere foot from my face and stared boldly at me. They seemed unafraid. Minnows skittered through the duckweed that floated along the banks in billowing rafts, like blankets of worsted green gauze.

Assouan, 1914
E.L. Butcher
Assouan is the favourite haunt of the Egyptian tourist, and enormous hotels have been built there in the last few years. A few miles to the south the great dam, or barrage, stretches its stony rampart across the river, and beyond poor Philae floats,* beautiful in her dying, on a waste of water when the Nile is high. It is a work worthy of the ancient Egyptians, but it may be questioned whether they should have planted it just there. On the island the pagan temples still lift their beautiful columns to the azure sky, but the Christian churches which succeeded them lie in indistinguishable ruin.

The river here was very beautiful at this point, with its many islands, its swift rapids, and broad levels of smooth water. Here is the oldest Nile water

---

* The building of the first dam across the Nile above Aswan in 1900 created a Nile 'lake' above it—just as the present High Dam created. The island of Philae was largely under this water for years before later developments brought it again above the Nile.

gauge, graven on the rocks by Pharaoh of old; here are inscriptions of many dates and many nationalities throughout the ages which have run their course since then. On one bank glass was made in very early times, and fragments may still be gathered from the desert.

Assouan, or the first cataract, was the southern boundary of Egypt almost all through the centuries which lie between the conquest of Egypt by the Moslems in 640 and the expeditions by which Mohammed Ali annexed the Soudan to Egypt in 1820. By that time the once-flourishing Christian kingdoms of the Soudan, who had opposed so determined a front to the Moslems that Amr gave up all idea of conquering the country, had disappeared. The slave trade which the Arabs had succeeded in establishing had led to all the usual horrors of war and massacre; little by little the flourishing towns and stately churches had been destroyed, and for some two hundred years before the expedition of Mohammed Ali the Soudan had been in the hands of a group of slave-traders, who called themselves sultans, and lived by the wholesale robbery and plunder of the dependent population, among whom the traces of past Christianity were few and far between.

The southern frontier, however, is not now at Assouan, or the cataract just above it, but practically at Wady Halfa, though the nominal boundary is the twenty-second parallel of latitude, so that we are still in Egyptian waters as we sail to Kalabsha, Dendur and Abu Simbel.

The High Dam, 2006
Rosemary Mahoney

Few travelers mentioned the inundation and its impact upon the life of Egypt, for most travelers came to Egypt over the winter months in Europe, arriving when the river was narrowing back from the flood.

The Aswan High Dam, built in 1964 just above the first dam, had radically changed the mood and pace of the Nile; it had brought the natural annual inundations to an end and had altered the style of Egyptian farming. Before the arrival of the dam, the Nile flooded once a year, allowing farmers only one opportunity to plant crops in the rich silt the receding river left behind.

Though the onset of the Nile's flood always remained constant, occurring usually in mid-June, the size of the flood did not, and for millennia predicting the amount of water the flood would bring had been one of the most important occupations of Egyptian life. Too little water meant drought, famine, and death, yet too much could be equally devastating. Unable to control or predict the behaviour of the river, Egyptians had been utterly at its mercy.

Ironing Linen, 1847

Harriet Martineau

This evening was so warm that Mrs Y. and I walked on the shore for some time without bonnet or shawl; the first and last occasion, no doubt of our doing so by moonlight on the 27th December. The next morning I rose early, to damp the folded linen; and I was ironing till dinner-time, that we might carry our sheets and towels in the best condition to the *kandjia*. No one would laugh at, or despise this who knew the importance, in hot countries, of the condition of linen; and none who have not tried can judge of the difference in comfort of ironed linen and that which is rough dried. By sparing a few hours per week, Mrs Y. and I made neat and comfortable the things washed by the crew; and when we saw the plight of other travellers—gentlemen in rough dried collars, and ladies in gowns which looked as if they had been merely wrung out of the wash-tub, we thought the little trouble our ironing cost us well bestowed. Everybody knows now to take English servants ruins everything—destroys all the ease and comfort of the journey; and the Arabs cannot iron.

The next stage of the Nile journey after Aswan—until the coming of first the British dam in 1900 and then the Aswan High Dam—was one of the adventures of the world . . .

Up the Cataract, 1847

Harriet Martineau

Such an event as the ascent of the Cataract can happen but once in one's life; and we would not hear of going ashore on any such plea as that the feat could be better seen from the shore. What I wanted was to feel it. I would have gone far to see a stranger's boat pulled up; but I would not refuse the fortune of being on board when I could. We began, however, with going ashore at the Rapid where we failed the evening before. The rope had been proved untrustworthy; and there was no other till we joined the Rais of the Cataract, with his cable and his posse. Our Reis put together three weak ropes, which were by no means equivalent to one strong one; but the attempt succeeded.

It was a curious scene—the appearing of the dusky natives on all the rocks around; the eager zeal of those who made themselves our guards, holding us by the arms, as if we were going to jail, and scarcely permitting us to set our feet to the ground, lest we should fall; and the daring plunges and divings of man or boy, to obtain our admiration or our backsheesh. A boy would come riding down a slope of roaring water as confidently as I would ride down a sand-hill on my ass. Their arms, in their fighting method of swimming, go round like the spokes of a wheel. Grinning boys pooled in the currents; and little seven-year-old savages must haul at the ropes, or ply their little poles when the kanjia approached a spike of rock, or dive to thrust their shoulders between the keel and any sunken obstacle; and after every such feat, they would pop up their dripping heads, and cry "baksheesh."

I felt the great peculiarity of this day to be my seeing, for the first, and probably the only time of my life, the perception of savage faculty; and truly it is an imposing sight. The quickness of movement and apprehension; the strength and suppleness of frame, and the power of experience in all concerned this day, contrasted strangely with the images of the bookworm and the professional man at home, who can scarcely use their own limbs or senses, or conceive of any control over external realities.

Up the Cataracts, January 7, 1850
Florence Nightingale

Everybody at Cairo dissuaded us from it; but let nobody come to Egypt without going up the Cataracts; they have never seen such an exhibition before, and never will again. It is quite as interesting, in its way, as Karnak in another, or Cairo in a third, as the most wonderful development of instinct I suppose the world contains. I thought it quite beautiful, and tears fill one's eyes when one sees the provision of God for the preservation of life, always answering exactly to its need in every country. In Europe, the intellectual developments are quite enough to preserve life, and accordingly we see instinct undeveloped. In America, the wild Indian tracks his way through a trackless forest, by an instinct to us quite as miraculous as clairvoyance, or anything we are pleased to call impossible; and in Egypt the wild Nubian rides on the wave, and treads upon the foam, quite as securely as the Indian in his forest. The strife of man with the elements—wind, earth and water—and his overcoming, was as grand an epic poem as any I ever read in Homer or Milton.

I should have expected to find the Triad of the Cataracts, Physical Skill, Strength and Rapidity.

Into Nubia, 1858
Emily Anne Beaufort

Miss Beaufort and her party changed to a smaller boat to continue up the Nile into Nubia. The journey south was very different then to our experience today. First the 'British' dam and then the High Dam changed the flow of the Nile. Before the dams the land rose steeply on both sides of the river; after the dams held back the river to distribute northward and the formation of Lake Nasser, the water rose up, making the landscape very different. Thus the descriptions of the journey before these changes is very different from the modern experience.

We ended that day with a row in the felucca near the foot of the Cataract, to enjoy the indescribable sight of that confusion of rocks, thrown about as if by hand, piled up and smoothed by the rushing water, shining and lustrous as coal and marble; the only two colours, the jet black basalt and the red porphyry, ornamented here and there with the vivid green of the little sont (mimosa) trees.

The desert looked strangely gay the next morning as we followed the same route from Assouan or Mahatta, for all the occupants of the six dahabeeyahs, then moored together, were on the same route, as well as four camels loaded with the furniture and provisions for our *kandjeh*—beds, basins, baths, and baskets, all piled up in confusion on the swaggering camels, while, hanging out over the top of one of them, a great wooden sofa, painted green, went wagging ludicrously along.

Our friends bade us adieu with a ringing cheer on the beautiful banks of Philae—ever-lovely Philae—and we sailed gaily on at 2 p.m. into Nubia, with eight of our own sailors under a Nubian Reis. Our new boat looked hopelessly unpromising and dirty, but we determined to make the best of it; and having made her look as nice as her old boards would permit, we gave ourselves up to watching the lovely scenes through which we were passing.

It is Egypt no longer, but something wholly different; the river seems to run more rapidly in its much narrower channel, and is of a deeper, clearer grey; the rocky hills rise abruptly on both sides, leaving on each bank only a narrow strip, but a few yards wide in many places, sometimes not even that, gay and bright with the vivid green of young lupins; then a fringe of palms, dom-palms, or castor-oil trees, a yard or two wide, and the dark red rock rises immediately behind them, or the sand of the desert closes upon the green, as if sternly saying, "Thus far, and no farther!" And thus it is throughout Nubia: scarcely anywhere does the cultivated land extend a quarter of a mile in width, often the rocks tumble down in heaps into the water.

Scarcely a village is to be seen, and but very few people, only one or two working singly among the lupins; a silence, almost deathly, reigns throughout the land, and the whole country seems, by a subversion of ideas, to consist of the river only—a snake-like kingdom of blue water set in green and yellow enamels. The boats with their singing crews are all gone; the birds

Frontier of Egypt and Nubia

have stayed behind in Egypt; there are no villages for the jackals to howl in; and the only sound that breaks upon the listening ear is that of the creaking sakiyahs and shadoofs at intervals.

And yet such is the beauty of the scene that Nubia is not melancholy; and so delicious is the air that breathing seems in itself a pleasure. The balmiest European summer's evening is raw and cold in comparison with the perfection of those Nubian nights; scarcely even cool, yet with nothing of the oppressive heat of the day, the evening air moves round one with a soft, sweet freshness as it bathes every sense at once in a dreamy but not languid feeling of pleasure, and charms sight, taste, touch and hearing with equal enjoyment.

The Adventure of the Cataract, January 25, 1882
Sophia de Franqueville

Before the dams were built boats had to be almost carried up the cataract, through the rushing, roaring water, by vast numbers of men, organised by the 'Sheik or Reis of the Cataract.' Now and then there was a serious accident . . .

Today we ought to have finished the first cataract, but after two hours' work our eighty men decamped with their Sheik as they were tired! Rather provoking when another hour would have finished their business; but they kindly promised to return with two hundred tomorrow and do *all* the rest of it! The *all* is a quarter of an hour's walking distance.

Yesterday at cock crow all our possessions on deck were cleared, the doors locked etc. . . . Then our own crew retired to the stern, and the pilot of the Cataract took possession of the rudder; the captain of the Cataract was in command; and the bows swarmed with Cataract sailors, and a very obstinate old Sheik supervised the whole. Soon blacks were swimming round the dahabeeyah for 'baksheesh' on queer rafts: their performance over, business began.

Our feluccas went to fetch men from the shore, and they were divided into companies on different rocks. Where they came from, I can't imagine, as they all suddenly hopped up and the banks were like a rabbit warren, swarming with men, old, middle-aged, young and boys. They shout, scream, talk, row, but that is almost all.

Ibrahim (their dragoman) says, in tones of disgust: "I don't like these Cataract people at all! All noise—not do any work."

The sand on our right and left is in quite bright golden heaps banked up. The rocks are, I think, basaltic, bare of any vegetation, only in the shallower pools there are large tufts of rushes. The chief cause of excitement consists in the tracking rope getting entangled or the end of the mast being struck against a rock. Oh! the shoutings, shriekings, howlings, and gesticulations! the boundings and leapings and flyings! It is simply killing,* and such a farce. . . . The pace at which the river goes is tremendous, not rushing down but rushing in eddies, whirling one another in the fastest of valses (waltzes), and in and out the river the folk go; one couple rushing past another and as smoothly as possible. It is an enchanting scene and very fascinating to watch.

Assouan and through the Lock, 1902
Emily Hornby

Miss Hornby and her party continued up the Nile through the locks of the new dam.

M. had gone on an expedition to a Coptic convent with a guide and a boat. At about 3:30 F. and I started in our boat with Ibrahim (their dragoman) and were rowed all around the island of Elephantine, saw the other side of the Savoy Hotel which is embowered in palm trees, very different to the arid bareness of the Cataract Hotel.[†] Still, I would fancy the latter was very healthy. To our right, on the mainland, on a high ridge of rock, was the Sheik's tomb, one of the objects of M.'s excursion. It looked a good pull, but rather a tempting path up to it, and I felt rather sorry not to have gone, but I was in Sunday clothes, and it was rather hot, and I also fancied seeing something of the river. We were rowed quite to the other end of the island, and then landed on the rocks for F. to make a sketch.

---

* 'Killing' was a slang term at the time for something that was very, very funny—making one laugh a very great deal.

† The Cataract Hotel had opened only one or two years before and its garden had not yet been completed.

Think we must have started about eleven. In about an hour came to the barrage, an enormous dam, stretching all across the river, of solid masonry. Some remains of the cataract along the right bank. The water was flowing through sluices at the bottom, they let it through by degrees. There is a narrow canal through for traffic, and a series of gates letting through a succession of locks, just like a regular canal. At the first gate there was a flight of steps up the barrier, and F. had just time to be hauled on them and go up. I delayed to finish my coffee and was too late. She came down a flight further on, and later when Ibrahim had come on board we all landed, and had quite a long walk on the connecting wall by the side of the canal, a tremendous width. Quantities of workmen throwing down blocks of stone, a very nice head engineer told us it was to strengthen the foundations. . . . We walked a long way and when we got back to the *Helene* [their dahabieh] found she had never stirred. We were nearly three hours getting through the locks. A steamer in front delayed us a good deal. Another time, of course, one would let the dahabieh go through by herself and ride on donkeys to Philae. It is a very interesting ride M. and F. say, about an hour, but we wanted to see the locks.

Once through we soon saw a quantity of rocky islets, and also realised that a fringe of green along the banks was submerged palm trees, and soon saw a quantity in the middle of the river looking like green islands in the distance. I had never heard of the destruction of palm trees among the devastation wrought by the dam. We turned a corner and Pharaoh's bed (on the island of Philae) came in sight, looking exactly like its pictures, except that it was surrounded by water, which did not spoil it in my eyes, as I had not seen it before. We anchored exactly opposite.

Reflections, 1930
Marta Bibescu

Princess Bibescu came to Philae during the period when it had been flooded in consequence of the building of the first dam above Aswan. Travelers floated through the temples by boat.

"Are there water lilies in Egypt?"

"Oh, as for them, certainly! They grow like weeds, by the thousand, in all the deep ditches and even in the Nile. If you stay until Egypt you will see them . . ."

But I see them now, they are omnipresent. On the capitals of Philae I have seen them in their real habitat. Because of the inundation of the temple, they are once more flowers on the surface of the water and in its mirror. At flood time, they have nocturnal immersion. I have seen them, too, in the temple of Luxor on the top of the outside columns in bud, as they live *before* sunrise. The architrave of the temple rests on the closed chalices, ready to open. And the capitals of the columns which surround the inside sanctuary, the Holy of Holies, where life itself is guarded, change. There, where the sun reveals itself, the chalices are open as if the sun looked on them and they saw the sun.

Left behind on Philae, 1818
Sarah Belzoni

When her husband, Giovanni Belzoni, went south on the journey that led to the opening of the great temple at Abu Simbel, he left Sarah on the island of Philae with their young Irish servant.

During Mr B.'s absence, I took my residence on the top of the temple of Osiris in that island, and with the help of some mud walls, I had enclosed two comfortable rooms. It was rumoured that there were thieves on the island opposite, though I rather think it was a trick to see what effect it might have upon me. . . . These people, when they see trunks or boxes belonging to Europeans, judge they are full of gold and silver, particularly after having seen such unnecessary things as spoons and forks of metal.

I was visited every day by the women inhabiting the different villages on the other side of the Nile; they used to cross on a ramouse, bringing sometimes one or two beads of cornelian antiques, or a little barley, some eggs and onions, getting in exchange glass beads or small looking-glasses.

My old acquantaince from the first year came to see me, particularly the friendly Zara, with the good old woman, who hailed me affectionately, and continued so too the last. The old woman was the merriest and best natured simple creature I ever met with; she would not have disgraced England itself;

she used to make many sensible remarks about our customs. Her husband and two fine lads were killed in a battle with another tribe. . . .

One day, on seeing some of our coarse cloth, Zara, in a very humble tone asked me, if I had got an old piece of cloth of the same kind to put on her head, as she had not got anything, she should be very happy. I told her I would look if I possessed such a thing, for I made it a rule, from dear bought experience, never to give anything on the moment it was asked for; on the next day I gave her a piece. I cannot describe the joy she expressed on receiving this present; but after examining it for some time, she said it was too clean, and would spoil her head, and she must make it dirty before she could use it. The reason she gave was, that being clean it would draw all the grease out of her hair, and particularly as all kind of fat, butter or oil, was very scarce and hard to be got; besides the beauty of the glitter of the fat used, it preserves the head against the burning heat of the sun.

The Temple of Isis, 1855
Lady Tobin
We re-entered the boat, and after passing through what is called the *third gate* of the Cataract, landed on the sacred isle of Philae. A short but steep ascent up a wooded bank led us to the great temple of Isis. This superb relic of an era when Philae was held in peculiar sanctity as one of the reputed burial places of Osiris, is considered by the learned as an elegant specimen of the lighter Ptolemaic architecture. It is in truth a noble ruin! The paintings upon the walls of the inner chambers—the sculpture and the painting of the columns and outer walls—still remain as perfect as they were thousands of years ago, and seem destined to be the admiration of ages and ages to come!* Here we behold, portrayed to the life—human figures—animals—and the customs and ceremonies of by gone days; with their undeciphered tales in clearly traced hieroglyphs! A staircase leads to small chambers in the wall of the eastern adytum; but a hurried glance was all we had to spare for what—even according to *tourists' rules*—ought to occupy four days. Some of the ceilings are painted dark blue, with white stars, to represent the heavens. We walked along the gallery extending from the

---

*   Sadly for many years, as a result of the hold back of the Nile by the early dam, the island of Philae lay under water and travelers sailed between the temple pillars in boats. When the island rose again from the Nile, these paintings were no longer "the admiration of ages."

View from Philae

propylon to the water's edge, and which *rests* upon a wall that formerly surrounded the island as a protection from the current. The view from hence,
as indeed from every part of Philae, is very fine. The temple of Esculapius,
with its columns and doorways yet perfect, stands at the end of the eastern
corridor in front of the great temple. The whole island is covered with
mounds and ruins of ancient edifices, whose fragments appear amongst the
mud hovels and scanty vegetation of the present day. Little more than an
hour's pleasant row before sunset, by the Western Channel as it is called,
to Assouan, brought us back in safety to our river *home*.

The Island from Above, 1873
Amelia Edwards
And now, returning to the roof of the temple, it is pleasant to breathe the
fresher air that comes with sunset—to see the island, in shape like an ancient
Egyptian shield, lying mapped out beneath one's feet. From here, we look
back upon the way we have come, and forward to the way we are going.
Northward lies the Cataract—a network of islets with flashes of river between.

Southward, the broad current comes on in one smooth glassy sheet, unbroken by a single rapid. How eagerly we turn our eyes that way; for yonder lie Abou Simbel and all the mysterious lands beyond the Cataracts! But we cannot see far, for the river curves away grandly to the right, and vanishes behind a range of granite hills. A similar chain hems in the opposite bank; while high above the palm-groves fringing the edge of the shore stand two ruined convents on two rocky prominences, like a couple of castles on the Rhine.

On the east bank opposite, a few mud houses and a group of superb carob trees mark the site of a village, the greater part of which lies hidden among palms. Behind this village opens a vast sand valley, like an arm of the sea from which the waters have retreated.

The Temple of Kalabsheh, 1851
Emily Hornby
Thursday, January 18th, 1851, 42nd day
Started earlier this morning, and before nine anchored close to the Temple of Kalabsheh. An immense temple close on the shore, a village close round it, and a strip of cultivated land. Quite glad to see it.

This temple is quite different to the others we have seen so far, it is supposed to have been destroyed by an earthquake, and all the halls are full of great masses of stone, quite difficult to get about. A Pylon at the entrance, then a court full of blocks of stone, then six pillars, and entrance between them to another hall, where there has been a great deal of colour, but it is very much defaced. Still, when one has looked a long time, a good deal comes out of their robes and crowns, and F. made a very pretty drawing of a female figure sitting on a lotus flower. On the portico there is a very famous Greek inscription about Silico, King of the Ethiopians; it looked quite indecipherable, but no doubt was much clearer in 1818 when it was first discovered [by travelers].

From here we went through the village, and up a hill, a good path, to Bet-el-Wadi, a very small temple cut out of the rock, but most interesting. The interior is supported by two fluted pillars, and there are niches with three seated statues in each, very much defaced. The inside pictures are also very much defaced—we had expected lovely coloured things from Miss Edwardes' descriptions, but could make out nothing.

The outside area is however most interesting. A long series of views. On one side the king in his chariot, bow in one hand, captives in another, held by the hair, his son breaking in with an axe the gate of a besieged city, all the people on the walls begging for mercy, a child tumbling over the wall.

Philae to Korosko,* 1873
Amelia Edwards

Sailing gently southward—the river opening wide before us, Philae dwindling in the rear—we feel that we are now fairly over the border; and that if Egypt was strange and far from home, Nubia is stranger and farther still. The Nile here flows deep and broad. The rocky heights that hem it in so close on either side are still black on the one hand, golden on the other. The banks are narrower than ever. The space in some places is little wider than a towing path. In others, there is barely room for a belt of date-palms and a slip of alluvial soil, every foot of which produces its precious growth of durra or barley. The steep verge beneath is green with lentils to the water's edge. As the river recedes, it leaves each day a margin of fresh, wet soil, in which the careful husbandman hastens to scratch a new furrow and sow another line of seeds. He cannot afford to let so much as an inch of that kindly mud lie idle.

Gliding along with half-filled sail, we observe how entirely the population seems to be regulated by the extent of arable soil. Where the inundation has room to spread, villages come thicker; more dusky figures are seen moving to and fro in the shade of the palms; more children race along the banks, shrieking for backshish. When the shelf of soil is narrowed, on the contrary, to a mere fringe of luminous green dividing the rock from the river, there is a startling absence of everything like life. Mile after mile drags its slow length along, uncheered by any sign of human life. When now and then a solitary native, armed with gun or spear, is seen striding along the edge of the desert, he only seems to make the general solitude more apparent.

The Tropic of Cancer, 1873
Amelia Edwards

About half way between Kalabsheh and Dendur, we enter the Tropic of Cancer. From this day till the day we repass that invisible boundary, there

---

* It is hard to realize as one cruises through Nubia on Lake Nasser today, how very different the Aswan High Dam has made the landscape, where once the Nile wound through steep banks and hills. At this time, before the Aswan High Dam lifted the water of the Nile up behind it, the shores of the Nile rose higher from the river than they do now. The great temple of Abu Simbel was lifted by the world—cooperating through the United Nations—so that its position should be that fixed by its original builders.

is a marked change in the atmospheric conditions under which we live. The days get gradually hotter, especially at noon, when the sun is almost vertical; but the freshness of the night and the chill of early morning are no more. Unless when a strong wind blows from the north, we no longer know what it is to need a shawl on the deck in the evening, or an extra covering on our beds towards dawn. We sleep with our cabin-windows open, and enjoy a delicious quality of temperature from sundown to sunrise. The days and nights, too, are of equal length.

Now, also, the Southern Cross and a second group of stars, which we conclude must form part of the Centaur, are visible between two and four every morning. They have been creeping up, a star at a time, for the last fortnight; but are still so low upon the eastern horizon that we can only see them when there comes a break in the mountain-chain on that side of the river. At the same time, our old familiar friends of the northern hemisphere, looking strangely distorted and out of their proper place, are fast disappearing on the opposite side of the heavens. Orion seems to be lying on his back, and the Great Bear to be standing on his tail; while Cassiopeia and a number of others have deserted *en masse*. The zenith, meanwhile, is but thinly furnished; so that we seem to have travelled away from one hemisphere, and not yet to have reached the other. As for the Southern Cross, we reserve our opinion until we get farther south. It would be treason to hint that we are disappointed in so famous a constellation.

Beyond Kalabsheh, 1873
Marianne North
Dakkeh I thought a still more picturesque place, with its black sheep and people huddled up in black woollen blankets, but Gertassee was the loveliest of all; only six columns left with one huge stone resting on the tops of two of them, placed on the summit of a hill standing quite alone, with other hills behind it and the blue river making a grand sweep beneath, and winding away into the far distance, edged with palm trees; the colours were all so pure and delicate it seemed too lovely for reality, like one of Claude's small pictures; here a nice black woman found her way up with her baby and sat by me as I worked, she examined the contents of all my pockets, but put everything carefully back. She fell in love with my paint brush, till I told her it was made of camel hair, when she thought less of it, "it was such a common animal, if it had only been a horse's or a pig's!"

As has been said earlier, the inundation lasted from September to December and the waters of the Nile poured out across the land, bringing fertility to the near-desert. Only after the inundation in December did most travelers set off up the Nile, and, thus, often moved into the next year while they were on their Nile journey.

The Girls, 1863
Lucie Duff Gordon

It is worth going to Nubia to see the girls. Up to twelve or thirteen they are dressed in a bead necklace and a leather fringe 4 inches wide round the loins, and anything so absolutely perfect as their shapes or so sweetly innocent as their look can't be conceived. My pilot's little girl came in the dress mentioned before carrying a present of cooked fish on her head and some fresh eggs; she was four years old and so *klug*.* I gave her a captain's biscuit and some figs, and the little pet sat with her legs tucked under it and ate it so *manierlich*† and was so long over it, and wrapped up some more white biscuit to take home in a little rag of a veil so carefully. I longed to steal her, she was such a darling.

Two beautiful Nubian women visited me in my boat, with hair in little plaits finished off with lumps yellow clay burnished with golden tags, soft, deep bronze skins, and lips and eyes worthy for Isis and Hathor. Their very dress and ornaments were the same as those represented in the tombs, and I felt inclined to ask them how many thousand years old they were. In their house I sat on an ancient Egyptian couch with the semi-circular head-rest, and drank out of crockery that looked antique, and they brought a present of dates in a basket such as you may see in the British Museum. They are dressed in drapery like Greek statues, and are as perfect, and have hard, bold faces, and, though far handsomer, lack the charm of the Arab women; and the men, except at Kalabshee and those from far up the country, are not such gentlemen as the Arabs.

---

* clever
† well-mannered

Dakkeh, Maharaka, Wady es Subua—and Abu Simbel, 1851
Emily Hornby

Went up to the temple about eight; others were there already.

An inner chamber with two lions, very like those at Mycenae, near the ground, another lion and baboon higher up. This temple is sacred to Thoth, who is represented as a baboon. More baboons in the main hall. Went with Ibrahim [their dragoman] to the top of the Pylon, sixty-nine steps. A most exquisite view, river winding a good deal in both directions. Some very curious hills on the Arabian side, might be pyramids, look quite volcanic. Bought some beads here.

On pretty briskly to Maharaka seven miles further. A most lovely row of columns, and a ruinous Pylon, with a relief of Isis sitting under a fig-tree.

They sailed on and anchored about five close under the temple of Wady es Subua.

We walked up to it, a good pull up soft sand. An alley of sphinxes led up to it, only two remain . . .

The next day we made very good progress and Abou Simbel began to appear about two o'clock. The others could see the colossal figures long before I did. They are most wonderful. The smaller temple of Nefertari comes first; we anchored just below the large one which has four colossal figures of Rameses II in front, two on each side of the doorway, all the temple itself excavated out of the solid rock. One of them has lost its head which is lying at its feet, the others are most perfect, beautiful calm features and lovely ears which are really three feet long. The doorway is approached by a corridor balustrade on each side covered with chains of captives, Syrians on the right, Ethiopians on the left; and next to the doorway on the sides of the thrones of the nearest Colossus, beautiful figures of Nile deities twining wreaths of lotus. Inside eight Osiride pillars, very superior to those at Gerf Hassan, pedestals much lower, faces almost perfect. . . . A smaller hall beyond and an inner sanctuary with four colossal seated figures, but too dark to see them.

Then went round . . . trying to see the wonderful things on the wall with candles. I could hardly make out anything. Then Ibrahim and I went to the other temple which has six huge figures, standing, four of Ramses II, and two of his Queen Nefertari in whose honour he built this temple. Here I could also see nothing of the interior decorations. Returned to the large temple and was delighted to see preparations for tea, which we all enjoyed thoroughly, on a table from the *Helene* just in front of the temple.

Then M. and I started up the huge mound of golden sand between the two temples. It was very soft and one had to drive one's feet deep in not to slip back. Ibrahim and one of the men followed us and helped us towards the end. There were a few easy rocks, and we were upon the level of the desert, quite dark stones here. They walked on towards a cairn over quite level ground . . . over flat fragments of dark red stone. Most splendid view, the windings of the Nile for miles, it disappeared and then appeared again, and boundless desert on each side; the air too delicious. Coming down was an affair of a very few minutes, and we stopped for a good look at the Colossi, when on a level with their calm unmoved faces. It was nearly dark when we got down.

M. [her sister] had seen in the guide books that about sunrise was the best time for seeing the temples, so I made an effort, though without much hope, and was actually off before the others, and in the temple soon after six, not waiting for any breakfast.

Most thankful I am I did, I could not believe it, the effect was magical. The sun poured right into the inner sanctuary, there were four Deities sitting in silent majesty, their faces rather defaced. All different crowns, one especially a very tall one, the crown of Upper Egypt.

Temples! Temples!, 1845
Isabel Romer

Temple upon temple! they followed each other in such rapid succession that I feared I should have a surfeit of them, and already felt the difficulty of digesting so many propyla as daily fell to my lot during the first days of our descent of the Nile. After seeing Maharraka and Dakkeh on the same day, we stopped in the evening to visit the Temple of Ghirsche Housseyn, a grand hemi-speos much in the style of Ibsamboul (Abu Simbel), dedicated by Rhamses Sesostris to the god Phtha, the Egyptian Vulcan.

The architecture of the interior chambers, like all rock-cut temples, has suffered little injury either from time or the ravages of a destroying enemy; but the constructed part of it, consisting of a pronaos of sandstone,

supported by colossal Caryatides, is in the most lamentable state of dilap-
idation. The position of Ghirsche Housseyn is magnificent, standing on
an eminence on the western bank of the Nile, facing the river, and surrounded by the Desert. Its general appearance as one enters the excavated
parts where the rays of the sun have never penetrated, is imposing and
solid to a degree. The fitful light thrown over lines of stupendous pillars
supporting colossal statues, by torches formed by ropes' ends, which,
tossed aloft by half-naked Nubians, assumed the appearance of fiery ser-
pents in the hands of demons, gave a fantastic and supernatural colouring
to the whole scene; and a multitude of bats, scared by the unwelcome glare
out of their dark retreats, and flitting madly about, like the spirits in Freis-
chutz, added in no small degree to the unearthly character of the place.
The closeness of the atmosphere in chambers which no current of air has
ever refreshed, the heat and smoke occasioned by the burning ropes, and
above all the abominable effluvium of the bats, produced such a stifling
sensation that I was glad to escape from them into the open air; but in
taking a last look at the chambers, with their colossal accessories penetrating far into the bowels of the rock, and remembering at the same time,
that, when this temple was erected, the use of iron was supposed to be unknown in Egypt, and gunpowder not even dreamed of, I was seized with
wondering awe of the people who could have achieved works of so stupendous a nature, as if by enchantment, without iron tools to hew, or gun-
powder to blast the solid rock.

Temples!, 1873
Amelia Edwards
There are fourteen temples between Abou Simbel and Philae; to say nothing of grottoes, tombs, and other ruins. As a rule, people begin to get tired
of Temples about this time, and vote them too plentiful. Meek travellers
go through them as a duty; but the greater number rebel.

For myself I was never bored by them. Though they had been twice
as many, I should not have wished them fewer. Miss Martineau tells how,
in this part of the river, she was scarcely satisfied to sit down to breakfast
without having first explored a Temple; but I could have breakfasted,
dined, supped on Temples. My appetite for them was insatiable, and grew
with what it fed upon. I went over them all. I took notes of them all. I
sketched them every one.

Towards Derr, 1861
M.L.M. Carey

I walked out with El Abiad to one of the curious-looking hills, but dinner-time, inexorable dinner time, obliged me to return without climbing it. Next morning, El Abiad and I started again before sunrise. He could not understand my pleasure in climbing these hard rocks, and wanted to carry me all the way himself. He would soon have changed his mind, had I allowed him to try, but he helped me along most gallantly, and looked at me with unfeigned astonishment, when he saw me at the top of the hill which I had pointed to as the object of my ambition. There I enjoyed the wildest, most extensive, and characteristic view of the desert land than I had yet seen. A vast extent of curiously-shaped rocky hills and mounds of sand, intermingled with the smooth pebbly plains mentioned above, was stretched before and around me. The narrow tracks along which the caravans from the interior wend their burning way could be traced on all sides, and looked parched and uninviting indeed, and the eyes rested with pleasure on the blue line of water, and the gaily painted 'Cairo' in the distance.

At eight a.m. we were off again, as soon as the milk for breakfast had arrived; we reached Derr at four p.m., passing by refreshing green plantations of beans, lupines, wheat, the castor-oil plant, and remarkably fine specimens of the date-palm. This district abounds in the date-trees, and between Korosko and Derr it is reckoned that 20, 000 of them are taxed; this being one of the regular taxes of the country.

Derr is quite a comfortable-looking town. It is the capital of Nubia, and is worthy the distinction, for the houses are much larger and better built than in any of its other towns. They all have doors, and at least the appearance of cleanliness. The streets, though three or four inches thick in unavoidable dust, are also very clean. There are large open spaces, 'squares' we might call them, planted round with date-trees, which Mohammed [her dragoman] said were used for the meetings of the 'Parliament,' by which grand title he designated any meeting of any kind, in village or town. The date-trees are all protected by little mud walls to the height of four or five feet, and in the centre of one of the squares is a large 'Egyptian fig-tree' (a species of sycamore).

Close on the river's bank is a Roman ruin, over-shadowed by one of these large trees, and now inhabited by some of the grandees of Derr. It is a picturesque object, and is backed by a large grove of beautiful palm-trees, all equally protected with walls like those in the square.

The Cemetery at Derr, 1845
Isabel Romer

After Isamboul, we had no eyes for the temple of Derr, so we rode into the town, which stands in a grove of stately palm-trees, the finest I have yet seen . . . As we rode through the cemetery we observed, amidst this poor and unciv-ilized people, an affecting custom which might well serve as an example to wealthier and more polished nations. The poverty of the Nubians does not admit of tombstones, and their graves are marked out either by an outline of pebbles, or by a rude fragment of stone placed at the head and foot; yet at every grave I noticed a bowl of water and an earthen pipkin filled with roast *dhoura* (Indian corn), and on asking Mohammed the meaning of such accessories to such a spot, he told me that it was the custom of the people here to place food for the poor every Friday on the graves of their friends and relations; thus con-ferring upon them, as it were, the prerogative of posthumous charity, and en-abling the starving poor to go and obtain a meal from the hands of the dead.

Today, if you sail across Lake Nasser, you share the experi-ence of earlier travelers as the great temple at Abu Simbel comes into sight. Through one warm afternoon I watched the temple facade approaching us—at first hardly recognis-able, then growing larger and even larger until it stood above us as we moored just on the edge of the wonderful site.

Other Tourists, 1897
E. M. Merrick

On one of our excursions to the temples, riding as usual on donkeys, we were overtaken by a party of Cook's excursionists, and as an American dashed past me he shouted out, "Ain't it sport, riding on a jackass?" That class of gentleman abounds up the Nile among the tourists; and I remember one, with whom we had a very casual acquaintance, remarking to me when I was feeling rather seedy at Assouan, "Well, you do look a worm. Guess Egypt don't suit you. You'll go home in a box likely." American expressions sound very funny to our ears. I heard a woman in Shepheard's verandah de-scribing a bonnet she had seen in church as being "real lovely; nothing but a wreath of bugs (butterflies) and an osprey."

A Mirage at Dakkeh, 1846
Harriet Martineau

While I was on top of the propylon of Dakkeh, I saw off to the northwest, a wide stretch of blue waters, with the reflection of shores and trees. Rather wondering how such a lake or reach of river could be there, while the Nile seemed to be flowing north-east, and observing that these waters were bluer than those of the river, I asked myself whether this could possibly be the mirage, by which I had promised myself never to be deceived. My first thought was of mirage; but a little further study nearly convinced me that it was real water—either a lake left by the inundation, or a reach of the river brought there by a sudden bend. I was still sufficiently uncertain to wish my friends to come up and see; though the reflection of the groves and clumps on the banks was as perfect as possible in every line. Just as I was going down to call my party, I saw a man's head and shoulders come up out of the midst of the lake: a very large head and shoulders—such as a man might have who was near at hand. The sensation was strange, and not very agreeable. The distant blue lake took itself off in flakes. The head and shoulders belonged to a man walking across the sand below; and the groves and clumps and well-cut banks resolved themselves into scrubby bushes, patches of coarse grass, and simple stones.

This was the best mirage I have ever seen, for its beauty and the completeness of the deception. I saw many afterwards in the Desert; and a very fine one in the plain of Damascus;* but my heart never beat again as it did on the top of the Dakkeh propylon. I had a noble view of the Desert and the Nile from that height; and it was only sixty-nine steps of winding stair that I had to ascend. Those propyla were the watch-towers and bulwarks of the temples in the old days, when the temples of the Deities were the fortifications of the country.

Approaching Abu Simbel, 1847
Harriet Martineau

I had been watching the winds and the hours in the fear that we should pass Aboo-Simbil in the dark. But when I came on deck, on the morning of the 4th, I found, to my great joy, that we were only a few miles from it, while a fresh breeze was carrying us well on our course. We passed it before

---

*   Harriet Martineau, after her journey through Egypt, crossed the northern desert to Sinai and from there traveled onward to Palestine and Syria.

breakfast. The façade is visible from a considerable distance; and as soon as it becomes visible, it fixes the eye by the singularity of such an object as this smoothed recess of the rugged rock. I found it unlike what I expected, and unlike, I thought, all the representations of it that I had seen. The portal looked low in proportion to the colossi; the façade was smaller, or at least narrower, than I had supposed; and the colossi much nearer together. The white wash which Champollion (it is said) left on the face of the northernmost colossus, has the curious effect of bringing out the expression of the countenance, so as to be seen far off. Nothing can be more strange than so extremely distinct a revelation of a face, in every feature, perhaps a mile off. . . . The expression of this colossus is very agreeable; it is so tranquil and cheerful.

Approaching Abu Simbel and Onward, 1873
Marianne North
We had been looking a long while through glasses at the distant hills for Aboo Simbel, when all in a moment we discovered the four gigantic figures

Abu-Simbal

of Ramses II, calmly looking down upon us from just above our heads, bathed in the golden sunset rays, and half smothered by golden sand; we all shouted with delight at finding them, and the sailors called out "Baksheesh!" and got it.

Soon after that we reached Wady Halfah, and mounted to the basalt rock of Abooseer, finding interesting dust-heaps and broken tiles belonging to the cities whose very names are lost, and the most extraordinary view of river and rocks, all higgledy-piggledy, covering miles of space below us and extending into the far distance, a few tamarisk bushes alone breaking the hard contrast of the colouring between the gold-coloured sand and the black rocks. . . .

Approaching Abou Simbel, 1873
Amelia Edwards

We were now only thirty-four miles from Abou Simbel; but making slow progress, and impatiently counting every foot of the way. The heat at times was great; frequent and fitful spells of Khamsin wind alternating with hot calm that tried the trackers sorely. Still we pushed forward, a few miles at a time, till by and by the flat-topped cliffs dropped out of sight and were again succeeded by volcanic peaks, some of which looked loftier than any of those about Dakkeh or Korosco.

Then the palms ceased, and the belt of cultivated land narrowed to a thread of green between the rocks and the water's edge; and at last there came an evening when we only wanted breeze enough to double two or three more bends in the river.

"Is it to be Abou Simbel tonight?" we asked, for the twentieth time before going down to dinner.

To which Reis Hassan replied, "Aiwah." (certainly)

But the pilot shook his head, and added, "Bokra." (tomorrow)

When we came up again, the moon had risen, but the breeze had dropped. Still we moved, impelled by a breath so faint that one could scarcely feel it. Presently even this failed. The sail collapsed; the pilot steered for the bank; the captain gave the word to go aloft—when a sudden puff from the north changed our fortunes, and sent us out again with a well-filled sail into the middle of the river.

None of us, I think, will be likely to forget the sustained excitement of the next three hours. As the moon climbed higher, a light more mysterious and unreal than the light of day filled and overflowed the wide expanse of river and desert. We could see the mountains of Abou Simbel standing as it seemed across our path, in the far distance—a lower one first; then a larger; then a series of receding heights, all close together, yet all distinctly separate.

That large one—the mountain of the Great temple—held us like a spell.

Waking at Abou Simbel, 1873
Amelia Edwards

It was wonderful to take every morning close under the steep bank, and, without lifting one's head from the pillow, to see that row of giant faces so close against the sky. They showed unearthly enough by moonlight; but not half so unearthly as in the grey of dawn. At that hour, the most solemn of the twenty-four, they wore a fixed and fatal look that was little less than appalling. As the sky warmed, this awful look was succeeded by a flush that mounted and seemed to glow—to smile—to be transfigured. Then came a flash, as of thought itself. It was the first instantaneous flash of the risen sun. It lasted less than a second. It was gone almost before one could say that it was there. The next moment, mountain, river, and sky, were distinct in the steady light of day; and the colossi—mere colossi now—sat serene and stony in the open sunshine.

Those Great Figures, 1850
Florence Nightingale

We clambered and slid through the avalanche of sand, which now separates the two temples. There they sit, the four mighty colossi, seventy feet high, facing the East with the image of the sun between them, the sandhill sloping up the chin of the northern-most colossus.

Sublime in the style of intellectual beauty; intellect without effort, without suffering. I would not call it intellectual either, it is so entirely opposed to that of the Jupiter Capitolinus; is more the beauty of the soul— not a feature is correct—but the whole effect is more expressive of spiritual grandeur than anything I could have imagined. It makes the impression upon one that thousands of voices do, uniting in one unanimous simultaneous feeling of enthusiasm or emotion, which is said to overcome the strongest man. Yet the figures are anything but beautiful; no anatomy; no proportion; it is a new language to learn, and we have no language to express it. Here I have the advantage; for being equally ignorant of the language of any art, I was as open to impression from them as from Greek or other art. The part of the rock smoothed for the temple face is about 100 feet to the highest row of ornament. Over the door is the image of the sun, and on either side an intaglio figure of the Great Rameses, offering, not burnt sacrifices, not even flowers, nor fruit, but a figure of Justice in his right hand.

What more refined idea of sacrifice could you have than this? Yet inside I was still more struck by the king offering justice to the God who gives him in return *life* and *purity* in either hand.

The door which is about twenty feet high, does not reach nearly up to the knee of the colossus.

Abou Simbel at Night, February, 1874
Marianne Brocklehurst
The moon is bright and we see the great figures of the temple plain enough a mile away. We land and struggle up the bank to the sand drift which once hid all, until Belzoni and others cleared it on one side* and brought to light the temple and gigantic statues sitting on each side of the door, as they had sat for 6000 years or so; four statues of King Rameses, each 70 feet high. One is fallen, the others very perfect, even the faces. Smaller figures, which reach only to their knees, would make decent statues anywhere else. The hall of the temple cut in the rock is supported by 16 figures of Osiris, 18 feet high. It leads into a sanctuary where four sitting statues are by the altar. Other chambers in the rock are all covered with bas reliefs of battles and chariots, the arks carried by the Egyptians into foreign countries and other curious subjects, very large and well executed, full of spirit. A good deal of colour is left on them. Faces all handsome and mild in expression. We were immensely impressed and think it the finest thing we have seen in the world. I suppose there is no temple so old or so grand anywhere.

Visitors in Nubia, 1817
Sarah Belzoni
On our arrival at Ybsambul I did not go ashore. The wife of Davoud Cacheff (the local governor), having heard there was a Frank (foreign) woman on board, sent a young negro girl on purpose to see what kind of animal I was: she was rather shy to come near me at first, but the men telling her if she came into the boat the *setti* [lady] would give her a bakshis,

---

* In 1818 the Italian Giovanni Belzoni and two British naval captains, Charles Irby and James Mangles, with the aid of Nubian and Egyptian workers, managed to dig through the sand and enter the temple. All three men wrote of their experiences in Egypt.

she came with reluctance. I gave her some beads, which instantly got the better of her fears, and she observed every thing on board minutely. Having kept her eyes fixed upon a half-pint basin, she jumped up and ran away. She returned in a few minutes, bringing me some dhoura bread and dates, telling me her mistress hoped I would not refuse to send her the beautiful basin, pointing to it; it was curious to see the anxiety the girl showed, for fear I should not give it to her: she made me understand her mistress had taken all the beads I had given her. I gave her some more, with the wonderful basin and a plate like it. The joy the poor thing felt on receiving it was such, that in her hurry to get out of the boat, she had nearly broken them.

. . . we stopped at the village of Eshke to transact some business with Hoseyn Cacheff. I remained on board while Mr B. went to visit him; during which time the women of the village with their children came running towards the boat; but some men belonging to the Cacheff would not let them approach, and those who pressed forward they beat, and at the others flung stones: on my seeing this I made a sign to the women to approach, and seemed in a great passion with the men for beating them; they were much pleased at the whiteness of my skin and the colour of my hair. To those who had few ornaments I gave beads for themselves and their children.

What pleased me most was they did not show any disposition to covetousness, or express any desire that I should give them any thing; they seemed perfectly content that I allowed them to see me, and imitated the action that I made to the men not to beat them. Those I gave beads to went away; I did not expect to see them again: they shortly after returned, bringing me some dhoura bread and dates, finer than I had ever seen before or since. I naturally concluded it was a demand for another bakshis.

According to the custom of the Arab women, on my giving them some beads, they took out what I had before given them, and kissing my hands, begged me to accept their presents, which I did; they then sent for more dates. I made them understand I gave them the beads only as remembrances of me, and not for the sake of getting anything in return. On seeing Mr B. and some of the Cacheff's men at a distance, they set up a great shout, and made me understand they must go. I was very sorry to part so soon with these women: their manners were much more friendly than I have ever met with. They watched the boat at a distance till we left the shore.

Entering the Great Temple, 1846
Harriet Martineau

The seriousness I plead for comes of itself into the mind of any thoughtful and feeling traveller, at such a moment as that of entering the great temple of Aboo-Simbil. I entered it at an advantageous moment, when the morning sunshine was reflected from the sand outside so as to cast a twilight even from the *adytum*, two hundred feet from the entrance. The four tall statues in the *adytum*, ranged behind the altar, were dimly visible; and I hastened to them, past the eight Osirides, through the next pillared hall, and across the corridor. And then I looked back, and saw beyond the dark halls and shadowy Osirides the golden sand-hill without, a corner of blue sky, and a gay group of the crew in the sunshine. It was like looking our upon life from the grave. When we left the temple, and the sun had shifted its place, we could no longer see the shrine. It is a great advantage to enter the temple first when the sun is rather low in the east.

The eight Osirides are perfectly alike, all bearing the crosier and flagellum, and standing up against huge square pillars, the other side of which are sculptured, as are all the walls around. The aisles behind the Osirides are so dark that we could not make out the devices without the help of torches; and the celebrated medallion picture of the siege would have missed us entirely, if one of the crew had not hoisted another on his shoulders, to hold a light above the height of their united statures. There we saw the walled town, and the proceedings of the besieged and besiegers, as they might have happened in the middle ages. . . . The battle scenes on the walls are all alive with strong warriors, flying foes, trampled victims, and whole companies of chariots. I observed that the chariot wheels were not mere disks, as we should have expected in so early an age, but had all six spokes. Every chariot wheel I saw in the country had six spokes, however early the date of the sculpture or painting. One figure on the south wall is admirable, a warrior in red, who is spearing one foe, while he has his foot on the head of another.

When we looked abroad from the entrance, the view was calm and sweet. A large island is in the midst of the river, and shows a sandy beach and cultivated interior. The black, peaked hills of the opposite desert close in to the south, leaving only a narrow passage for the river. It was nearly evening before we put off from the bank below the temple. It had been an animating and delightful day; and I found myself beginning to understand the pleasure of "temple-haunting"; a pleasure which so grew upon us that we felt great grief when it came to an end. I, for one, had suspected beforehand that this work would soon become on of mere duty or routine; but we found, even before we left Nubia, that we were hardly satisfied to sit down the breakfast without having explored a temple.

The Transformation of Abu Simbel, 1988
Bettina Selby

> *The vast changes which were brought to Abu Simbel and Nubia in the 1960s in order to create Lake Nasser mean that the land we see today is very different from that through which earlier travelers passed. Selby found this in some way disappointing—to me, this great work, which brought nations all over the world together to care for one of Egypt's great treasures, is a marvel in itself.*

Abu Simbel is another multi-million dollar engineering marvel. As the waters of the new lake rose, the whole colossal structure of Egypt's most famous temple was injected with resin and sawn into a thousand blocks, which were put together three hundred yards away from the original cliff-face site. A huge dome disguised as a mountain was specially constructed to receive them. The visitor can walk about inside the hollow hill and wonder at the feat. He can walk around the four colossi of Ramses the Second at the entrance and stroll through the halls and never find a trace of where it was all stuck together exactly as it was. He can then do the same with the great companion temple of Nefertari, Ramses the Second's wife, and if he is as keen on engineering feats as my guide Moussa Mohammed was, he will be amply rewarded for the two-hundred mile journey there. If, however, he has gone to see a great temple, he might well be disappointed, Abu Simbel is yet another well-preserved museum; as at Philae, the spirit of the place is buried beneath the water.

A Mighty Abode, 1907
Norma Lorimer

It is a mighty and awesome sanctuary—a mighty abode of an almighty god.

At the beginning of each new day the sun penetrates the darkness of the temple and illuminates it right up to the very sanctuary. It is at sunrise only that the darkness of the four great halls is broken; it is at sunrise only that the whole building is suddenly lit up as though with a thousand lamps. The light is the light of the sun-god who carries in his advent the promise of Horus.

If you sit in the temple of Abou Simbel in the stillness of the dawn, with the might and majesty of the building enfolding you like the waters of a silent sea, and there await the coming of the sun, you will see the hawk-headed Harmachis step forward from his niche above the door to greet the god as he mounts the bank of golden sand.

Slowly he will pass under the great porch, which is guarded by four kingly figures, and enter the pillared hall, deep-bellied in the rock. There he will walk between the sixteen giant statues of Osiris, which are lined up like a royal bodyguard along his route to the shrine. At the holy of holies Ptah, the ancient god of Memphis, and Amon and Rameses and Harmachis are all seated in expectant attitudes awaiting his coming.

In the great stillness you can feel his presence like the presence of a king in whose being there is all majesty, power and dominion.

The beauty of Abou Simbel is its simplicity—its simplicity and strength. Its simplicity humbles and exalts you, its strength overwhelms you. It is its simple majesty that places it as high above other temples made by man's hands as the heavens are high above you.

The Furthest Point, 1847
Harriet Martineau

The next morning was almost as cold as the night; but we preferred this to heat, as our business today was to ride through the desert to the rock of Abooseer—the furthest point of our African travel. Before breakfast, the gentlemen took short walk on shore, being carried over the intervening mud.

They saw a small village and a school of six scholars. . . . The lesson was from the Koran; and the master delivered it in a chanting voice.

Two extremely small asses were brought down, to cross with us to the western bank. We crossed in a ferry boat, whose sail did not correspond very well with the climate. It was like a lace veil mended with ticking. Our first visit was to the scanty remains of an interesting old temple near the landing-place.

We rode to the foot of the rock of Abooseer, and then ascended it—in rather heavy spirits, knowing that was to be our last look southwards. The summit was breezy and charming. I looked down the precipice on which I stood, and saw a sheer descent to the Nile of two hundred feet. The waters were gushing past the foot of this almost perpendicular crag; and from holes of its strata flew out flocks of pigeons, blue in the sunshine. . . . The whole scene was composed of desert, river and black basaltic rocks. . . . To the north-east, the river winds away, blue and full, between sands. Two white sails were on it at the moment. From the river, a level sand extended to the soft-tinted Arabian hills, whose varied forms and broken lights and shadows were on the horizon nearly from the north round to the south-east. These level sands then give place to a black rugged surface, which extends to where two summits, today of a bright amethyst hue—close the circuit of vision. These summits are at a considerable distance on the way to Dongola. . . .

There is a host of names carved on the accessible side of Abooseer. We looked with interest at Belzoni's and some few others. We cut ours with a nail and a hammer. Here, and here only, I left my name. On this wild rock, and at the limit of our range of travel, it seemed not only natural, by right to some who may come after us. Our names will not be found in any temple or tomb.* If we ever do such a thing, may our names be pub-licly held up to shame, as I am disposed to publish those of the carvers and scribblers who have forfeited their right to privacy by inscribing their names where they can never be effaced.

The time arrived when we must go. It was with a heavy heart that I quitted the rock, turned my back on the south, and rode away.

The Great Rock at Abouseer, 1874
Marianne Brocklehurst
Wednesday, February 4 Three feluccas sail up to the Rock of Abouseer. We scramble up through the deep sand and have a fine view of the cataracts and rocks, a strange lot of little islands of sand and lumps of black, highly pol-ished granite which we have just passed. The rapids are not so strong as at the 1st Cataract, but shallower. No dahabeeyah can get up. Everything goes on by camels. Dongola is a four days' ride from here. Unfortunately, the wind was high and the air full of sand and we could not see much of the dis-tant view of the hills above Dongola which we ought to have done.

---

* In the nineteenth century many travelers carved their named on the monuments of Egypt.

This is a grand rock, 200 feet above the river, and to quote Mr Murray*
is "the Ultima Thule of most Nile voyagers". It has names of the illustrious
cut all over it. We saw Peytherick, Tatton Sykes, F.W. Holland amongst the
rest. This is all very well here but it is abominable to disfigure the temples
and tombs and we were grieved to see the great name of Murray itself con-
fronting us largely on the grand figure, the first as you enter the temple of
Abou Simbel. We had a rough hard pull back again [5 miles] and a dangerous crossing of the river at last, the waves and wind high against us.

Up the Second Cataract, 1861
M.L.M. Carey

The row-boat which accompanied the 'cangia' was put off, with two men
in it, taking with them one end of a long rope which was fastened to the dahabeeh, and by which they were to tow the larger vessel along, when they
had tied it to one of the rocks. The grisly Reis of these cataracts[†] rose at the
bow of the vessel, and directed his men by voice and hand. One man, in
Nubian costume, jumped into the water, swam with the end of another rope
between his teeth, and then jumping from point to point, fastened it to the
rocks, and pulled upon it with all his might to help us up. On a smaller scale,
the whole scene of the First Cataracts was re-enacted, till the 'cangia' was
safely moored in a sheltered nook, under the famous rock of 'Abousir'. We
had been four hours on our journey, and before proceeding any further, it
was necessary to strengthen ourselves with some of the substantial luncheon
which Mohamed had prepared for us. Sandwiches, that is to say, a small flat
loaf of bread, slashed up into thick slices, radiating from one point like a
fan, between each of which is placed a supply of cold turkey, the remains of
our now regularly established Sunday dinner; dates, dried figs, wine . . .

And now we left the boat. The rock of Abousir rose almost perpendicularly on the bank overlooking the black and green porphyry rocks of the
Cataracts. [They were faced with the problem of lifting the two invalids of
their party over the rough land.] Two pair of strong arms interlaced to form
a sedan, raised each of them from the ground; and after a few halts for
breathing-time to bearers and burdens, they were safely landed on the top
of the rock of Abousir.

---

* She refers to *Murray's Guide to Egypt*.
† The Reis of the cataract was the man in charge of arranging the hauling of the boats
up—or down—his stretch of the river. Mrs. Carey's use of the word 'grisly' means
elderly, grey haired.

We stood at last on the rock of Abousir with the Second Cataracts of the Nile at our feet. From left to right, as far as the eye can reach, it follows the thickly studded groups of black or dark green porphyry rocks, with which the bed of the river is broken up. The blue water winds and rushes in rapids and eddies, in and out and round them all, making a low, roaring, splashing sound, which, when the river is full, is heard at a great distance. In the far horizon, a silver line of light marks where the Nile again pursues a placid course, until it shows again its turbulent career in the Third Cataracts at Semneh. Vessels of moderate size may pass the Second Cataracts at the time of the high Nile, in the months of August and September; but later in the year this barrier is impassable, so that all further explorations must then be made by land on dromedaries.

Wadi Halfa, January 22, 1844
Countess Hahn Hahn
Few Europeans, dear brother, receive letters from their sisters dated from *Wadi Halfa*. You shall be one of the privileged. I am now within the tropics, near the second—the great—cataract of the Nile, and on the southern frontier of Nubia. All this I know. But what countries and what people are my neighbours, that I do know but very indistinctly; for I have no map, no book, nothing with me at all that refers to Nubia; and therefore, respecting neighbourhood and neighbours, I can tell you only that eighteen days' journey on a camel would take me to Dongola, and eighteen more to Sennaar, and that Cordovan and Darfur are at still greater distances. In this country they reckon by camel-marches . . .

Wadee Halfeh, 1861
M.L.M. Carey
The village of Wadee Halfeh is a straggling one, shaded by very fine date-palms, but rejoicing in such a quantity of dust, and castor-oily inhabitants as to afford little temptation to frequent visits. The sand-bank by which our boat was moored was far more enjoyable. It was a very extensive one, covered with white sand, like sea-sand; and by careful picking and choosing, we could find a firm footing upon it even for the crutches, so that (the invalid) Cousin Phil turned out for a constitutional regularly twice a day. A small dahabieh was moored here belonging to four young men who had forsaken their boat at Assouan, and gone on camels into the desert to Dongola. . . . The other vessels at Wadee Halfeh, on our arrival there, were cargo-boats, near which bales of goods were being constantly deposited

from the backs of kneeling camels that had come down in long files from the interior.

Later Mrs. Carey had an unusual experience . . .

Mohamed's heart had for some time been set upon taking me out for a serenade in the small boat, with 'music on the water', as he termed it. At Wadee Halfeh I agreed to go.

The full band, with tom-tom, tambourines, drums, and fifes, were packed as tightly as they could be packed, in the further end of the boat; and there was just room enough for me, and Sarah who attended me, to sit in the stern. How astonished my friends at home would have been could they have seen me and my companions. There was only a half-moon, so that it was not a light night, only a portion of the outlines of the figures of the dark musicians, their sparkling eyes and shining teeth when they opened their mouths to sing, the ornamental portions of their instruments upon which the light of the moon struck, and the dancing reflection on the waters, were perceptible in the surrounding dimness. The men were in high spirits, delighted with their own noise, and with the honour conferred upon them. They sang in full chorus as we rowed along, saluting every dahabeeh on our road so lustily, that their inmates rushed to the deck or the windows, to see what could be going on. The wild sounds nearly deafened us, and the pale moon looked down again from above in silent amaze, I am sure, at the savage din which dared thus to cross her reflection on the still waters.

The Arabs went through the whole of their catalogue of songs in succession with unabated vigour to the end, and hardly would they allow us to escape, when we returned to the dahabeeh, having had enough and to spare their serenading.

Two Cultures to Wadi Halfa, 1988
Bettina Selby

Most of the deck space of the Wadi Halfa steamer was reserved for prayers. Only the men prayed, standing in a line shoulder to shoulder on the mats spread out specially for them, their shoes and sandals placed neatly around the edges. They went through the prescribed Moslem ritual making the deep obeisances, foreheads touching the ground while trying not to look at the distracting sight of young Western men and women lounging about the periphery in scanty clothing. The bikinis and bare torsos were not unsuitable for the weather, which was growing noticeably hotter by the hour, but were insensitive in this part of the world, where people consider bare flesh to be immoral and even the men keep their legs covered. There were about thirty of these sun-worshipping whites, mostly fairly young Britons and Australians on a bus tour through Africa. I had seen their vehicle, looking rather like a moon buggy, with its wide smooth tyres. It was lashed onto a barge steaming up the lake ahead of us, and I think that it may have sunk somewhere in the middle because, although I spent three days in Wadi Halfa, it had still not arrived when I left. By then the passengers were becoming extremely irritated with one another as well as with the local people.

Turning North, 1862
M.L.M. Carey

Thursday, January 17th At ten a.m. the 'Cairo' started on her way home. She would be some time about this said journey home; still the sound was pleasant to the ear, and whatever the rest of the party, out of respect to antiquity perhaps, or from any other cause, may have hidden each in their own bosom, there was one face whose features decidedly shortened, and one pair of feet that skimmed the deck for joy at the thought of returning to the civilised world again; and they were those of honest Sarah (her maid). Visions of civilised society, European hotels, and no more ironing days in the scorching sun, with the true English home drawing gradually nearer, floated before her brain as she sat watching the newly arranged scenery of the dahabieh.

The twelve rowers sat at the oars, and pulled with hearty good will, for they were going home too. Their manner of rowing is very curious and picturesque. They rise from their seats at every stroke, stand upright on the desk as they dip the oars in the water, re-seat themselves, letting the left foot return into the hold, while the right rests on the deck, and pull a long double stroke, singing in chorus as they row.

They have several different 'pulls,' as Mohamed [their guide] calls them, and a particular song or chant is adapted to each of them. That from which we started from Wadee Halfeh, he proudly announced as "the oldest 'pull' of all! Three hundred years for this song!" In one they prolong the stroke so much, and pull with such vigour, that they literally throw themselves flat upon their backs on the deck before lifting the oars out of the water; and there was one very quiet and still longer stroke, with a peculiarly low and solemn chant belonging to it, which they called "the man-of-war pull," and which was used now and then as a show-off, but the men did not enjoy it much.

When there is a gentle or a fair wind they will row all day long, stopping only three times to take their meals and to rest. It is hard work, but in general they show no signs of fatigue, and will, on an emergency, continue rowing all night for a little extra 'baksheesh.' The wind, however, is so constantly contrary, that they have much idle time on their hands, to make up for the hard days of rowing. At such times the oars are laid aside, and the dahabeeh drifts down with the stream; the deck is immediately covered with sleeping forms, lying about it in all directions; or, should the men find the weather cold, they pop down each into his hole, and either disappearing altogether, or, leaving a head and pair of shoulders only visible above, they begin munching leeks and onions. A breath of fair wind springs up, the steersman shouts, and a few of the sleeping forms start up to unfurl the small sail at the bow, to furl it again perhaps in the course of ten minutes, and to disappear once more into the hold, until another shout brings them suddenly back again, to row with might and main till the pilot orders them to cease, when down they all tumble as before.

Crocodiles! 1873
Amelia Edwards

Our pilot leaned forward on the tiller, put his finger to his lips, and whispered—"Crocodilo!" The Painter, the Idle Man and the Writer were all on deck, and not one believed him. They had seen too many of these snags already, and were not going to let themselves again be excited about nothing.

The pilot pointed to the cabin where L. and the Little Lady were indulging in that minor vice called afternoon tea.

"Sitteh!" said he. "Call Sitteh! Crocodilo!"

We examined the object through our glasses. We laughed the pilot to scorn. It was the worst imitation of a crocodile we had yet seen.

All at once the palm-trunk lifted its head, cocked its tail, found its legs, set off running, wriggling, undulating down the slope with incredible rapidity, and was gone before we could utter an exclamation.

We three had a bad time when the other two came up and found that we had seen our first crocodile without them.

A sandbank which we passed next morning was scored all over with fresh trails, and looked as if it had been the scene of a crocodile-parliament. There must have been at least twenty or thirty members present at the sitting; and the freshness of the marks showed that they had only just dispersed.

Ramses Statues, 1846
Harriet Martineau

On her way down the Nile, Miss Martineau's party and other groups stopped again at Abu Simbel.

The faces of Rameses outside (precisely alike) are placid and cheerful, full of moral grace: but the eight Osirides within (precisely the same too) are more. They are full of soul. It is a mistake to suppose that the expression of a face must be injured by its features being colossal. In Egypt may be seen that a mouth three feet wide may be as delicate, and a nostril which spans a foot as sensitive in expression as any marble bust of our day. It is very wonderful, but it is quite true.

Met on Our Way, 1873
Amelia Edwards

I shall not soon forget an Abyssinian caravan which we met one day just coming out of Mahatta. It consisted of seventy camels laden with elephant tusks. The tusks, which were about fourteen feet in length, were packed in half-dozens and sewn up in buffalo hides. Each camels was hung with two loads, one at either side of the hump. There must have been about eight hundred and forty tusks in all. Beside each shambling beast strode a bare-footed Nubian. Following these on the back of a gigantic camel, came a hunting leopard in a wooden cage, and a wild cat in a basket. Last of all marched a coal-black Abyssinian nearly seven feet in height, magnificently shawled and turbaned, with a huge scimitar dangling by his side, and in his belt a pair of enormous inlaid seventeenth-century pistols, such as would have become the holsters of Prince Rupert. This elaborate warrior represented the guard of the caravan. The hunting leopard and the wild cat were for Prince Hassan, the third son of the Viceroy. The ivory was for exportation.

Anything more picturesque than this procession, with its dust driving before it in clouds, and the children following it out of the village, it would be difficult to conceive.

Coming Downstream—After the Inundation, 1862
M.L.M. Carey

The river had, of course, fallen considerably since we passed up, in the month of November; the appearance of the banks was completely changed; no more dhoura was to be seen; wheat was now growing on plains which were then under water; the river was at times quite narrow, and flowed through small passages between intervening banks, formed by its rich alluvial deposits, which are no sooner left dry than they are prepared for fresh crops of cucumbers and water-melons.

Since our leaving Sioot, these banks had gradually increased in number and size, and careful navigation was required to avoid them. The dragoman's wary eye was never off the water, and now he warned the Reis, as night drew on, to stop the vessel if he did not "know the water." The Reis said he "knew the water quite well," and presently, with three considerable lurches, we stuck fast. Mohamed paced the deck or sat upon the steps in a most unenviable state of mind. I believe he thought we were there for a week; and so we might have been had not assistance come opportunely in our distress. Moreover, Mohamed considered that, although the whole fleet of the Nile should stick once a week, the "best boat on the Nile" had no business "sticking" at all.

Every man on board, the Reis, steersman, and all, got into the water to try and move the heavy weight. At length we floated, but for two minutes only; in we were again, deeper than before. Loud calls upon 'Allah' and 'Mohamed' resounded through the gloom; the men renewed their exertions with almost superhuman force, but it would not do, and there we must have remained had not a cargo boat passed and lent us the aid of her crew.

Down the Cataract, March 1874
Marianne Brocklehurst

Miss Brocklehurst gave one of the most detailed and carefully observed accounts of the fearful experience of coming down the cataract from above Aswan.

Up at six, on deck, boarded by the Reis and his men, the *shellaleel*. As our old Reis remarked, "Twenty to row, thirty to scream and ten to direct."

They row us gently down to the head of the cataract, which is no sham this time, and a different passage to the one we came up. We saw before us a narrow passage between high granite rocks where the water is regularly roaring for about three hundred yards and with a sudden rush and a bound we are in for it.

The great boat gathers fresh impetus every moment, the very Arabs forget to scream for some moments, and just at the last, when we seem to be tearing straight down upon the wall of rocks before us, the steersmen (four of them) give us a good twist and we turn sharp to the left and escape with our lives. The Arabs then gave themselves up to extravagant demonstrations of joy, seized the turbans of some of our men, and salaamed and shook hands with us. They began these manifestations rather too soon and by getting in front of the pilots, who could not see, we narrowly escaped a great rock in the middle of the rapid towards the end, which as it was we bumped and scraped against considerably and might have got a very similar hole in our side to that the poor crocodile had. After this grand go, we sailed in smooth water for some minutes and then had another rush down another rapid, not so long nor so sheer as the first but sufficiently dangerous, as was proved by the dahabeeyah *Dongola* which followed us and got a great hole through her on the rocks of this second rapid, causing a stoppage of two days for repairs before she could be brought to Assouan. We, more fortunate, were now well over our troubles and we glided pleasantly down to Assouan in an hour and a half. The scenery is of course very striking and grand and the morning sunlight made it beautiful. We had all enjoyed our shoot tremendously and after paying our backsheesh, bazaaring and calling on the Governor, who was holding court as usual under a sycamore tree at the gate of the town . . .

Last Hours at Philae, 1873
Amelia Edwards

On her way north Miss Edwards spent a day alone full of memories at Philae.

We spent eight enchanted days at Philae; and it so happened that when the afternoon of the eighth came round, that for the last few hours, I was alone on the island. Alone, that is to say, with only a sailor in attendance, which was virtually solitude; and Philae is a place to which solitude adds an inexpressible touch of pathos and remoteness.

It has been a hot day, and there is dead calm on the river. My last sketch finished, I wander slowly round from spot to spot, saying farewell to 'Pharoah's Bed'—to the Painted Columns—to every terrace, and palm, and shrine, and familiar point of view. I peek once again into the mystic chamber of Osiris. I see the sunset for the last time from the roof of the Temple of Isis. Then, when all that lustrous flush of rose and gold has died away, comes the warm afterglow.

No words can paint the melancholy beauty of Philae at this hour. The surrounding mountains stand out jagged and purple against a pale amber sky. The Nile is glassy. Not a breath, not a bubble, troubles the inverted landscape. Every palm is twofold; every stone is doubled. The big boulders in mid-stream are reflected so perfectly that it is impossible to tell where the rock ends and the water begins. The Temples, meanwhile, have turned to a subdued golden bronze; and the pylons are peopled with shapes that glow with fantastic life, and look ready to step down from their places.

The solitude is perfect, and there is a magical stillness in the air. I hear a mother crooning to her baby on the neighbouring island—a sparrow twittering in its little nest in the capital of a column below my feet—a vulture screaming plaintively among the rocks in the far distance.

I look; I listen; I promise myself that I will remember it all the years to come—all the solemn hills, these silent colonnades, these deep, quiet spaces of shadow, these sleeping palms. Lingering till it is all but dark, I at last bid them farewell, fearing lest I behold them no more.

After the Inundation, 1846
Harriet Martineau

In the afternoon, between Eilethyia and Isna, we passed five boats with European flags: one of which was Russian, and the rest English. The Russian countess was an Englishwoman, moreover. I could not but hope that these travellers would not pronounce decisively on the scenery of Egypt, as observed from their boats; for they were too late in the season to see much without the effort of going ashore. The river had sunk so much that we hardly recognised some districts, whose aspect appeared totally altered from what it was a few weeks before. . . .

6

Northward down the Nile

In the days of sail the travelers' boats had been driven south by the wind from the north at the end of the year. When the time came to return, their boats were carried northwards by the flow of the river. Often they were in Nubia at the turn of the year—and, thus, the date of their return was in a new year. On the journey south less time was allowed by their reis for stopping, but once they turned north again they could stop more often, and moored at the towns including Luxor (the Thebes of the past) and the great sites of the West bank which they had passed wistfully as they sailed south to Nubia.

Here, we follow travelers from Aswan northwards down the Nile. Luxor provides so much interest that it is covered in a separate chapter.

North from Assouan, 1855
Lady Tobin
We were under weigh during the night, and soon after breakfast reached Komombo—where we remained twenty-four

hours, to give the Reis an opportunity of seeing his wife and children, who resided there. We walked to the famous Temple over a strip of parched ground, between the cracks of which lupins were sprung up—and along the edge of a field which some Arabs were preparing for cultivation. Near this field was a fine cotton plantation, where several Nubian slaves—the happiest of Egypt's population, for they are generally well treated and have nothing to lose—were busily employed.

The Temple of Komombo is still for the most part embedded in the sand. It was founded in the reign of Ptolemy Philometer, and is singular among the existing temples of Egypt in having a double entrance and two parallel sanctuaries. Among an admirably preserved sculpture and painting on the walls, friezes, and columns of this majestic ruin, one ceiling attracted our notice from its extremely distinct and fresh appearance—the colours retaining all their pristine brilliancy. Close by, towering above the river, is an edifice erected upon an artificial platform. It is now in so a ruinous state that very little can be traced of its original plan.

On the evening of Friday, November 11th, we anchored at Edfou. We saw during the day three crocodiles and some storks.

A few minutes' walk early the next morning—through fields of millet, beans, lupins, and *bamiahs*—brought us to a wide canal, across which we were safely carried by three of our sailors, who contrived to make a capital *arm-chair* with their hands and arms. We had to pass a manufactory of earthen jars, and along a street of the miserable town of Edfou, before we found ourselves in front of the Temple so worthy of its fame.

From the summit of the massive gateway we looked down upon the noble court (now used as a granary) with its yet perfect rows of columns— and the rich fertile valley of the Nile. The river here makes a very considerable bend.

Kom Ombos, 1844
Countess Hahn Hahn

The Egyptian temples have fallen prey to sand and the ravages of man far more than the Nubian. The sites of the former gave them over to the sand, whilst they offered convenient habitations to a whole village of populous land. The splendid temple of Kom Ombos succumbed to the sand on one side, and to the mud-washings of the Nile on the other. Where the river makes a sharp bend, and has a high perpendicular bank, lies this temple, visible from afar, domineering over an extensive region, and looking like the corpse of a king laid out in royal state.

We visited it towards sunset, and the purple rays majestically illuminated it, as candelabra light up a catafalque. Later rose the moon, causing the lovely forms even more distinctly to step forth, the ruins to sink back in deeper gloom, and giving the broad desert the aspect of a winding-sheet; add to this, the solid silence all around, and the tranquil Nile softly flowing at our feet, and you have one of the finest pictures which this journey yielded me.

You would like to hear something of the temple itself. Only conceive! The ante-hall alone stands upright, and in such a way that pillars are buried in the sand to the half of their height. The four rooms which follow it are lost up to the frieze, and the cross-beam stone blocks, twenty to twenty-two feet in length, have sunk down. In order to look closely at the hieroglyphics, the designs, and the well-preserved colours, I knelt upon the sand which reaches above the door-cornice, and found upon the frieze remarkably well formed escutcheons of the time of Ptolemy.

A smaller temple exhibits at present only heaps of ruins, whilst a lonely pylon stands close upon the high and rugged bank, and seems to await the fate which must have befallen his companions; they, no doubt, fell together as the earth loosened with the overflow, and rolled down the declivity. Earlier destruction has probably been warded off by a wall, which restrained the advancing waters. The deserted pylon looks very melancholy; they generally stand in pairs, like twin-brothers, faithfully together keeping the long watch.

Night Noises on the Nile, 2006
Rosemary Mahoney

Dogs quibbled in the dark distance. Donkeys screeched in hysterical fits that sometimes lasted a full minute. Herons squawked and muttered along the riverbank. Fish—or perhaps some other, more sinister, creature—splashed and gurgled around the hull of the boat. At 4:45 a.m. the call to prayer began in the many mosques of nearby Kom Ombo, an insistent din, like the throbbing discord of a bees' nest. Many voices vibrated from the same general vicinity, no two in step with each other. Technically, believers were required to rise and begin praying now, but not a soul in the camp stirred. Amr and Wa'il and all the other felucca men snored on. I was always a little disappointed that the call to prayer never seemed to provoke an immediate response from anyone I had acquainted myself with in Egypt. I, however, was highly conscious of it, even enamoured of it, and had fallen into the habit of humming its pleasant tune, probably blasphemously, under my breath wherever I went.

Rowing down the Nile, 2006
Rosemary Mahoney

Traveling alone in a small fisherman's boat from Aswan, Rosemary Mahoney set out rowing down the Nile early one morning.

The river had a grass green hue at this hour and felt supple and comfortable beneath me, like a down mattress. On the track that ran along the rubbly east bank at the foot of some sandy reddish cliffs, the train to Cairo clattered and whistled, stirring up a twister of dust behind it. Herons gargled in the bushes overhanging the river. Near noon the call to prayer began to emanate from beyond great stands of banana trees all along the banks; from this distance it was a melancholy lowing sound, warped occasionally by the idle wind. I stayed close to the west bank and rowed steadily while the sun crept higher in the sky. The current seemed to move faster the farther I got from Aswan. I was breathless with expectation, happiness and anxiety.

Down the middle of the river I rowed, feeling that I was not floating but flying. No one shouted at me because there was no one there to see me. The river was delightfully empty. This was not like any other body of water I had rowed on. I knew how far this water had travelled through time and space, and what in the world it had inspired. Because the Nile idly, mindlessly slid down the incline of the African continent, human beings had been able to develop civilization; sitting on top of this water was like being united with my origins.

The land that lay along the bank had changed in the century and more that divided Rosemary Mahoney from earlier travelers—although some scenes were little changed.

Women in black walked slowly along the river-banks with jugs on their heads, disappearing in and out of stands of eucalyptus trees and all along the banks I saw children tending fires in fields, burning the stubble of crops—a diabolical job to have to perform in such heat. The fields were rectangular and evenly divided by irrigation canals and mounds of black earth. Beyond the fields were the caramel coloured hills and the huge expanse of roasting desert rubble. There were mud-brick villages here, with houses painted yellow and blue, and men riding donkeys, and crumbling mud-brick walls, and brown sheep trotting through the dust beneath stands of date palms. I saw a white camel lying by the river-bank with his nose lifted high in the air and a man in nothing but an enormous white turban and white underwear standing scare-crow still in the middle of a flooded field. I saw mud-brick graves in the distance—rectangular mounds of earth with palm fronds stuck into them as markers—and boys carrying hoes on their shoulders and girls carrying brittle cornstalks on theirs. These were exactly the scenes of ancient Egyptian life depicted over and over on the walls of ruined temples. A gunshot rang out in a banana grove, and a hundred white birds flew up out of the greenery with sharp cries of alarm.

Esne, 1844
Countess Hahn-Hahn
Esne is the first town after Assuan, and has its own manufactories: for instance, the manufacture of small pipe-bowls, which are made in millions, of red clay. The town is altogether Eastern: the crooked streets, windowless houses, dirty bazaars and many coffee-rooms. I saw a snake-charmer there: Heaven, how disgusting! Five snakes wound themselves around his arms, attached themselves to his fingers, bent and twisted themselves in his hands. I did not know that they were venomous; they are always hideous.

The Alme Dancers, 1861
M.L.M. Carey
[At Esna] the streets of the present town are almost on a level with the roof of the portico [of the temple], and the wretched hovels of the natives are built so close upon the beautiful ruins that they hide them completely. . . . In the evening we went with Mohammed [their dragoman] to what he called 'a private house' that we might see the 'alme' dance. The 'private house' was little more than a mud hovel. The space in which the girls danced could hardly have been five foot square; the spectators, mounted on the raised seat against the wall, were seated on their own chairs, which had been

brought with them from the boat. A bed with mosquito curtains was at one extremity of the apartment; a divan at the other. The instrumental and vocal performers crowded at the little open door-way; and a small oil lamp, hanging from the ceiling, was the only light provided, to illuminate the darkness. Had we not brought our own lantern with us, little indeed should we have seen of the performance. The 'alme' dance with their bodies rather than their feet, making a series of contortions, shakings and joltings, which suggest the idea that the figures of these girls consist of two distinct parts, which have very little to do with one another.

They shuffle their naked feet along the ground in a most inelegant manner, keeping time to the music which is being played for them. One of the girls played with small brass cymbals, a pair of which she held in each hand; her companion raised one hand to her head, at times as though in grief, at others spying through her fingers with most impudent looks, while the other arm was fixed akimbo on her side. There were regular figures to the dance; the performers seemed to follow the music according to their own inclination, and at the conclusion of the exercise they looked as hot and tired as might be expected after such unnatural exertions . . .

Dancing-Girls

The dress of the 'alme' is always gay and handsome. They wore on this occasion striped India silk, and necklaces of gold coins, crocodiles, and other forms, all in gold. Their fez caps were sewn all over with small money; a handsome crown piece of solid gold fastened the rich black silk tassel; and a number of long braids of silk, equally covered with coins, forty of them at least, dangled behind the tiny plaits of their black hair, which between the silk braids and the tassel of the fez, were very little seen.

We were sufficiently pleased with these curiosities to be enabled to express truthful admiration and satisfaction, notwithstanding the sensations of disgust and pity which the dancing itself could not fail to raise in a European lady's mind. We were glad to have seen it, but were equally sure that we should never wish to witness it again; though the fiddler and his fiddle we would most gladly have captured and taken away with us.

Honest Sarah's sense of propriety received even a greater shock than ours [she was their English maid], and her looks of undisguised horror were an amusing part of the play: indeed I am not sure that they had not their effect in increasing the impudent looks of the 'alme,' which were towards the conclusion mostly aimed at her. But Sarah could not get over a great number of the daily sights she saw in this strange land, as her averted eyes and frequent sudden disappearances into the depths of the cabin abundantly testified. But we will not quarrel with her for this; it is a fault on the right side. And we like her all the better for her true English modesty.

Delays and an Accident, 1858
Emily Hornby
Got up early for El Kab, and then heard there was not time for us to stop there, as the tug was bound to be at Luxor this evening, which we had never understood. However, there was no help for it, and personally, I was not sorry, as I had rather a cough, and was glad of a quiet day. Passed Esneh. Quite an important town, with some good houses, evidently belonging to Europeans, and a railway station. Temple rather hard to distinguish, there is so little of it above ground. A great many palm-trees about. Several dahabiehs anchored, and a good deal of shipping. On the opposite side, the Arabian side, a range of pale pink hills. Expected to be at Luxor about four. Meant to dine at hotel and have quite a festive evening, but twice got upon sand-banks, and were a long time getting off, so soon that was hopeless.

Finally, about seven, just before dinner, heard loud yells on deck, and then a tremendous crash. Quite thought the crew had mutinied, and that we were going to be murdered; but Ibrahim rushed into the saloon, saying, "Ladies, do not be frightened!" It appeared the tug had insisted on going on after dark, against advice, got upon another sand-bank, and pulled us after her right upon another boat already stranded there, with a large anchor hanging outside. The anchor had gone right through the side of the saloon, and across the corner into M.'s cabin. She was lying on the bed, and it must have gone within an inch of her head. We cannot be too thankful for such a providential escape. We now anchored for the night; the broken glass was cleared away, and we were left with half one side of the saloon open.

Women along the River, 2006
Rosemary Mahoney

I had seen notably few women on the river. There had been a couple washing clothes or walking along the banks with baskets on their heads, disappearing in and out of clumps of trees in their long black gowns, but I had seen many more birds than women. I saw herons, egrets, kingfishers, black-and-white hoopoes with harlequinesque markings and fanning red crests, green bee-eaters, hovering kestrels, and scores of unidentifiable buteos soaring high above the river.

Alone on the River, 2006
Rosemary Mahoney

I anchored my boat and stepped onto a beach littered with small shells. After sitting so long on the water, I was unsteady on my feet; everything seemed to sway beneath me. I walked the length of the beach—the length of a football field—and back again, and then sat in the shade of a large bush. The shade formed an oval exactly the size of my body, and as the shifting sun forced the shade to slide around the bush, I had to slide with it. A pair of stone curlews, shorebirds slightly bigger than crows, fluttered out of the sky and landed near me on the beach; they had long yellow legs and shocked-looking bright yellow eyes as big as a human's, and they stared at me in a spooky, hypnotized way. Dragonflies floated drunkenly by. Whole rafts of water hyacinths hurried past like feathery green mattresses set loose on the current. The sky looked galvanized in the east, a broiled greyish white, though directly above me it was turquoise blue. I sat happily for an hour, drank a bottle of water, and tried to figure out where I was. I guessed I was twenty miles or so from Qena. I was exhausted. The palms of my hands were raw. I felt the heat pushing me toward the earth, and eventually I lay down in the sand, using my shoes as a pillow.

Two boys passed not many feet away. Her boat moored at the edge of the river didn't attract their attention—it was too common a sight, the sort used by every fisherman in Egypt.

Dangers Ahead, 1836
Sarah Haight
Before we arrived at Siout [Asyut] we were hailed by a boat from Cairo, and from her learned that the plague had made its appearance in almost every town along the river. This information, of course, put an end to our land expeditions. Fortunately, the same boat had on board for us a good supply of provisions, sent by our provident Cairo landlord, Mr Hill, with a store of fine oranges for me. Our greatest solicitude after the unpleasant intelligence of the plague, was in reference to the strict quarantine which it became necessary for us to keep, and the impossibility of preventing our Arab boatmen from mixing with their friends along the river. For the last week we never went on shore in the vicinity of any habitation.

Such Great Heat, 1862
M.L.M. Carey
We emerged from the sepulchres into the open air under the broiling sun, and finding just sufficient shade to accommodate us beneath the wall of the rocky entrance, we spread our shawls on the sand, and sat down to luncheon. The Arabs would taste nothing, because it was Ramadan: even a little boy to whom an orange was offered put it away until the evening feast.

The degree of heat which we experienced here would in an English climate have induced extreme languor and loss of spirits; but the bracing air of Egypt produced a totally different effect. Although the exposure to it was at times painful, or even dangerous, inducing headaches and burning feverishness in those with whom it did not quite agree, yet we never felt languid during any part of our journey, and we noticed an unusually even flow of spirits in all the travellers on the Nile, not excepting the invalids. It was not often that my companions [of whom two were in Egypt for their health] found the heat of Egypt unpleasantly great; but on this occasion it was agreed on all sides that 'painful' would not be too strong a term to apply to our ride back from Apis to the dahabieh, although both Apis and Memnon

had furnished ample food for thought, and although we passed by many re-
freshingly green fields of wheat and clover, and large tracts of the brilliant
yellow 'selgum.'

As a kind caution to future visitors, it may be worth while to mention, that
on our return to the dahabieh it was discovered that some few squadrons of
the 'light infantry'* of Egypt had returned along with each one of us, collected
no doubt from the sand or near the catacombs. Other bands were evidently
making their presence known on the lower deck, as its busy appearance soon
testified. The troops of the enemy were fortunately discovered before their
intended onslaught had begun, and we warn all travellers to keep the visit to
Sakkara for their return from the Cataracts. Although extra ablutions will be
found necessary after the shortest excursion on shore (or even without it),
had this been our first instead of our last but one, and that one to the Pyramids
of Geezeh, from which I believe the whole army of Egypt could not have de-
terred us, our antiquarian zeal would have suffered materially.

The Great Statue and Ants, 1874
Marianne North

We stopped at Memphis, and rode about the wonderful palm forest, all
strewn with statues and bits of polished granite; one large one of Ramses
II, lying flat on its nose, which is the same shape as that at Abu Simbel, perfectly beautiful but a trifle too long, perhaps, and with an absurd look of
the Prince of Wales about it. Mr S. said it was intended to be looked at from
below, so that if we were to stick H.R.H. on the top of an exceedingly high
pedestal he might perhaps look beautiful and majestic too, who knows?

I sat down on the ground to make a sketch of the distant Sakkarah Pyramids, and presently I found a long procession of ants walking over me,
and discovered myself to be in the middle of an ant-road of about thirty
yards long, a clear well-trodden path. My sailor wanted to break it up, but
I would not let him, which pleased some old Arabs near, and they showed
me the end of the road, where all the little creatures took their loads into
a very small hole, and disappeared; almost as curious and difficult a work
as the pyramids themselves, about which we, the higher educated animals,
think so much, and a far more useful work, for the pyramid merely sheltered the bones of one man, the ants nest sheltered the food of a whole
colony, and themselves too.

---

* By "light infantry" Mrs. Carey means the fleas which infested people in Egypt.

I found another colony of ants the nest day at the very top of old Cheop's tomb, thriving probably on the remains of Frank* picnics.

Back in Cairo, 1854
Lady Tobin
We bade adieu to our dahabieh on Thursday, December 8th, and drove in an open carriage to Shepheard's Hotel. It was market day at Boulak. An immense number of loaded camels were standing or lying in an open space to our left, and we passed many more on the road. The hotel is the largest I ever saw; with its handsome stone staircases, wide corridors, and lofty apartments. There are good baths too, and a well supplied *table d'hote*. On the other hand, the beds are by no means so free from *creeping things* as they might be with proper care, and the attendance is woefully deficient. Certainly what *we* call good servants must be extremely scarce in Egypt.

The constant arrival of passengers to and from India [crossing to and from Suez] keeps up an unceasing bustle and excitement. Young and old, married and single, black *ayahs* and English nurserymaids, sickly squalling children, yellow faces and dowdy dresses, disappointed hopes and ardent expectations—all assemble here! Of mere *tourists*, the Americans are at present the most numerous. They leave their own country with a fixed resolve to *see* so much and *spend* so much within a specified time, and almost invariably perform to a hair's breadth what they have undertaken.

Returning North to Alexandria, 1850
Florence Nightingale
We did not get to Atfeh [where they would board the boat for Alexandria] till ten o'clock, too late to bid adieu to our solemn Nile; who, indeed, had been all that day as ugly and as contrary as it was possible to be. There was the wretched sick woman to be carried. Mrs X's spoilt child would not part from its wax doll. What was to be done? A good-natured man took charge of the doll and the child, and I took charge of his baggage, as being the least helpless thing of the two, and of Mrs X.

At last we arrived at the Mahmoudieh Canal—you have to walk across to the boat, as they do not open the locks at night. If anybody could have drawn that scene, how good it would have been. The imperious old Smyrniote, with her blue cockade in the foreground; the miserable Benzik,

---

* Frank—the word for a foreigner throughout the Near East at the time.

with the dog in his arms, which it became a *tour de force* to be able to hold; behind, helpless females not daring to step across the plank. At last Mrs X and I were left alone on the shore. Paola came. "Take Mrs X," I heroically cried: "I will not stir from the hat-box of the man who has taken charge of the doll."

At last we were all lodged on board the Mahmoudieh boat, where you sit bolt upward all night on benches round the cabin, with a large company of biting animals of every description. The moon shone, the horses, each mounted by a wild Arab, galloped—for you are towed by horses—and we went along merrily, only occasionally going aground, owing to the lowness of the water. At breakfast the old Smyrniote ate enough for ten men's dinners. It was too cold and too ugly to go on deck. We reached Alexandria about twelve, and spent the rest of the day in making ourselves clean, and seeing after that wretched Frenchwoman.

The news from Greece was bad; and all thought it best and shortest to go to Corfu by the Trieste boat—do our quarantine there, instead of perhaps two quarantines at Smyrna and Syra—and get the latest news of Athens.

Adieu to Cairo, April, 1874
Marianne Brocklehurst
Adieu to Cairo. After all our wanderings we look back upon it as the most enchanting city in the world, with its narrow streets, its party coloured mosques and minarets far sweeter than those of Constantinople or Damascus, its shady, gleamy bazaars and motley coloured crowds. We shall never see they like again! Oh Cairo!

We journey together (by train) to Alexandria, are very sleepy and very cross with an ugly looking fat Egyptian who gets in unexpectedly. We try to turn him out with the help of dragoman Abas and don't succeed. He turns out indeed to be Governor of Alexandria and talks English as well as we do. He brought the first hippopotamus to England, he says, and we became very friendly in the long run, and very well we do perhaps!! At Alexandria, Abbats Hotel is full and we sleep in new rooms in damp beds and (my companion) suffers for it afterwards and all the way through Syria.

Sunday, April 19
We stop all day at Port Said, picnicking on the banks of the Suez Canal, picking up coral from the Red Sea and prowling on the shore of Lake Manzalee, where dead flamingos lie about on the sand. A good passage we had, and another in prospect, and so goodbye to old Egypt!

7

Luxor and the West Bank— the Thebes of Old

 *As today, after Alexandria and Cairo, most travelers' main experience of Egypt is in Luxor—on both the East and the West banks. However, many travelers in the days of sail stopped only briefly at Luxor when going south, spending a much longer time there and on the west bank while sailing north—carried along by the flow of the river toward the end of their time in Egypt.*

Arrival at Thebes, 1817
Sarah Belzoni

Mrs. Belzoni, at an early stage of her life in Egypt, was returning from Aswan to Luxor so that her husband, Giovanni, could arrange the collection from the west bank of the great head of Ramses II which now dominates the Egyptian halls of the British Museum. Mrs Belzoni was

161

not, in the terms of her days, 'a lady' and her experiences of
Egypt were very different from those told here by most of the
other women—who were 'ladies.' When the Belzonis arrived
in Luxor from their journey to the south and her husband set
about his 'business' of removing—in a larger boat, the vast
bust of Ramses, he lodged her at Luxor with a local family.

We at last reached Luxor. Still there was no rest for the soles of our feet.
There was no boat to take the great colossal head on board; and, notwithstanding this poor accommodation, we were obliged to set off for Gheneh.
We had no sooner arrived there than we were obliged to return, as there was
a large boat pressed for the use of the Bashaw, wherein some Franks had taken
their passage as far as Aswan, which boat was promised for Mr B. for the head.
We tied our little boat to the large one. We had come down well enough with
the stream in our miserable bark; but on going against it we had not set off
twenty minutes when the Arabs began to cry out most dreadfully: in a moment we found the boat was half full of water. Fortunately the large boat, per-
ceiving our danger, ran to land immediately, and we went on board of it.

The next morning we arrived at the wished for haven, Mr B. had but just
time to put me in a house, where he was informed that there would be a room
on the top for me; he was then obliged to sail for Esneh to secure the boat.

This was the first time I had ever been left alone with the Arabs without
an interpreter or a European, with about twenty Arab words in my mouth.
What they denominated a room, consisted of four walls open to the sky, full
of dates put to dry in the sun, an oven in one corner, a water jar, and a fireplace
of three bricks for a pot to stand on, without a chimney; and this place not to
myself, as it was an apartment for the women. I never in my life felt so isolated
and miserable, in a violent fever, exposed to the burning sun; beside the tor-
ment to have all the women of the village coming out of curiosity to see me.

At last I began seriously to think of enclosing one corner of this place
for myself: fortunately it happened to be market day; I sent to buy some
mats, and with the help of the women (I was going to say), who did more
harm than good, I made me a comfortable little room, inclosed and covered
over; I had all my things taken in. Beside the pleasure to be by myself, I had
the additional luxury of two ounces of tea, which I had received from Cairo
on the return of a courier. I felt more content at that moment than I now
should in the finest palace of Europe.

I had just begun to enjoy a little repose, when I had an attack of opthalmia.* During the first ten days a virulent humour discharged from my eyes; I had not any thing to apply to them: I could not bear the light. I used to filter the water to wash them. Whenever the women saw me washing them with water they would all set up a cry telling me it was very bad, and that it was my washing them every morning that had made them so. In Nubia they had the same idea.

My eyes were determined not to be cured so easily: blest with the comforts of Job, the women told me in twenty days perhaps I might get better; but if not in that time, it would go on for forty days—and finished by crying *Malash* (no matter). Instead of being better at the end of twenty days, I became totally blind. I cannot describe the agony I felt on the occasion; I thought I had lost my sight for ever. My situation was not an enviable one, the women still crying *Malash*. The last stage of the disorder was truly dreadful; the eyelids lost their power, I could not lift them up; this was another blow. The women boiled garlic in water to steam my eyes over: it is possible it might have done some good, though I did not feel the effect immediately. I found their experience in this matter perfectly correct; the eyelids began to gain strength, and by degrees, at the end of forty days I could see a little. After getting well of this attack, I made it a rule to wash my eyes daily with water mixed with aqua vitae, which strengthened them much: if ever I found them inclined to a relapse, I made the wash stronger, and kept washing them several times a day: it never failed to cure them; though I never had my eyes as strong as they had been before.

Arrival at Thebes, 1824
Anne Katherine Elwood

Mrs. Elwood was traveling to India with her husband, an East India Company officer, and had sailed south to Luxor, but would soon turn north again to cross the desert to the Red Sea.

About noon, the Reis began to look out for a large sycamore, the landmark by which he was to recognise Thebes. A cangia was moored in its neighbour-

---

* At this time and for many decades after ophthalmia was widespread in Egypt, causing permanent blindness to many.

hood, and a tent was picturesquely pitched beneath its friendly shade, in the neighbourhood of a water-mill. These were the property of Mr Hay, who with Mr Bonomi,* had been residing here for some time, amusing himself with making excavations and discoveries. Scarcely had we come to anchor, ere we were beset by wild-looking natives, offering necklaces, scarabaei, and other curiosities for sale, with the same eagerness with which the Waterloo people bring relics to travellers.† Our gravity was quite put to flight by the sudden entrance of a cat—through the window. Had she been alive she would have been invaluable, on account of the rats which infested the Cangia; but this was a staid old mouser, of the time of Pharaoh perchance, looking as demure and as wise, however, as any of the tabbies of the present day, though probably three thousand years had rolled over her head in her mummy form. We took possession of her, and of some of the other curiosities, which were here offered in such profusion that they seemed to lose their value by their numbers.

Later they crossed the Nile to view the temple of Luxor and were soon surrounded by the local Cacheff and his follow-ers—who "peeped in at the doors and windows of the boat, eyeing me with as much curiosity as we should view a rhinoceros or hippopotamus." Accompanied by "a strange and motley group" they visited Luxor temple.

This majestic building is nearly choked with modern huts, heaps of sand, and mounds of rubbish, broken pottery, dirt, and filth. In many of the walls, sticks are inserted for the accom-modation of pigeons, which bird is particularly venerated by Mahometans, as the life of their Prophet was once saved by a dove; and these, together with the circular pots, resembling men's heads, peeping over the battlement walls, had a most singular effect.

---

* Robert Hay (1799–1863), fascinated by Belzoni's published account of his travels, de-cided to travel in the Near East and Egypt in 1824, taking Joseph Bonomi there as his artist. He published Illustrations of Cairo in 1840. Joseph Bonomi (1796–1878), a trained artist, went to Egypt with Hay, but worked and traveled with others there.
† By 'the Waterloo people' she means the people who collected things from the bat-tleground of the great battle and sold them to tourists who went to see the scene.

At the principal entrance of the Temple stand two noble obelisks, in perfect preservation, with colossal figures, in a sitting position, half imbedded in the sand. After passing through a majestic Propylon, we saw some fine sculpture and paintings, representing battle-scenes.

Arriving at Thebes, 1847
Harriet Martineau

At last we were at Thebes—in the afternoon of this Tuesday, the 19th of January. We were very happy, for there was no hurry. On either hand lay the plain of Thebes, and before us there was leisure to explore it. We stayed eight days—giving five to the western bank and three to the eastern. We made, we thought, good use of our time, exploring daily as much as we could without plunging ourselves into too much fatigue and excitement. What the excitement is can be known only to those who have spent successive days in penetrating the recesses of the palaces, and burying themselves in the tombs of the Pharaohs, who lived among the hundred gates of this metropolis of the world before the Hebrew infant was laid among the nests of the Nile water-fowl. Perhaps some hint of what the interest of Thebes is, may be derived from such poor account as I am able to give of what we saw there; but I shall tell only what I saw, and nothing of what I felt. That can be spoken of nowhere but on the spot.

That first evening we attempted nothing beyond a little stroll on the shore at sunset. The first thing we saw was a throng of boats—five English flags and one Russian. Some were just departing, and others went the next day. Thebes is the last place in the world where one wishes for society: so I dare say every party of the whole throng was longing to see the rest sail away.

Luxor Temple—Far and Near, 1843
Countess Hahn Hahn

We had seen the temple of Luxor in the morning, and we had it besides always before our eyes, since it lies close upon the Nile, consisting of three halls of columns—a colossal one, and two smaller—which produces a grand effect at a distance, as well as when you are near to them. Viewed at a distance, particularly from the other bank, and by the light of evening, with the Arabian mountains as background, and the broad and silent Nile as foreground, these pillared halls have the mythological character of a picture by Claude Lorraine. You do not know to what point of earth it actually belongs, so dreamy is the vapour, so ideal the colouring, with which it is enveloped—and yet one is firmly persuaded that upon the earth it may be found.

Obelisk and Propylon

Standing close to Luxor you are doomed to behold its charms disappearing before the most loathsome of loathsome realities. By the side of this obelisk, which is and will remain the admiration of all times, which is wrought in granite with the delicacy and sharpness of a cameo—by its side, and amongst the four granite colossi and pylons—that royal entry to palaces and temples, as far as the end of the pillared halls, the village has nestled, crept and built itself up; it is an abomination to wind one's way through such filth. What a desecration of pillars, temples and sacred things! Under such circumstances, to be buried more than half in rubbish is an advantage. The obelisk is free. It was probably dug out when its companion was taken to Paris.* I have driven perhaps twenty times along the Place de la Concorde, and that obelisk has always appeared to me to overload the spot rather than ornament it. Now I know why. Egyptian architecture is from one casting. If its columns and pylons, and the whole arrangement of the building, rendered palpable to the senses, energy, endurance and strength, so do the obelisks, elevating their slim forms as monoliths, sixty, seventy, eighty feet high, elegantly and distinctly, by the side of those mighty and dark forms, show that strength may have also grace. . . .

---

* One of the obelisks before the temple—which we see in early pictures—was removed and taken to Paris to be set up in the Place de la Concorde where it stands today.

I rejoice that I had the good taste not to fall into ecstasies at the obelisk in Paris because it drew its origin from Thebes. There it is utterly unfitting, as it is here in harmony with all that surrounds it. Two colossi are buried up the breast, two even to the covering of the head. The pylons looked as if decaying; a mosque, and a children's school—in which boys were very assiduously reading, with a measured rocking movement of the upper part of the body—are leaning against them.

Recording the Past, 1930
Marta Bibescu
An American clung to the wall of the temple like a climbing rose in the sunlight. He was copying the symbols and will be there everyday for six years. These vestiges of another race are to be carried to a museum in the New World.

When people have arrived at a certain level in the scale of human values, they begin to delve into Egypt.

The Antiquity Dealers, 1836
Sarah Haight
The Pasha had for some time since forbidden, under very heavy penalties, any excavation or search for antiquities and treasures to be made in any part of his dominions, giving as a reason that the *fellahs* neglected the cultivation of the soil, and, consequently, curtailed his revenues. Another reason is alleged for this arbitrary order; it is, that several collections of Egyptian antiquities have been sold in England lately at enormous prices by private speculators. This has excited the old Shylock's cupidity, and he has forbidden the exportation from the country of the least article of *virtu*. The Greek's house* was watched day and night by some of his arguses. We thought, however, that by a little backshee soporific, the guards might be put *hors de combat*. The old Greek was too much in fear of bastinado to break the law, and the negotiation resulted much to our disappointment.

Our principal object was to obtain one of the beautifully ornamented mummy-cases, with its Pharaoh or pontiff within it untouched. He showed my husband a great number which he obtained some time previous, but dared not part with one. All that could be obtained were the spoils of one beautiful female mummy, supposed to have been a person of great distinction. . . .

---

* This was the historic house was on the west bank of the Nile near Gourna where early travelers met and shared their experiences. It was pulled down for development a few years ago.

Trade in Antiquities, 1874
Amelia Edwards

The tourists longed to collect Egyptian 'antiquities' and the local people were happy to oblige. If a laborer found a genuine ancient object it seemed like 'a gift from God'; if backstreet traders could create 'antiquities' the travelers might well go home content. . . .

Forgers, diggers, and dealers play, meanwhile into one another's hands, and drive a roaring trade. Your dahabeeyah, as I have just shown, is beset from the moment you moor till the moment you pole off again from the shore. The boy who drives your donkey, the guide who pilots you among the tombs, the half-naked Fellah who flings down his hoe as you pass, and runs beside you for a mile across the plain, have one and all an 'anteekah' to dispose of. The turbaned official who comes, attended by his secretary and pipe-bearer, to pay you a visit of ceremony, warns you against imposition, and hints at genuine treasures to which he alone possesses the key. The gentlemanly native who sits next to you at dinner has a wonderful scarab in his pocket. In short, every man, woman and child about the place is bent on selling a bargain; and the bargain, in ninety-nine cases out of a hundred, is valuable in so far as it represents the industry of Luxor—but no farther. A good thing, of course, is to be had occasionally; but the good thing never comes to the surface as long as a market can be found for the bad one. It is only when the dealer finds he has to do with an experienced customer, that he produces the best he has.

Flourishing as it is, the trade of Luxor labours, however, under some uncomfortable restrictions. Private excavation being prohibited, the digger lives in dread of being found out by the Governor. The forger, who has nothing to fear from the Governor, lives in dread of being found out by the tourist. As for the dealer, whether he sells an antique or an imitation, he is equally liable to punishment. In one case he commits an offence against the state; and in the other, he obtains money under false pretences. Meanwhile the Governor deals out such even-handed justice as he can, and does his best to enforce the law on both side of the river.

Luxor, a Modern City, 1907
Norma Lorimer

Luxor as we see it is but the modern Moslem city which has raised itself primarily for the benefit of tourists upon the site of ancient Thebes.

We arrived at Luxor at sunset. . . .

In coming to Luxor I did not know that the Sahara, the touchstone of my childish imaginings, was there, that the plain of Thebes lay under its great stillness.

"Do you know what lies on the summit of these smiling hills?" Mohammed [her guide] looked across the Nile. We were standing on a terraced garden high above the blue waters, a garden with white steps and white colonnades, as Italian as a Roman palace perched above the bay of Balae. "If you climbed to the topmost peak of those high hills which melt into the clear blue, you would find yourself on the rim of the Sahara, the great mid-desert of Africa."

Seeing Thebes, 1874
Marianne North

We worked hard at Thebes, where the distances are too great for hurry, having to hide from one great sight to the other over the burning plain, on which the harvest was then going on; the first day we 'did' the tombs of the kings, the Memnonium and Colossi; I felt quite fit to be pickled and mummified when I escaped from the tombs, which were far too archaeological for modern humanity. I hate walking where I cannot see my feet, or being hauled about even by the gentlest of Arab guides, but as I fell flat on my back once, argument and remonstrance were of no use, and I was hauled in by one hand, holding a candle in the other; of course we were astounded by the amount of careful painting done in miles of darkness before electric light or gas were invented, and how we rejoiced when we got into the air and sun again!

Sunday, March 4; Monday, March 5 1858
Emily Hornby

Miss Hornby's journal reveals much of the everyday life of a Nile journey, which a published account would probably leave out.

Luxor from the Water

Arrived at Luxor about nine. Anchored opposite side, just in front of the temple. Crossed in felucca for church. Service at 10:30; church very full. Very interesting service about Sodom and Gomorrah; the clergyman has been deciphering Babylonian manuscripts . . . Holy Communion. . . . Luncheon at hotel. Very good. Back to the dahabieh for tea. Wrote some more letters and cards. Back in boat for evening church at six. Posted letters in hotel.

M. and I started on donkeys at eight, with Ibrahim, for the tombs of the kings.

First crossed sand, then crossed railway and canal bridges, and some way along a road, a dry canal on one side, cornfields on the other.

The Last Night of 1849
Florence Nightingale

Writing to her parents in England . . .

Did you listen to the old year passing away and think of me? Where do you think I heard it sigh out its soul? In the dim unearthly colonnades of Karnak, which stood and watched it, motionless, silent, and awful, as they had done for thousands of years, to whom, no doubt, thousands of years seem but as a day. Would that I could call up Karnak before your eyes for one moment, but it "is beyond expression."

No one could trust themselves with their imagination alone there. Gigantic shadows spring up one every side . . . and they look out from among the columns, and you feel as terror-stricken to be there, miserable intruder, among these mighty dead, as if you had awakened the angel of the Last Day. Imagine six columns on either side, of which the last is almost out of sight, though they stand very near each other, while you look up to the stars from between them, as you would from a deep narrow gorge in the Alps, and then, passing through 160 of these, ranged in eight aisles on either side, the end choked up with heaps of rubbish, this rubbish consisting of stones twenty or thirty feet long, so that it looks like a mountain fallen to ruin, not a temple.

Florence Nightingale and her companions returned to Karnak during their stay at Luxor.

In the evening we went to Karnak; the night was dark, the moon had betrayed us. No one can describe the desolation of riding over the desert by night; at home one's imagination used to rest in a smooth desert: this was all, as usual tumbled about; but we could see little. All I know is that one man held me on behind, while another led my ass; and the blasts of sand in your face, though there was no breath of a wind, where the only thing stirring beside ourselves and the stirring of the wild dogs all around us, which sounded like the spirits of the old, Efreet Egyptians let loose. . . .

Then we stood under the pylon, whose top reaches heaven; men passed between the propyla into the vast atrium; one single column still stood there, not wringing its hands, but raising its unearthly head among the stars, and watching calmly and ceaselessly the course, not of years, but of periods . . .

At Home in Luxor, 1864
Lucie Duff Gordon

For some years Lady Duff Gordon settled in a house on the east bank at Luxor, where she was called on by all the foreign travelers along the Nile, and associated closely with the local dignitaries.

The view all around my house is magnificent on every side, over the Nile in front facing north-west, and over a splendid range of green and distant orange bluff hills to the south-east, where I have a spacious covered terrace. It is rough and dusty to the extreme, but will be very pleasant. Mustapha came in just now to offer the loan of his horse, and to ask me to go to the mosque in a few nights to see the illumination in honour of a great Sheykh . . . I asked whether my presence might not offend any Muslimeen, and he would not hear of such a thing. The sun set while he was here, and he asked if I would object to him praying in my presence, and went though his four *rekahs* very comfortably on my carpet. Now I am settled in my Theban palace, it seems more and more beautiful, and I am quite melancholy that you cannot be here to enjoy it. The house is very large and has good thick walls, the comfort of which we feel today for it blows a hurricane; but indoors it is not at all cold. I have glass windows and doors to some of the rooms. It is a lovely dwelling. Two funny little owls as big as my fist live in the wall under my window, and come up and peep in, walking on tip-toe, and looking inquisitive like the owls in the hieroglyphics; and a splendid horus (the sacred hawk) frequents my lofty balcony. . . .

The Temple of Luxor, 1845
Isabel Romer

And so we retired to rest to dream of obelisks and sphinxes, and awoke to behold the sun rising above the colossal pillars of the Temple of Luxor, and tingeing with rosy light the summit of the lovely obelisk of pale red granite, whose sister has been transported from this sublime solitude to adorn the Place de la Concorde in Paris.

A fragment of fourteen gigantic columns faces the river: this was my first view of the architecture of ancient Egypt, and—shall I confess the truth to you?—while lost in astonishment at the might and massiveness of what I beheld, I could not detect in the emotions they excited any of that delighted admiration which has filled me with enthusiasm at the sight of monuments far less imposing.

"This is *stupendous*, indeed," said I to myself, "but is it *beautiful?*" and candour answered No!

We scarcely allowed ourselves time to breakfast before we were on shore. Early as the hour was, the sun had already such power that the sand actually scorched my feet; but on we went, valiantly braving that inconvenience, and the suffocating clouds of dust raised by a ragged troop of Arabs, who immediately surrounded us with the usual clamour for *backshish*; and soon we stood within the Temple of Luxor, alas! so chocked up with an Arab village that we could neither comprehend its disposition nor trace out its outline.

We could understand nothing but the portions taken by us in detail as we passed along them, carefully picking our steps that we might not crush to death some pigeon so tame that it would not move out of our way, or some brood of tiny chickens just emancipated from the egg-shell, or some new-born lamb or kid, or some naked infant sprawling in the sand. Here, an old ram butted at us from his dark corner, as if to call our attention to the living type of the Ram-headed Deity multiplied in the hieroglyphics around us; there, a crouching woman twitched our garments as her outstretched hand spoke eloquently of her wants; and all fraternizing together in the greatest apparent harmony, and enjoying the same degree of freedom, man and brute alike, in the most wretched attempt at human habitations which I ever beheld. Such is the distracting picture that presents itself in the interior of this once proud sanctuary of the Pharaohs.

The gigantic colonnade which we had beheld from the river consists in a double row of seven columns, each eleven feet and a half in diameter, covered with hieroglyphics and surmounted by capitals representing the leafy summit of the palm-tree. The quantity of sand and rubbish which more than a thousand years of abandonment has accumulated around the base of these pillars, has raised the level of the soil to about one half of their original height. This very much detracts from the harmony of their appearance, for they are now not sufficiently lofty for their bulk; but it is easy to imagine what must have been the noble symmetry of those columns when free from the degrading encroachments which time and neglect had gathered . . .

Mud Huts in the Temple, 1849
Florence Nightingale

✍

Miss Nightingale stopped briefly at Luxor on her way upstream.

✍

We left Thebes at twelve yesterday, after having stayed there a night. The view of the whole temple of Luxor from the poop, as you sail away, is beautiful—the plan of it being less disturbed by the mud huts. What the disturbance of these is, morally and physically, no one can describe. It is not the bodily misery that shocks one: I have seen greater than that in London. On the contrary, the huts in Luxor temple were each full of calves, turkeys, hens, goats, camels, together with their men and women; the corn which the women were grinding was excellent, the breads in the oven were of the whitest, finest flour, and as well baked as yours. If it *had* been physical misery, one could have borne it—it was the moral degradation, the voluntary debasement, which was so hideous. To see those columns lifting their heads to the sky even now, when half buried, and carrying one's eyes naturally on high, and to see human beings choosing darkness rather than light, building their doorways four feet high or less, choosing to crawl upon the ground like reptiles, to live in a place where they could not stand upright, when the temple roof above their heads was all they needed!

Already from a long distance we could see the huge statues of Memnon brooding over the sunny plain. We rode past a sakiya with its dripping wheel and quiet oxen resting in the sun; we passed a herd of black goats and kids led by a woman who, as we came up, held a fold of her black draperies across her face. A boy then approached, idly driving before him a sheep with a coat of curly bronze wool. He sang, he stopped to look at us, and he stopped to look at a group of children who sat in the shade of the swishing sugar-cane. They smiled, lifted their dark eyes shyly as we rode past; the smaller of them were clad only in beads and girdles of fresh green grass; chewed bits of sugar-cane were littered all around them. . . .

A Ride to El-Karnak, 1847
Harriet Martineau

After breakfast, we rode away to El-Karnak, the sun coming out, but the wind rising so as to cover us with dust, and render the examination of the external structures less easy than we would have wished.

The road from El-Uksur to El-Karnak once lay, as everybody knows, between sphinxes, standing six feet apart, for a mile and a half. Those which remain, headless, encumbered, and extending only a quarter of a mile, are still very imposing. Then come pylons, propyla, halls, obelisks, temples, groves of columns, and masses of ruins, oppressive to see, and much more to remember. I think I must say nothing about them. They must be sacred to the eyes that see them; I mean, incapable to be communicated to others. Those that have not seen El-Karnak know nearly as much as can be told when they remember that here are the largest buildings, and the most extensive ruins in the known world: and that the great hall is 329 feet by 170, and 85 feet high, containing 134 columns, the 12 central ones of which are 12 feet in diameter, and the others not much smaller; the whole of this forest of columns being gay with colours, and studded with sculptures.

Of this hall the central roof is gone, and part of the lateral covering. The columns are falling, and at an accelerated rate. There is saltpetre in the stone; and the occasional damp from the ground cause corrosion of these mighty masses near the bases. They fall, one by one, and these leaning wrecks, propped up by some accident which must give way, have a very mournful aspect. We cannot but look forward to the successive fall of these incomparable pillars, as that of the trees of a forest undermined by springs. These will sink under a waste of sand, as those into the swamp, to be perhaps found again after thousands of years, and traced out curiously—a fossil forest of the mind.

Carried to Karnak and to the Other Side, 1854
Lady Tobin

The Tobins had met the Egyptologist Heinrich Brugsch (1827–1894) who had been sent to Egypt by the Prussian government a year or so before, worked on various sites and became Prussian Consul in Cairo in 1864. He guided them around some of the sites of Luxor.

. . . late in the day, Miss A. and myself were each placed in a sort of litter—borne aloft on the shoulders of our strong and active sailors, who chanted all the way—and proceeded to Karnak across the plain; advancing by that wondrous Avenue of Sphinxes which formerly extended from the gateway of the Great Temple to Luxor!

Mr Bruksh who acted as our cicerone—giving us the advantage of his graphic descriptions, and the facility with which he deciphered hieroglyph-ics—had contrived to make himself very comfortable in his classical dwelling, whose interior walls were rich in elaborate sculpture; and where both Champollion and Gardner Wilkinson had lived before him.

We actually *saw* but very little of the ruins! It seemed a hard case to be compelled to *grope* about Karnak, but there was no help for it. We took tea with Mr Bruksh, and *tried* to look at his drawings and some curious old Coptic manuscripts which he had purchased. In spite of various drawbacks we really enjoyed the cool evening air; and aided by a bright moon and the glimmer of our torches were soon safely carried on board the *Clothilde*.

In the morning Mr Bruksh joined our early breakfast, and we crossed the river to the western bank. The litters were again put to requisition, and a hard day's work I fear it must have been for the twelve Arabs who bore them; although they now and then rested for a short time, and were relieved by others occasionally. The sun's glare prevented my seeing much of the wild and desolate track, and narrow gorge by which we approached the Tombs of the Kings.

The tomb opened by Belzoni is considered far superior and in much more perfect preservation than any yet discovered at Thebes: it is entered by descending a rather steep staircase. The paintings on the walls are as clear and brilliant, and their outlines as distinct and sharp as they ever were. I cannot describe them; suffice it to say we had the full benefit of Mr Bruksh's valuable explanations. . . .

Thence we proceeded to the Temple Palace of Ramses II, the fragments of whose colossal statue lie scattered around its pedestal. This stupendous monu-ment of Egyptian sculpture was wrought at Syene [Aswan] and transported to Thebes, 188 miles distant, in a finished state!—since the quarry where it was hewn can yet be distinctly traced. This statue—one single piece of granite—weighed one hundred and eighty seven tons, five and a half hundred weight! How could any human power destroy such a colossus at a period when gun-powder was unknown? is the still unanswered question of every traveller.

The Road to Karnak, 1873
Amelia Edwards

In the afternoon we took donkeys, and rode out to Karnak. Our way lay through the bazaar, which was the poorest we had yet seen. . . .

Approach to Karnak

Next came the straggling suburb where the dancing girls most do congregate. These damsels, in gaudy garments of emerald green, bright rose, and flaming yellow, were squatting outside their cabins or lounging unveiled about the thresholds of two or three dismal dens of cafes in the market-place. They showed their teeth, and laughed familiarly in our faces. Their eyebrows were painted to meet on the bridge of the nose; their eyes were blackened round with kohl; their cheeks were extravagantly rouged; their hair was gummed, and greased, and festooned upon their foreheads, and plaited all over in innumerable tails. Never before had we seen anything in female form so hideous. One of these houris was black; and she looked quite beautiful in her blackness, compared with the painting and plastering of her companions.

We now left the village behind, and rode out across a wide plain, barren and hillocky in some parts; overgrown in others with coarse halfeh grass; and dotted here and there with clumps of palms. The Nile lay low and out of sight, so that the valley seemed to stretch away uninterruptedly to the mountains on both sides. Now leaving to the left a Sheyk's tomb, topped by a little cupola and shaded by a group of tamarisks; now following the bed of a dry watercourse; now skirting shapeless mounds that indicated the site of ruins unexplored, the road, uneven but direct, led straight to Karnak. . . . Then our way dipped into a sandy groove bordered by mud-walls and plantations of dwarf-palms. All at once this groove widened, became a stately avenue guarded by a double file of shattered sphinxes, and led towards a lofty pylon standing up alone against the sky.

The Unrivalled Ruins of Karnak, 1859
Emily Anne Beaufort

The more fortunate chance would be to have a fine moonlight view after becoming well-acquainted with the plan of the ruins; but even under seeing the disadvantage of seeing what we did not properly understand, it was a scene that impressed itself upon the mind for ever; the deep black shadows concealing much of the brokenness and decay, and the splendid light illuminating, with a sort of tender glory, the massive columns, immense pylons, and slender obelisks. By this light it was only and altogether beautiful and lovely; but one needs the sunshine and blue sky to bring out the stupendous proportions of these unrivalled ruins.

Perhaps few spots on earth could be more solemnly beautiful than the centre aisle in the Great Hall, with the six gigantic columns between the sixty-one attendant columns on either side, the moonlight piercing through the open clerestory of delicate tracery against the dark sky, turning the obelisk, ninety-two feet high, at one end of the aisle, into a silver needle, rising with a stern grace against the ruined temple behind it; and at the other end illuminating a single column, standing alone in the centre of a vast square, between giant pylons and huge walls, with its capital complete, its shaft uninjured, seeming almost livingly sorrowful in its loneliness.

View from Karnak, 1907
Norma Lorimer

Last night I visited the temple of Amon at Karnak by sunset—in Egypt it is either night or day, there is no gloaming, and there from my vantage point on the summit of a high pylon, I heard Rachael still weeping for her child.

From the temple gateway I saw the land of the Nile stretching like a ribband of yellow light far to the right, and far to the left; and across the river the pink cliffs of Thebes, or "the mountains of coffins," as the ancients called the vast necropolis of their city; and behind these cliffs these the entrance to the famous valley which runs back to the high hills of the desert—that valley of the tombs where the Pharaohs lie buried in sepulchres large enough for churches. I watched the darkness fall upon the temple-strewn plain, which we today call Thebes; and when my eyes recrossed the river I saw one Moslem minaret rise alone in the yellow light from the gay city of Luxor; while all above me and around me there was the stupendous light of Egypt.

In the darkness beneath, for only the heavens held that mysterious night, lay crouching figures of sphinxes guarding lonely temple paths, and little hamlets huddled beneath tall palm trees and humble mosques, with no city wealth to spend on costly minarets, and white saint's tombs speaking of peace and holiness.

Reflecting at Karnak, 1925
Annie Quibell

Karnak has had a different history from Luxor, as it lay far out of the modern town and never was built over. But is has suffered more than Luxor, for it said to have been in a great part destroyed by one of the severe earthquakes which occasionally have visited Egypt. Even without that catastrophe, the total neglect of more than two thousand years would be enough to explain the very great deal of damage. It was the task of M. Legrain,* who spent twenty-eight years at Karnak, to set up again the forest of columns which compose the Hypostyle Hall and to carry out a great amount of restoration in the rest of the temple.

So the visitor of today sees a Karnak much more like what it originally was than any of the early travellers did. The Temple had been well planned and its history worked out, so that it is possible for those who take sufficient trouble, to understand a great deal about it. It is well worth while for everyone to get hold of its main divisions, especially the limits of the older temple, which was built and completed in the Eighteenth Dynasty, and the immense additions which were made in the Nineteenth. The one was before Tell el Amarna; the other after it, when Amen of Thebes had come back to his own and to greater glory than he had ever had before.

Besides these two principal parts of the temple, there were many later additions and many subsidiary temples and pylons built round it at every period down to the Romans. It is a difficult and confusing place; even after all we can read about it and see of it in repeated visits, we are left with a feeling of amazement at its vastness rather than whole-hearted admiration of its beauty. It is very, very fascinating to spend time there and to explore, day by day, more of the halls and temples and gradually to find the solemnity of the place grow on us as we begin to understand it, till we come to realise what the central shrine of such a temple meant, and we enter it with a kind

---

* Georges Legrain (1865–1917) was a French Egyptologist who worked around Aswan and in 1895 started working at Karnak and was Chief Inspector of Antiquities at Luxor.

of awe and see the stone pedestal inside, where the sacred Barque rested, close guarded by massive doors.

Last Scenes at Luxor, 1847
Harriet Martineau

The finest impression, or the most memorable, which we obtained at El-Karnak was derived from our moonlight visit, that last evening. There is no questioning of any style of art, if only massive, when its results are seen by moonlight. Then, spaces and distances become what the mind desiderates; and drawbacks are lost in shade. Here, the mournful piles of fragments were turned into masses of shade; and the barbaric colouring disappeared. Some capricious, but exquisite lights were let in through crevices in the roof and walls of the side chambers. Then, there were the falling columns and their shadows in the great hall, and the long vistas ending in ruins; and the profound silence in this shadowy place, striking upon the heart. In the depth of this stillness, when no one moved or spoke, the shadow of an eagle on the wing above fell upon the moonlit aisle, and skimmed its whole length.

It was with heavy hearts and little inclination to speak that we turned, on our way home, to take a last view of the pylons of Karnak. The moonlit plain lay, with the river in its midst, within the girdles of the mountains. Here was enthroned the human intellect when humanity was elsewhere scarcely emerging from chaos.

Travelers at Luxor soon turned their time and attention to the 'other side,' the west bank of the Nile with its temples and the Valley of the Kings.

To the 'Other Side,' 2006
Rosemary Mahoney

By walking to the sites on the west bank, Rosemary Mahoney astonished the local people.

It was true that very few tourists actually walked from the ferry landing to the Ramesseum or the Temple of Hatshepsut, but I couldn't understand why. It wasn't far and the walk was interesting with its mud huts and dusty palms and ancient-looking plows being dragged along by enormous water buffalo. I had walked along the tops of irrigation mounds through the green fields of wheat and alfalfa and sugar cane and had met farmers and bullocks and children along the way. The two Colossi of Memnon rose up on my left with their huge fractured hands nesting primly on their huge thighs; they sat straight backed, like two bad boys sent to sit in the corner of a classroom.

Across the Luxor Nile there was the Ramesseum, the Temple of Ramses II, and the Valley of the Kings, the enormous pharaonic cemetery. Just as at Elephantine Island (at Aswan), walking across the desert on the west bank of Luxor became an exciting adventure when you realised that all that crumbling rubble under your feet was composed of bits of ancient pottery, human kneecaps, strips of linen winding-sheets, and scraps of painted wooden sarcophagi. You could walk across the open plain below the Temple of Hatshepsut and stumble on the mud-brick walls of the dwellings of ancient tomb builders. Strewn about the crumbling walls lay the builders' broken teacups, pot handles, and bits of painted jugs. The dust was pink with the powder of crushed pots. Like Amelia Edwards and that whole band of nineteenth century travellers, the more I found of these colourful chunks of crockery and wood, bits of plate painted in yellow and red, the more I wanted to find.

The Colossi, 1850
Florence Nightingale
There is nothing horrid in the death bed of Thebes.

When I see the evening sun making golden the tips of her violet crown—her amethyst diadem of hills, which sits so royally upon her noble brow—the words perpetually come into my head—

Her destiny's accomplished—her time of work is done
She dwelleth in the golden home, her faithful toil has won.

And the pastoral life of the few Arabs here looks more like a new world that is beginning—an infant world springing out of her ashes, than a dying and helpless old age.

Well, we climbed up on the pedestals of the Colossi, and copied a few Greek and Latin inscriptions, which told how, in the times of this Emperor or that Ptolemy, "I heard the Memnon once in the first hour." But, as I am

The Two Colossi

only writing my real and individual impressions, I must confess that I cannot understand people raving about these Colossi. The faces are so utterly
gone, that to talk about any expression is absurd, and to compare them
with the Ramses Colossi at Abu Simbel is to compare the Torso with the
Apollo Belvedere; if size is the object, the Abu Simbel Colossi are two feet
the biggest; but I don't see how an ugly thing put into a solar microscope
is made handsome. At Thebes one can afford to be disappointed in one
thing—even in a great thing; otherwise I should be mad with myself at
having felt so little about these Colossi. But they are such sightless, shapeless ruins, they look like sightless Lear after the storm—as if the lightning
of heaven had rested upon them, and made them the awful ruins you see;
as if Amunoph had been the author of some fearful secret crime, and this
was the vengeance of God making all secret things manifest, blighting
them with some Macbeth's doom.

The Valley of the Kings, 1827
Wolfradine Minutoli
We soon after entered the sacred city, which contains the last remains of
those ancient kings, whose works we still admire. Steep and barren rocks

confine the road which formerly led to this abode of peace. The ancient kings of Egypt certainly could not have chosen a more secluded and mournful spot, or one more favourable to meditation. Loose and scattered stones now render the access to them difficult.

Nothing disturbs the silence of this place, not even the humming of a single insect; in fact, none could exist in this desert spot. The farther you advance the more frightful is the appearance of these rocks, which at last present immense surfaces quite perpendicular. It is in a manner between two walls, formed by nature, that we have to proceed for a whole hour; the mind feels oppressed, and divided between a sensation of fear and expectation. But soon new wonders succeed all those which we have before admired and described, rivet our attention, and, as it were, complete our knowledge of these extraordinary people. It must be owned, that it is not until we have visited the tombs of the kings that we can form a just idea of the high degree of civilization, luxury, and multifarious knowledge of the ancient Egyptians.

I visited four of these tombs; the most magnificent is undoubtedly the one the entrance of which was discovered by Belzoni. A long vault or gallery, hewn in the rock, leads to the different apartments, and thence to the principal chamber, which contained the superb alabaster sarcophagus, which has since been sent to England by Mr Salt.*

On both sides of the entrance gallery are small cabinets, containing fresco paintings, so extremely beautiful and brilliant, that they look as if they had just received the last touch from an artist's pencil. They are for the most part scenes of domestic life, rural occupations, the different trades, represented with all the utensils necessary for their exercise, allegories and arabesques of the most tasteful designs. The ceilings are painted as in our most elegant apartments; and if the authenticity of these tombs were not indisputable, we should be tempted to apprehend some deception, so astonishing does it appear that time should have respected works which were completed so many centuries ago.

---

* The walls at the entrance are covered with "numerous hieroglyphics." Dr Ricci, who had copied them for William Bankes, "counted as many as two and twenty thousand." The sarcophagus became a matter of dispute between Henry Salt, the British Consul, and Belzoni, and after their deaths Sarah Belzoni sold it in London and it is today displayed in the Soane Museum in London's Lincoln's Inn Fields.

"Belzoni's Tomb," 1824
Anne Katherine Elwood

Mrs. Elwood entered the cave (in the Valley of the Kings) lately discovered by Giovanni Belzoni. The British Consul, Henry Salt, had had a door placed near the entrance to keep out the external air.

I thought of Aladdin and his cave, as from a painted corridor we passed into a room filled with spirited sketches, and then by another staircase we found ourselves in a large subterranean hall, and a handsome arched room, where stood the alabaster sarcophagus. One of the lateral apartments has a projection all round, and was termed from thence by Belzoni 'the side-board room:' it was, when first discovered, full of small figures of perfumed wood, from six to ten inches long, covered with hieroglyphics, many of which are still remaining. The walls of all are covered with the most spirited paintings, the colours as fresh and as vivid as if finished yesterday, and it was with difficulty we could believe they were some thousand years old.

One room is in an unfinished state, and, from this circumstance, is, perhaps, more startling and affecting than those which are completed, for it has the appearance of having been just left by the workmen, who were intending shortly to return to complete their performances. There was something wonderfully striking, and even awful, in thus traversing these majestic suites of subterranean apartments, excavated in the bowels of the earth; and I really could have fancied myself visiting some of the palaces of the Arabian Nights, constructed by magicians or genii.

Our Arab attendants were highly delighted with all they saw, and one of them particularly devoted himself to me, and insisted on being my squire wherever I went, amused us considerably by his way of doing the honours. He was particularly pleased with a huge ox in a procession, to which he turned my attention, making a chucking noise, as if to bid it to go on; as Michael Angelo exclaimed 'cammina' to the equestrian statue of Marcus Antoninus; and when, after examining the figures with mature deliberation, he and his companions had discovered their eyes, noses, mouth, etc with the greatest joy and glee they pointed them out to us, expressively touching their own features at the same time, as if doubting our capacity to comprehend

The Hall of Beauty

them; and upon some of the party writing their names upon the wall, they immediately fell to imitating them, by scribbling something also, as if they thought it was some magical ceremony.

Into the Tombs, 1828
Sarah Lushington

Mrs. Lushington suffered greatly from oppression on entering the tombs—caused by the lowness of the roof, and being under the ground, but was soon able to enjoy all the 'strange and novel sights.'

After leaving this tomb, we visited that opened so long ago by Bruce,* supposed to be the tomb of Ramses III; it was also exceedingly curious, and in tolerable preservation. The whole of the walls are covered with paintings;

---

* James Bruce (1730–94) who traveled through Egypt on his way to Ethiopia in 1768.

and there I beheld tables, chairs and sideboards, patterns of embossed silk and chintz, drapery with folds and fringe, precisely as an upholsterer would have fitted up a room when Egyptian furniture was in vogue. Indeed, it was an amusement to us all when I discovered some patterns exactly similar to those which I had sent, only seven years before, to a gentleman of our party.

Praise for the Paintings, 1828
Sarah Lushington

In company with John Gardner Wilkinson, author of Murray's Guide to Egypt and other books, who they had met by chance, the Lushingtons visited the Tombs of the Kings on the west bank.

The paintings, with colours as vivid as those of any modern artists, and the engravings, in alto and basso-relievo, in perfect preservation did not delight me so much as an unfinished chamber, the walls of which were covered with drawings previously to their being cut in the stone. These were mere outlines in black or red, but sketched with such boldness and lightness, that the more I looked the more I admired. Scarcely can I yet believe the hand that traced them to have been dead so many centuries. Many of the figures are as large as life, and though mere outlines, wrought with as much expression as a finished painting.

No book could better have portrayed the usages of the Egyptians than these tombs. Everything is described: in one chamber, preparing and dressing the meat, boiling the cauldron, making the bread, lighting the fire, fetching water. Another chamber presents scenes in a garden, a boy being beaten for stealing fruit, a canal, pleasure-boats, fruit, flowers, the process of various arts, such as sculpturing, painting, mixing colours, etc.

After seeing two more tombs I was compelled to return home from fatigue . . .

Mummies, 1828
Sarah Lushington
In the evening, I accepted the invitation of Signor Piccinini, a Lucchese, in the service of the Swedish Consul at Alexandria, who had resided about nine

years at Thebes, to see the opening of a mummy, that I might myself take out the scarabaeus, or any such sacred ornament as might be found in the coffin. The Signor's dwelling was nothing more than a mud hut in the hills of Gournoo. I ascended to the only apartment by a few steps; this room contained his couch, his arms, his wine, his few drawings, and all his worldly goods. The window shutters, steps, and floor, were composed of mummy coffins, painted with hieroglyphical figures, perhaps four thousand years old; and it was curious to observe the profuse expenditure of materials to which I had been accustomed to attach ideas of value, from seeing them only in museums and collections of antiquities.

I had accompanied Signor Piccinini with great glee, thinking what a fine thing it would be to tell my friends in England. What my notions of opening a mummy were I cannot define—something, however, very classical and antique—certainly anything but what it proved in reality.

Half a dozen Arabs were standing around, panting under heat, dust, and fatigue. They had only just brought in their burthern, and were watching with eager look the examination of its contents, (their profits depending upon the value of the prize), while the candles which they held to assist the search lighted up their anxious countenances.

The outside case of the mummy was covered with hieroglyphics, and the inner one consisted of a figure as large as life, with the face and eyes painted like a mask. On lifting up this cover, nothing was seen but a mass of dark yellow cloth, which, though it must have consisted of at least fifty folds, yielded like sand to the merciless hand of the operator, and the skeleton appeared to view. It was some time before I could recover from the horror with which the scene impressed me; I saw no more, but this little was sufficient to make me consider the employment as disgusting as that of a resurrection man, and the manner of performing is not less unfeeling. It may be called the pursuit of science, but to me it appeared nothing more than rifling the dead for the sake of the trifling ornaments with which the corpse is generally buried.

This, indeed, was the fact; for the moment it was ascertained that the mummy contained no ornament, the skeleton, together with the papyrus, on which were inscribed numerous distinct hieroglyphics, and the other materials, was cast forth as worthless rubbish. Sufficient papyrus and relics have been procured for the interests of science; and I think it would redound to the Pasha's credit if he were to issue an edict, to clear his country from these mummy scavengers. He had, indeed, ordered all the corpses to be re-interred; but, according to evident demonstration, this order was habitually disregarded.

Scarabaei are scarce; a few were brought us by the Fellahs, while wandering about the ruins, though none of value. Ancient coins are procurable in abundance, but they are too numerous to prove curious, and they had certainly no beauty to attract us to be purchasers.

Ancient Firewood, 1827
Wolfradine Minutoli

The following day we continued our journey. Being in want of wood, the Arabs supplied us with a considerable quantity, consisting of the remains of mummy cases, among which were some very valuable pieces which my husband saved from the auto-da-fe. The grave inhabitants of ancient Egypt certainly never suspected the use which would be made of their last abode. The mummy cases are made of sycamore wood, which is extremely hard.*

This tree resembles our oak; it is a pity that it is now hardly ever met with in Upper Egypt, where it must have been plentiful, to judge by the use that was made of it. The smell of the wood that we burnt was almost intolerable; it was covered with bitumen and varnish, which strongly affect the nerves—this at least is the effect it produced upon me, and we were all punished for having thus disturbed the last repose of the dead. In a country, however, so destitute of fuel as Egypt, we were obliged to content ourselves with that which necessity had procured us. In many parts of the country, they even use camels' dung, which, mixed with straw, and dried in the sun, is made to serve instead of fuel.

Searching for Mummies, and Celebrating, 1855
Lady Tobin

We lunched . . . and then turned towards that range of sandstone hills, whose sides are honeycombed by the enormous Necropolis of ancient Thebes.

We dismounted at a spot beyond which our donkeys could not keep their footing; and scrambled up a most toilsome ascent composed of rock, loose stones, gravel and sand—in the vain hope of finding a large mummy pit, described by Mr Bruksh as being easy of entrance, and full of mummies of men, women and children. Our guide led us from one pit or cavern to another; but they were all so dark and apparently impenetrable, that we

---

* A present was made to Mrs. Minutoli at Thebes of a small workbox of this wood, which was discovered in the catacombs. It was in such good preservation, that on opening it, winders with thread on them were found inside.

were on the point of abandoning our object altogether; when Captain Holden allowed himself to be carried by some Arabs down a yawning chasm, to the threshold of one of these sepulchres, where he beheld a confused assemblage of mummies and painted sarcophagi; but the dust and effluvia prevented his remaining more than an instant. Greatly disappointed, we with difficulty retraced our steps; and after a fruitless examination of some other tombs, we were told by our guide—who either was, or *pretended* to be ignorant of what we wanted—that he knew of a mummy pit, the mouth of which, although narrow, *might* be entered; and that it contained large chambers full of mummies! Nearly exhausted with heat and fatigue we at length reached the base of a very steep hill, where our conductor called a halt and pointed upwards. I am ashamed to confess that I suffered all the rest of my party to proceed on foot, myself staying behind with the donkeys and Antonio. . . .

The rest of the party discovered a narrow entrance which the guide assured them led to the *promised chambers*. They accordingly took off some of their clothes, and one by one, on their hands and knees down the sloping passage, and *squeezed* themselves through a hole two feet square into a dark room—beyond which were doubtless *others*, for the Arabs had come provided with candles. The heat and stench were so exceedingly overpowering that they could not take more than a momentary glance at the mummies—whole and mutilated—which surrounded them above, below and on all sides!

We had had a fatiguing day, and felt refreshed by a cool breeze from the river, for it was near sunset when we reached the dahabieh.

The Valley of the Kings, Tuesday, January 1930
Marta Bibescu

I visit Howard Carter, who is going to take me to the tomb of the Living King, whom American ladies at the Winter Palace Hotel dub familiarly as "the poor little man Tut."

Carter had written me to arrange a time. I called for him at his dwelling in the desert. It is just a cube of mud with a rectangular garden formed by the shadow of the house. His studio window opens out into daylight. This is where he reads Balzac.

In the mountain necropolis, I am first honoured with admission to the laboratory. It is an empty tomb with fresco paintings, furnished with wooden tables, a stove, and a soldering lamp. Carter works here to get the coating of rosin from his treasures.

Mr Lucas, his laboratory assistant, is heating the golden trappings of the mummy in a flame to melt the aromatic gums incrusting it. It is a long, patient task.

This spectacled sage shows me a bird on a golden plaque no larger than the nail on my little finger. The artificer has used five different enamels to colour the feathers.

I saw his bouquet also. I held it in my hands. They found it when they opened the tomb, placed upright at the foot of the sarcophagus.

It was made of olive and willow branches, cornflowers, blue nympheas and belladonna berries. They have all kept their form and have not quite lost their colours.

Travelers continued northward from Luxor to Cairo and onward to Alexandria, stopping occasionally along the way.

8
Egypt Beyond the Nile— the Desert

 Egypt is made up of the narrow green, grow-
ing, heavily populated strip on either side of
the Nile—and desert. The desert or near-
desert stretching on either side of the river and
into the Sinai Peninsula makes up a greater
part of Egypt than does the fertile lands beside
the Nile. Not all travelers ventured into the desert—nor do they
today—but for those who travel in these dry lands there is a different—and often exciting—experience.

The Desert, 1843
Countess Hahn-Hahn

*The Countess came to Egypt through the desert
from Palestine.*

Oh, believe me, dear mother, the desert is very tedious! If you can call to mind how the country looked between Berlin and Strelitz, before the road reached to the Baltic, you may form some notion of the desert. Sand, sand, and nothing but sand; or where water appeared amongst it—a green oasis. But suppose you were borne upon a camel, and then tell me that *ennui* would not accompany you the whole distance. A desert remains a desert. The majority of people who come hither are so delighted at finding themselves upon the top of a camel in the desert of *Arabia*, upon the celebrated isthmus of *Suez*, which united two quarters of the world, that every thing about them looks interesting, and bright colours are imparted even to the desert. I tell you the simple and unvarnished truth. . . .

The Almost Waterless Desert, 1926
Winifred Blackman

The natural barriers of Egypt have enabled the inhabitants, particularly those of the upper country, to live in comparative isolation throughout the whole of their history. On the north side lies the sea, along the east and west side stretch vast, almost waterless deserts, while to the south ingress by way of the Nile, is impeded by a series of cataracts. . . .

The noontime break

The vast solitudes of the deserts are terrifying to the country folk, most of whom, up to the present day, cannot be induce to traverse even the fringes of those wastes after sunset. Fear of hyenas and, still more, fear of *afarit*, forbids any man to venture beyond the cultivation at night. The ordinary peasant, unless he is obliged to remain in the fields either to protect his crops or to watch over his sheep and goats, returns to his village before sunset, remaining there until just before the dawn of the following day.

The Frst Day Out, 1899
Emily Hornby

Often the scenes travelers observed as they crossed the Sinai desert called to their memory scenes from the Old Testament of the Bible.

The Arabs and camels were all crouched round a little Arab village quite near behind a fence of brushwood, some children were about. I had some hot milk and toast for breakfast—it answers better than anything. It was most interesting to see them load the camels. The bedding etc was all rolled up and put into square sacks closed by a flap. I could fancy Joseph's brothers had that kind. A network of strong rope is laid across the camel, which is kneeling down and grunting very much, a package slung on each side, the ends brought across the camel's back and laced up.

I was perfectly comfortable on my camel . . . We were each led by a very nice Arab. I have tried in vain to learn their names, I must write them down tomorrow. The whole procession was led by a baby camel which seemed to be quite following its own devices.

We followed the line of the Red Sea, glittering to our right, a line of mauve hills beyond; the desert was exactly like the sea shore, sometimes stones about, sometimes not. To our amazement we saw posts, and heard they were the telegraph line to Sinai. . . . We plodded steadily on for four hours—it was not at all hot—and then pulled up for a halt, on what seemed a peculiarly flat and shelterless piece of sand, but there were some tufts of coarse herbage, not grass, but a sort of little shrub, on which they said the camels could graze. They also handed to me this morning two sorts of yellow flowers, growing close to the ground, which the said camels like very much. The little boys kept gathering bundles and handing them to them.

Our luncheon tent was put up in a second, our saddles arranged as arm-chairs, and we were thoroughly comfortable. Luncheon followed: sardines, hard-boiled eggs, cold chicken, cheese and pickled onions—which they think a great delicacy, and I am very fond of myself. Onion is bussal in Arabic. Wine and coffee afterwards, oranges and raisins. We rested nearly all the hottest part of the day, but it was still very hot when we started.

Day in the Desert, 1847
Harriet Martineau

At four o'clock in the morning, or earlier, Alee brought a light into our tent. Our tin basins had been filled the night before, and a pitcher of water and tin cups placed on the table. I always slept in what is called Levinge's bag—an inexpressible comfort. Without it, I believe I should scarcely have slept at all; but, as it was, I lay down every night, absolutely secure from insects of every kind. The flies might hang in clusters, like bees, on the tent pole; the beetles might run over the floor, and the earwigs and fleas skip among the camel furniture; in my bag, under its wide airy canopy, I was safe from them all, and from all fancies about them. It did not take me above five minutes a day to put up and take down my canopy; a small price to pay for comfort and good sleep.

As soon as we opened our tent door, while I was taking down my bag, and the gimlets which screwed into the tent poles, and served us for pegs to hang our things on, Alee carried out our table and its trestles and the camp-stools, and Abasis laid the cloth for our open-air breakfast. We sat down to it at five or soon after, when the stars were growing pale, and the translucent dawn began to shine behind the eastern ridges, or perhaps to disclose the sheeny sun. While we were at our meal, we saw one after another of the other four parties come forth from their tents, and sit down to table—the two bachelor companions being always the last. They were generally sitting down just when I was walking off in advance, with my courbash (hide whip) and bag, containing map, book, note-book, goggles and fan.

By this time the tents were down, in due succession; the camels were groaning and snarling, and the Arabs loading them—with an occasional quarrel and fight, for variety.

Having learned from Alee or the Sheik which way I was to go, I wandered forth; and many a glorious view I had of the sunshine breaking in among the mountain fissures, while the busy and noisy camp yet lay in deep shadow below. One by one the company would mount and follow. . . When the sunshine reached me, or I had walked enough for the present, I put on my goggles, pulled my broad-brimmed hat over my eyes, and signed to my watchful camel driver. Then down went the beast on its knees, and my driver set his foot on its neck while I sprang on, and settled myself with my stirrup and between my cushions, and stowed my comforts about me. When I had firm hold of the peg before and the peg behind, the creature was allowed to rise, and I sustained its three jerks—two forward and one backward—as well as I could.

The Changing Desert from the Red Sea, 1877
Lady Annie Brassey

> *Returning from a journey that had taken them on their sailing ship the 'Sunbeam' around the world from Britain's Isle of Wight in July 1876 through West Africa, Rio de Janeiro, across the Pacific to Honolulu, Japan, Singapore, Ceylon and Yemen, the Brassey family sailed up the stormy Red Sea to Suez, landing at 6 p.m. on 25 April, 1877.*

At the Canal Company's office the 'Sunbeam' was entered on the Company's books, and arrangements were made with the chief pilot for tomorrow, while the children amused themselves riding a pony up and down, and jumping over the little brooks, and I strolled about admiring the growth of vegetation since we were last here in 1869. . . .

Thursday, April 26th Such a sunrise as this morning's you could see only in Arabia or Egypt. There is a peculiarity about desert colouring at sunrise and sunset that can never be seen anywhere else. We had sundry visitors during the early morning, and before ten o'clock we were in the Canal and steaming on at regulation speed. As the sun rose the heat became intense, 96° in the shade under the double awnings. So far from there being a cool breeze to temper it, a hot wind blew from the desert, like the blast from a furnace. I stood on the bridge as long as I could bear the heat, to look at the strange desert view, which could be seen to great advantage in going through at the top of the high water. Sand, sand everywhere; here a train of camels, there a few Arab tents, now a whole party shifting their place of abode; a group of women washing, or a drove of buffaloes in a small tributary stream.

Friday, April 27th Another glorious sunrise. This is a beautiful climate, though there is scarcely any rain, only one very slight shower has occurred during the last three years at Suez, but the soil of the desert after the Nile overflow brings forth tenfold. . . . We had an excellent breakfast, and left by the eleven o'clock train for Cairo. . . . The change in the face of the country since we were last here eight years ago is transformed into one large oasis of undulating fields of waving corn, where there used to be nothing but whirlwinds of sand. All this had been effected by irrigation. The wealth of Egypt ought to greatly increase. How the people managed to live before is a mystery. Now every field is full of labourers reaping and stacking corn, women gleaning, and in some places the patient, ugly black buffaloes ploughing the stubble for fresh crops.

The Land that Surrounds Us, 1879
Isabella Bird

> *Miss Bird was on her way toward Europe after a long jour-ney in the Far East. She made arrangements in Cairo to travel alone with her Bedouin guides on pilgrimage through the Sinai desert. She expresses with her usual wry humour the problems of mounting a camel—in a long skirt . . .*

All this region looks like the level beach of a sea. The Red Sea must have covered it at one time. It is hard sand and gravel, and as easy to walk upon as a gravel walk. When I can walk no farther, my camel, with much difficulty and many objurgations, is made to lie down. Hassan stands at one side and the sheykh on the other, and with Hassan's help I attempt to take a flying leap into the middle of the saddle. Sometimes this is successful the first time, and if it is Hassan puts an arm in front of me and the sheikh puts an arm behind me, and the dreaded moment arrives, which I am more cowardly about each time. The camel, with a jerk which might dislocate one's neck, jumps on his knees, nearly throwing me backwards, then another violent jerk brings him to his haunches, and would throw me over his head, but for Hassan's arm, then, the forward movement is arrested by another jerk which sets him on his four legs and leaves me breathless on the lofty elevation of his hump. This process is reversed as one dismounts, and it is repeated six times daily!

But things are not always so comparatively smooth, for just I am prepared to spring the brute makes a snarling lunge with his teeth, either at me or his driver, or just as I am half way up jerks himself up on his four legs, and the whole process has to be gone over again. Yesterday I had just touched the saddle when by rapid movement he threw me off sidewise, and this morning jerking himself up before I had clutched firm hold of the saddle, he threw me over his shoulder and bruised me a great deal.

After being mounted the caravan straggles in single file, Hassan bringing up the rear, my camel being led, and then for four or five hours we crawl over the burning, glaring sand. I now understand what is meant [in the Bible] by "As a hireling earnestly desireth the shadow." At 8:30 a.m. the shadow of my driver is fully eight feet long, and as the morning wears by it shortens to something a little over two feet; then I know that noon has come.

Dawn in the Desert, 1827
Sarah Lushington

Mrs. Lushington was returning from India through the Red Sea, crossing the desert from the sea to the Nile.

Our second place of encampment was truly singular, our tents being pitched in a sort of circus, about two miles in extent, completely closed in (except at two passages) by rugged mountains, part of which rose above our heads almost perpendicularly. I left my bed before daylight, when the whole camp was buried in sleep, and indulged my astonishment at the novel spectacle of tents surrounded by numerous camels, with their drivers and burthens, ranged in a circle, according to the position of their respective masters. I wondered to find myself thus tranquilly situated in the Desert, whose difficulties had been so magnified; and I looked up to the canopy of the stars, the view of which was so remarkably bounded by the belt of mountains, with feelings which I shall not now attempt to recall in their original intenseness.

I cannot imagine that any climate in the world can excel that of the Desert at the season we crossed it.

No Water in the Desert, 1876
Isabella Bird

Not often do we read women complaining of the experiences of travel, and Miss Bird was the most experienced of travelers, but at this point in her journey she was not at all happy.

The water had been hardly drinkable at noon, and at night, when I asked for rice, Hassan's gloomy countenance grew yet more gloomy, and he said there was not water enough: the Bedaween had stolen it. Being unable to have either rice or chocolate, what I had in the morning having been made of *saltish* water, possibly from Marah, I supped on raisins and chocolate paste only.

Of course there was not any water for washing either that night or the next morning—a discomfort under any circumstances, and an actual hardship in these. When I lay down I asked Hassan to bring me all the water that there was, and he presently reappeared with a most glum and clouded face, bringing a teacup nearly full of a thick, dark-coloured fluid like the refuse stream of a dye-work, and, putting it down by me, said, "You get all; you very ill." Then, smelling it, he said, with a look of infinite disgust, "*Stinks.*" I felt as if I could drink up the Nile, and as I raised myself on my elbow frequently during the night and sipped this foetid decoction of goat's hide (from the water-carrying bag) in teaspoonfuls, the suffering hourly increased. I was really ill and I wondered if I could remain sane until the afternoon of the next day, twenty hours later, when we would reach the wells of the Wady Feiran.

All the watery texts of the Bible came to my memory, and those beautiful words—"A pure river of water of life, clear as crystal" absolutely tortured me.

Desert and Water, March 1911
Lady Evelyn Cobbold

Our baggage camels are groaning under more than their usual load, as four of them are commandeered to carry water alone. The water is carried in big clay jars of graceful design, which have never altered in shape for many centuries. Instead of corks, the necks of the jars are stopped with green leaves, and, though exposed to the rays of the African sun when carried in nets on the camels' backs, the water is always cold—thanks to the porous quality of the clay.

Every drop of water required for household purposes is brought away from the river or canals in these earthen jars by the women. From time immemorial the women have trooped down to the water's edge with these 'goollahs' on their heads—a long line of graceful figures, in flowing black garments. Arrived at the river's bank, each woman tucks up her skirts and wades into the stream to fill her jar. These goollahs when full weigh about forty pounds, and with this load on their heads, the women climb the steep bank and walk erect with easy gait back to the village, often a mile or two away. It is pretty to watch the incessant stream of veiled women softly coming and going, their inscrutable eyes never glancing to right or left, as they silently pursue their way, a vision of the changeless East.

The Khamsin, 1848
Harriet Martineau

Miss Martineau was traveling through the Sinai Desert when her party faced the experience of a desert storm—the khamsin.

Today we had experience of the Khamsin. When the heat had become so intolerable that all moved forward silently in dull patience, some with a secret wonder whether they should ever breathe easily, or feel any muscular strength again, a strong wind sprang up suddenly from the south. Though it was as hot as a blast from an oven, and carried clouds of sand with it, I must say I felt a great relief. I was aware that the sensation of relief could not last; for the drying quality of this wind was extraordinary, and immediately felt this upon the skin. Still, the sensations under the evaporation were those of relief for the moment; and before they were over, we stopped, and could get under the shelter of our tents. The thirst which this wind caused was of course great; but we had plenty of water and oranges. I was surprised, after all I had read, to see how like thick fog an atmosphere full of sand can be. The sand was not course enough to be felt pattering upon the face, though it accumulated in the fold of one's dress; but it filled the air so completely as to veil the sunshine, and to hide altogether the western boundary of the wadee, and all before us. The eastern mountains, near whose base we were travelling, rose dim and ghostly through this dry hot haze. We have proceeded to the Wadee Gharendel, where there is a small spring and a palm or two; but this wind caused us to halt sooner, for the advantage of a sheltering sandhill.

Arriving at the Convent of Sinai, 1847
Harriet Martineau

There is nothing like the words written down at the time; so here are those of my journal of that date: "Paths through the tamarisks; and Arab tents, and black goats and swathed goat-herds; and the first sunshine dropping in through the mountain clefts, golden beyond description, and making golden the waving palm tops in the illuminated nook I look down upon. On turning round, I saw our loaded camels coming winding through the tall stems behind me, and their drivers among the trees. How must Feiran (if then like what it is now) have appeared to the Israelites after wandering in the arid places of the Desert! But it is not fertile, as some authors say, who mean by that it is cultivated. I saw nothing grown by husbandry; and the soil is sandy as elsewhere. Tender grass and cresses spring in the brook; and there are tufts of herbage and weeds in the rock-clefts: but the palms are unpruned, and all is wild, however sweet. As we pursued the wadee, the vegetation subsided into the usual Desert tufts; and the way was hot and dry. Our last views of Mount Serbal were very fine as it towered, all in lilac hues and blue shadows, above the nearer mountains behind us. Before us were rising all the morning, the peaks of the Sinai nucleus."

It was this that made that Saturday, the 6th of March, a remarkable day to us. On this day, we travelled from Wadee Feiran to Mount Sinai, and at night we rested in the convent.

There are deserts on both sides of the Nile through which travelers have to go to reach the oases. Here, Norma Lorimer visits an oasis to the west of the Nile.

Dawn at Khargeh Oasis, May 1908
Norma Lorimer

It was in the early mornings and at night that I felt the mystery and spell of the desert most profoundly.

At Khargeh, I was always awake before dawn, if I had ever been to sleep at all—which was not often, for camel-riding by day under a tropical sun with the thermometer at 108° in the shade is not conducive to sleep at night—and I used to stand at the little window in my room and watch through the sliding wooden shutters for the mysterious approach of dawn. I used to watch it "come up like thunder," as Kipling says, come up over the desert, and with it always the same train of camels draped with white sheepskins.

In the grey light the white-turbaned heads of the riders as they appeared over the horizon line reminded me of the company of Wise Men who followed the star to Bethlehem.

I liked those soft cool hours before the world began, before the open wilderness was blazing with light; I liked it, for as yet the flies had not invaded my castle, and I could think—think as I never can think when life is a battle against flies and glare. At dawn the flies of the day before lie stupefied heaps round my window ledges, intoxicated with the river of Keating's powder I had poured out for them.

In that desert dawn there was always but one noise to break the stillness: the angry roar of the camels as they were forced to kneel for packing and unpacking. Camels, I soon discovered, are the barn-door cocks of the desert.

Sakara and the Apis Cemetery, 1861
M.L.M. Carey

Returning down river from Nubia as far south as beyond Wadi Halfa, Mrs. Carey and her party reached Sakara.

. . . little remains to be seen besides the colossal granite figure of Ramses the Great, which lies, broken and prostrate, on the ground in a hollow that is filled with water at the high Nile. The face lies downwards; the features are still perfect, and surpass even the colossi at Aboo-Simbel in their soft, placid expression. . . .

A number of pyramids rise on the plain beyond. Those of Dashoor are the largest; they were beyond our reach, but we managed to get close to the principal one of the Sakara group. The nearer we approached the smaller it seemed, yet its dimensions are about 351 feet on two sides, and 394 on the other two. We could not perceive any entrance; it presents the appearance of five giant steps, its several stories having lost their outer casing. Our guides next directed us to some catacombs at a short distance, concerning which they could tell us nothing more distinct than that "all English, French and Italians go to see it," and therefore that we must go too. From our guide-books we inferred that we had come to the celebrated 'Apis Cemetery.' Long underground passages were hewn in the rock, crossing each other at right angles mid-way. On either side were deep recesses, lined like the passages with masonry, and arched over at the top. In each of these were a very large, handsome sarcophagus of black granite, highly polished, and measuring 12 feet 5 inches long, by 7 feet 6 ½ inches wide, and being 7 feet 8 inches in height without the lid, which is of the same material, coped above and making the whole height 11 feet. These lids were all pushed a little on one side, thus showing the interior of the now empty sarcophagi.

They counted twenty-five sarcophagi, and many others remained still bricked up and unopened.

Human sarcophagi seemed but common-place in our eyes compared to those of Apis, the actual existence and sight of which now clothed with reality to our minds the strange stories of the honours paid by reasoning human beings to the unreasoning beasts of the field....

We emerged from the sepulchres into the open air under the broiling sun, and finding just sufficient shade to accommodate us beneath the wall of the rocky entrance, we spread our shawls on the sand, and sat down to luncheon. The Arabs would taste nothing, because it was Ramadan: even a little boy to whom an orange was offered put it away till the evening feast.

Beyond the Desert—and an Afreet, 1911
Lady Evelyn Cobbold

We make our way through the desert till an opening in the hills shows us the Pyramid of Medum, first seen glowing like a pink pearl against the faint blue sky of evening.

We are once more in sight of the Nile. Beyond the Pyramid, on the other side of the river, stretches the Arabian Desert, and the Mokattam Hills rise like a great amphitheatre, showing ridge upon ridge of deep mauve, yellow, and rose, changing from moment to moment so completely that new mountains and colours seem to replace those just vanished. We camp within a few miles of this relic of a long-past age, older than the Pyramids at Ghiseh, built by King Snefru about four thousand years BC.

Slowly we journey through this mysterious land, whose every grain of golden sand is steeped in history.

Towards nightfall we pass near a large cemetery on the edge of the desert. Our watchman, Reched, being weary and wishing to make a short cut, carelessly walks through it, thereby tempting the powers of evil, with the unfortunate result that in the distance he sees a woman in white. He then knows that an afreet has entered into him. His "blood changes," and from having been a happy, sunny youth, he became dejected, haggard, nervous.

The Arabs realise that he is possessed, but hope, as the afreet has only just entered him, that a holy man will be found with a charm potent enough to exorcise the evil spirit.

All Arabs firmly believe in the existence of these genii or afreets who, as taught by the Koran, are an intermediate order of creatures who eat and drink, live and die, and in many ways resemble mankind. There are good and evil genii, and they can make themselves visible under the guise of animals, and more especially snakes. When passing through dark alleys, graveyards or likely haunts of the evil ones, an Arab will recite a verse of the Koran to protect himself. At the great Day of Resurrection, the genii and animals will appear, as well as men.

Approaching the Nile at Last, 1844
Countess Hahn Hahn

The German countess was traveling from Palestine into Egypt across the desert.

At noon we perceived a dark line at the horizon. As soon as the camel-dri-vers caught sight of it, they began to dance for joy; and their monotonous song sounded louder than I had ever heard it. The line was the great palm-forest of Salahyeh, behind which a branch of the Nile flows, and we were now in Lower Egypt. Four hours elapsed, however, before we reached it. Single clay huts, with enclosures of palm leaves for goats, sheep and poultry, lay along the edge of the forest, which is regularly planted, and supplied with ditches for the purposes of irrigation . . .

Her caravan traveled on for two days.

The next morning, however, the 30th November, was lovely. From this spot the character of the country alters, or rather is changed by man; for the whole of Egypt would be a barren desert if the overflow of the Nile were not assisted, and, by means of canals, dams, sluices, and ditches spread over the soil, upon which the gradually receding waters deposit their fruitful slime, or whose plantations they nourish. Where no water penetrates, the desert takes undisturbed possession of the soil; and so it happens that, with-out transition, it passes over at once from sterility to paradise.

They advanced three hours . . .

By the side of a field of cotton in bloom and upon the other side stood water that had overflowed, flat and motionless like our forest-waters, and palms, nebeks, and sycamores, were reflected silently and clearly in them.

The Travelers:
Brief Biographies

Emily Anne Beaufort (1826–87), daughter of the creator of the Beaufort Wind Scale, married Viscount Strangford, organized a hospital for Turkish soldiers during the Crimean War, and traveled widely. She went with her sister to Egypt in 1858, after their father's death.

Sarah Belzoni (1785–1870) married the famed Egyptian explorer and excavator Giovanni Belzoni in 1803 and accompanied him on his travels in Egypt and Nubia from 1815. She also traveled on her own in Egypt and to Palestine. She contributed her own account of her experiences to his *Narrative of the Operations and Recent Discoveries . . . in Egypt.*

Matilda Bethune-Edwards (1836–1919), cousin of the better known Amelia Edwards, was also a writer of novels, children's books and accounts of her travels, mainly around the Mediterranean.

Marta Bibescu (1888–1973), the beautiful and talented daughter of Romanian aristocrats, traveled in Egypt in 1930, and wrote skilful sketches of her experiences there.

Eileen Bigland (1898–1970) was a journalist and travel writer—usually visiting places not popular with tourists. She journeyed in Egypt in 1948 before it became a tourist 'honey-pot.'

Isabella Bird (Mrs. Bishop) (1831–1904) was the greatest of Victorian travel writers. From England, she went to America and Canada as a young woman, and later traveled to Australia, Hawaii, and again to America. She went to China and Malaysia and returning from that journey, she visited Egypt and went on pilgrimage to Sinai.

Winifred Blackman (1872–1950) was an anthropologist who spent much of her working life in Upper Egypt engaged in studies of the lives of the Fellahin. The results of her studies make an important understanding of the ordinary rural Egyptian people.

Lady Annie Brassey (1839–87), described as "one of the most agreeable of lady voyagers," went round the world by sea in 1876–77 with her husband and children on their large private yacht. They visited Egypt and the Mediterranean.

Marianne Brocklehurst (1832–98) visited Egypt four times between 1873 and 1896 and made a considerable collection of antiquities, now in Macclesfield Museum.

E.L. Butcher (fl. 1914) lived in Egypt as the wife of a churchman. Her insights into the country are added to by photographs at a time when the inundation still flowed through the buildings at Philae, the temple at Abu Simbel was close to the river, and there were many working boats on the Nile.

M.L.M. Carey (fl. 1860), writer and artist, traveled cheerfully on the Nile with her elderly cousin, his invalid daughter and two English servants. She published her account illustrated with her lively pictures.

Ellen Chennells (fl. 1865) was employed in the 1860s by the Egyptian royal family to work with the ladies of the harem. She traveled with the Viceroy of Egypt on the royal yacht.

Mary Chubb (1903–2003) accompanied the Egypt Exploration Society's dig at Tell-al-Amarna in 1930 and also spent a season digging in Syria. She wrote two fascinating and sensitive books about her experiences.

Lady Evelyn Cobbold (1867–1963) spent much of her childhood in Morocco, where she became attracted to Islam. She spent periods in Egypt, particularly the Fayoum, and went officially on pilgrimage to Mecca as a Muslim.

Lucie Duff Gordon (1821–69), owing to ill health lived for a time in South Africa and then in Egypt, where she died and was buried in Cairo. She lived in Luxor and became very much a member of Egyptian society there. She wrote regularly to her family and these letters were published both in her life and after her death.

Amelia Edwards (1831–92) was a writer who went to Egypt almost casually in 1873–74, publishing a good account of her journey. She was fascinated, but disturbed, by the casual exploitation of Egypt's past. She became deeply involved in Egyptology, working for the creation of the Egypt Exploration Society to carry out disciplined research in exploring and recording the standing monuments. She lectured on the subject of Egyptology and devoted most of her life to these matters.

Anne Katherine Elwood (fl. 1840) accompanied her East India Company employed husband to India, traveling through Egypt in 1825–26. When they returned to England she wrote about her journey and her life in India as well as an important book about women authors.

Eliza Fay (1756–1816) was a very adventurous woman. She accompanied her husband to India in 1799 through Egypt and the Red Sea. They separated, but she worked on in India on various business ventures.

Sophia de Frankeville (fl. 1880) was the daughter of the Lord Chancellor of Great Britain. She traveled through Egypt and on through Sinai to Petra and Syria.

Constance Gordon Cumming (1837–1924) wrote a number of books about her travels visiting brothers, sisters and other relations around the world. She traveled through Egypt in 1868 to India, where her sister lived.

Countess Ida Hahn Hahn (1805–80) was a divorced German aristocrat and novelist who traveled in the Near East with a male partner in the mid-1840s. She converted to Catholicism, established a convent in Germany, and lived there for the rest of her life.

Sarah Haight (1808–81) was an American who traveled widely with her husband, a well-to-do New York merchant. They visited Egypt in 1836.

Emily Hornby (d. 1906) traveled to Sinai and Petra in 1899 and 1901, and sailed the Nile with her sisters in 1906. Her journal of this Nile journey was published by her sisters as a memorial to her.

Norma Lorimer (fl. 1907–15) was traveling on her own through North Africa and Egypt in 1907. Her account of that journey is described from her diary.

Sarah Lushington (d. 1839) was the wife of an Indian army officer with whom she traveled through Egypt on their return to England, giving guidance for ladies intending to brave the 'Overland Route.'

Rosemary Mahoney (b. 1961) is an American traveler and writer who in 2006 determined to row a fisherman's skiff down the Nile from Aswan—having become familiar with the accounts of earlier travelers.

Harriet Martineau (1802–76) suffered from bad health and deafness but this did not stop her becoming an important economist and traveling widely in America (1834-36) and the Near East in 1848—often showing her interest in the economy of the country.

E.W. Merrick (fl. 1900) was a portrait painter who, in Egypt, painted the American journalist-explorer H.M. Stanley and also the Khedivah. She went to India and became a successful artist there.

Wolfradine Minutoli (1794–1868), as a young bride, accompanied her Prussian husband, on a scientific mission to Egypt, and published her account of the journey in English in 1827.

Florence Nightingale (1820–1910) visited Egypt with friends and possibly there took the momentous decision to train as a nurse—a profession thought unsuitable by her parents. Put in charge of nursing during the Crimean War, Florence became a great heroine.

Marianne North (1830–90) was a traveler with a good sense of humor and one of the most intrepid of the 'Victorian lady travelers.' She traveled with her widowed father until he died in 1869. After a year she set off around the world to paint as many of the plants of the tropics that she could find. Her work is on display in a special gallery in London's Kew Gardens.

Ida Pfeiffer (1797–1858) was born Ida Reyer in Vienna. After an unhappy marriage and motherhood, she set out to travel in 1842, first to the Holy Land and Egypt, then to Norway, Brazil, Chile, China, India, Baghdad, Constantinople, and, after a few years, to Cape Town, Borneo, New Orleans, and London.

Sophia Poole (1804–91) was the sister of the Arabist Edward Lane. She lived with him and her two sons in Egypt for many years and published *The Englishwoman in Egypt* when she returned to England.

Annie Quibell (1862–1927) lived for many years in Egypt as an excavator and draftsman with the great Egyptologist, Flinders Petrie. She married James Quibell, Keeper of the Egyptian Museum and later Secretary General of the Egyptian Antiquities Service.

Isabella Romer (c. 1805–52) separated from her husband and traveled in the East, and published an account of her travels in two volumes in 1846.

Bettina Selby (1934–) has cycled through different parts of the world, writing about her experiences—which are very different from those who travel more augustly.

Lady Tobin (fl. 1840–60) visited the Middle East twice with her husband. She wrote and illustrated an account of their first journey.

Mary Whately (1824–89) was the daughter of the Archbishop of Dublin, where she worked among the poor, particularly in schools. In the early 1870s she went to Egypt and set up schools for poor Egyptian girls, traveled as a missionary on the Nile with her Syrian colleagues, and wrote several books about her experiences.

Bibliography

Bartlett, W.H. *The Nile Boat; or, Glimpses of the Land of Egypt.* 2nd ed. London: Arthur Hall, Virtue, and Co., 1850.

Beaufort, Emily Anne. *Egyptian Sepulchres and Syrian Tombs.* London: Longman, Green and Roberts, 1861.

Belzoni, Sarah. "Mrs Belzoni's Trifling Account," in *Narrative of Operations and Recent Discoveries.* London: John Murray, 1828.

Bethune-Edwardes, Mathilda. *Reminiscences.* London: G. Redway, 1898.

Bibescu, Marta. *Egyptian Day.* New York: Harcourt, Brace and Company, 1936.

Bigland, Eileen. *Journey to Egypt.* London: Jarrolds, 1948.

Bird, Isabella. "A Pilgrimage to Sinai," in *The Leisure Hour.* London, February–April, 1886.

Blackman, Winifred. *The Fellahin of Egypt.* London: Harrap, 1927.

Brassey, Lady Annie. *A Voyage in the Sunbeam.* London: Longman, Green and Roberts, 1878.

Brocklehurst, Marianne. *Miss Brocklehurst on the Nile: Diary of a Victorian Traveller on the Nile;* repr. Disley, Cheshire: Millrace, 2004.

211

Butcher, E.L. *Things Seen in Egypt.* London: Seeley Service, 1914.

Carey, M.L.M. *Four Months in a Dahabeeh or a Narrative of a Winter on the Nile.* London: Booth, 1863.

Chennells, Ellen. *Recollections of an Egyptian Princess.* London: Blackwood, 1893.

Chubb, Mary. *Nefertiti Lived Here*; repr. London: Libri Publications, 1998.

Cobbold, Lady Evelyn. *Wayfarers in the Libyan Desert.* London: Arthur L. Humphreys, 1912.

Duff Gordon, Lucie. *Letters from Egypt.* London: Macmillan, 1875; repr. London: Virago Travellers, 1983.

Edwards, Amelia. *A Thousand Miles up the Nile.* London: Longmans Green, 1877.

Elwood, Anne Katherine. *Narrative of a Journey Overland to India, and a Voyage Home 1825-8.* London: Colbourne and Bentley, 1830.

Fay, Eliza. *Original Letters from India (1779–1815).* Edited by E.M. Forster. London: The Hogarth Press, 1986.

de Franqueville, Sophia (Sophia Mathilda Palmer). *On the Nile.* London: self-published, 1889.

Countess Hahn Hahn. *Letters from the Orient or Travels in Turkey, Egypt and the Holy Land.* London: J. Ollivier, 1845.

Haag, Michael. *Discovery Guide to Egypt.* London: Hippocrene Books, 1990.

Haight, Sarah. *Letters from the Old World by a Lady of New York.* New York: Harper and Brothers, 1840.

Hornby, Emily. *A Nile Journal.* Liverpool: J.A. Thompson and Co., 1908.

———. *Sinai and Petra: The Journals of Emily Hornby in 1899 and 1901.* London: James Nisbet and Co. Ltd, 1902.

Lorimer, Norma. *By the Waters of Egypt.* London: Methuen and Co., 1909.

Lushington, Sarah. *Narrative of a Journey from Calcutta to Europe.* London: John Murray, 1829.

Mahoney, Rosemary. *Down the Nile Alone in a Fisherman's Skiff.* New York: Little Brown and Co., 2007.

Martineau, Harriet. *Eastern Life, Present and Past.* Philadelphia: Lea and Blanchard, 1848.

Merrick, E.M. *With a Palette in Eastern Places.* London: Sampson Low, 1899.

Minutoli, Wolfradine. *Recollections of Egypt.* London: Treuttel and Würtz 1827.

Nightingale, Florence. *Letters from Egypt 1849–1850.* Edited by Anthony Sattin. London: Barrie and Jenkins, 1987.

North, Marianne. *Reminiscences of a Happy Life.* London: Macmillan, 1898.

Pfeiffer, Ida. *Voyage to the Holy Land, Egypt and Italy*. London: Ingram, Cooke and Co., 1853.

Poole, Sophia. *The Englishwoman in Egypt*. Edited by Azza Kararah. Cairo: The American University in Cairo Press, 2003.

Quibell, Annie A. *A Wayfarer in Egypt*. London: Methuen and Co, 1925.

Romer, Isabel. *A Pilgrimage to the Temples and Tombs of Egypt, Nubia and Palestine*. London: Richard Bentley, 1846.

Selby, Bettina. *Riding the Desert Trail by Bicycle to the Source of the Nile*. London: Abacus, 1983.

Smith Lewis, Agnes. *In the Shadow of Sinai*. Cambridge: Cambridge University Press, 1898; repr. Brighton: Alpha Press, 1999.

Stevens, E.S. *My Sudan Year*. 1912; repr. London: Darf Publishers, 1985.

Tobin, Lady Katherine. *Shadow of the East*. London: n.p., 1855.

Whately, Mary. *Letters from Egypt to Plain Folks at Home*. London: n.p., 1879.

———. *Among the Huts in Egypt: Scenes from Real Life*. London: Seeley, Jackson, and Halliday, 1871.

Index of Travelers